A

Gift for

:

from

AUTHENTIC AMISH COOKING

COOKING
with the
HORSE & BUGGY
PEOPLE II

Sharing a Second Serving of Favorites
from 207 Amish Women of Holmes County, Ohio

Compiled by Henry and Amanda Mast

Carlisle Press
WALNUT CREEK

Layout and Design by Virginia Beachy, Rachel Coblentz,
  Teresa Hochstetler, Charity Miller, Miriam Miller

Cover Art by Wayne Troyer

Text Art by Mary Yoder

ISBN 1-890050-62-8

For a complete Carlisle Press catalog call 1-800-852-4482.

2673 TR 421
Sugarcreek, OH 44681

Carlisle Press
WALNUT CREEK

Contents

LIST OF ABBREVIATIONS USED

oz.— ounce	sm.— small
lb.— pound(s)	c.— cup
tsp.— teaspoon	pt.— pint
Tbsp.— tablespoon	qt.— quart

Acknowledgments

A special thank you to all the ladies that took time to share recipes to make this book possible!

With the girls' help we spent many a joyful evening sorting through recipes. It was very interesting because we all like to try new recipes, although there are some older ones which hold special memories.

So when you are enjoying these tasteful recipes, don't give us the honor, because we are only humans, but *"praise God, from whom all blessings flow,"* and be thankful for our sharing, caring community.

Respectfully,

The Masts

Introduction

I n 1986 the first volume of *Cooking with the Horse & Buggy People* was published. For 15 years and 100,000 copies later it is still a faithful standby for the Amish as well as thousands of others who enjoy good homemade meals.

Seeing how much cooks everywhere enjoyed Cooking with the Horse and Buggy People Volume I, Amanda Mast and her friends have opened their well-used recipe boxes and stirred up another batch of favorites.

Tested and perfected with years or everyday use these family heirlooms are shared with you in hopes that they'll not only make cooking new and refreshing for you, but will delight even the most discriminating taste palate.

Nestled in the idyll landscape of peaceful hills and valleys, the Amish women whos recipes are featured in this book live in the world's largest Amish community—Holmes County, Ohio. Holmes County has been home sweet home to five and sometimes six generations of Amish families often living on the same four square miles as their ancestors who migrated here in the early 1800s.

We hope that by sharing a valuable part of our heritage we'll encourage you to share yours; by treasuring ours– we'll remind you to treasure yours; remembering ours– helping you remember yours.

Here's 207 Amish women wishing you health, happiness, good friends, plenty of sunshine, and joy. And of course, a delicious homecooked meal with a generous second helping!

My favorites

Notes

Notes

Breads & Rolls

Bread

3/4 c. sugar
3/4 c. flour
1 Tbsp. salt
4 Tbsp. instant potato flakes
3 1/2 c. warm water
2 Tbsp. or 2 pkt. dry yeast
3/4 c. vegetable oil
2 c. whole wheat flour
6 c. white flour

Mix sugar, flour, salt, and potato flakes. Add water. Stir well and add yeast. Let set until it rises a bit, then add oil. Mix well. Add flour. Mix well. Let rise until double in size, then work out into pans. Let rise. Bake at 300° for 30 minutes.

Katie Mae Troyer

Bread

2/3 c. warm water
1 1/2 Tbsp. yeast
1 tsp. sugar
2 c. warm water
1/2 c. sugar
1/3 c. oil
2 1/2 tsp. salt
7 1/2 c. flour

Mix 2/3 c. warm water, yeast, and 1 tsp. sugar. Combine 2 c. warm water, 1/2 c. sugar, oil, and salt. Add yeast mixture and work well. Add flour. Work until dough is no longer sticky. You may need to add a little more flour while working. Cover and let rise until double in size. Work down. Let rise again, then work out into pans. Let rise again. Bake at 350° for 20 minutes. Yields 3 loaves.

Mrs. Wayne Yoder

Bread

1 1/2 c. boiling water
2 Tbsp. shortening
2 tsp. salt
1 c. oats
1 Tbsp. yeast
3/4 c. warm water
1/4 c. molasses
1/4 c. brown sugar
4–5 c. flour

Mix boiling water, shortening, salt, and oats. Cool slightly. Dissolve yeast in warm water. Sprinkle with sugar. Add oat mixture and remaining ingredients. Bake for 30–35 minutes. Yields 2 loaves.

Mrs. Levi Yoder

Bread

3/4 c. flour
1/4 c. sugar
1/4 c. brown sugar
1 Tbsp. salt
3/4 c. vegetable oil
2 c. cold water
1 c. boiling water
2 Tbsp. yeast
7–8 c. flour

Mix 3/4 c. flour, sugar, and salt. Add cold water, boiling water, and yeast. Let rise slightly. Add oil and flour. Let rise for 30 minutes. Punch down. Let rise for another 30 minutes. Punch down. Let rise for 1 hour. Shape into 4 loaves. Let rise and bake at 350° for 20–30 minutes. If brown bread is desired, you may use some brown flour.

Mrs. Emanuel J. Miller

Whole Wheat Bread

3 c. warm water
3 eggs, beaten
1 1/2 Tbsp. yeast
3/4 c. honey
3/4 c. Crisco
2 Tbsp. salt
3 c. wheat flour

Mix water, eggs, yeast, honey, Crisco, and salt. Beat in flour with egg beater until smooth. Add more wheat flour and knead until smooth. Let set in a warm place and punch down every 10 minutes for 1 hour. Let rise again, then shape into 4 loaves. Bake as regular bread. Be sure to beat with egg beater and punch down every 10 minutes as directed! This is just as soft as white bread.

Mrs. Raymond Wengerd

Homemade Bread

1/2 c. sugar
1/8 c. salt
1/8 c. yeast
1/2 c. lard or Wesson oil
3 1/2 c. warm water

Add flour until it reaches desired consistency. If you want whole wheat bread, use 3 c. whole wheat flour, and additional white flour. Yields 4 loaves.

Mrs. Mahlon R. Yoder

Light Brown Bread

³/₄ c. plus 3 Tbsp. sugar
2 tsp. salt
1¹/₂ c. vegetable oil
3 c. hot water
2 c. whole wheat flour
1¹/₂ c. lukewarm water
3¹/₂ Tbsp. yeast
3 tsp. sugar
8¹/₂ c. Thesco flour

Mix first five ingredients with a wire whisk. Let cool until lukewarm. Mix next three ingredients and 1¹/₂ c. Thesco flour with a wire whisk. Combine both mixtures. Add remaining flour. Yields 6 loaves.
Mrs. Harry M. Miller

White Bread

1¹/₂ Tbsp. yeast
1 Tbsp. salt
¹/₃ c. sugar
6 c. Thesco flour
¹/₄ c. lukewarm water
¹/₃ c. oil
2 c. hot water

Dissolve yeast in lukewarm water. Set aside. Mix together hot water, oil, salt, and sugar. Cool. When cool, add yeast mixture. Stir, then add half of flour. Stir, then add remaining flour. Work dough. Let rise until double, about 1 hour. Punch down and divide into 3 separate pieces. Put into pans. Let rise until double in size. Bake at 350° for 20 minutes. Let cool slightly. Put into bags while still warm so they steam will soften it.
Mrs. David Miller

Super Bread

2 Tbsp. sugar
1 tsp. salt
2 c. hot water
¹/₃ c. vegetable oil
1 Tbsp. yeast
¹/₂ c. whole wheat flour (optional)

Mix everything together except flour and yeast. Sprinkle yeast on top and stir a little so yeast dissolves. Let set for 30 minutes. If wheat flour is used, add and let set for 30 minutes. Add enough white flour so dough doesn't stick to your hands while kneading, about 5 cups.
Mrs. Roman R. Miller

Hillbilly Bread

4 c. warm water
3 Tbsp. yeast
4 c. whole wheat flour
1 c. warm water
1 c. oil
1 c. sugar
4 tsp. salt

Combine 4 c. warm water, yeast, and flour in a large mixing bowl. Mix well. Set aside in a warm place for 30–45 minutes. Add 1 c. warm water, oil, sugar, and salt. Add white flour until dough is the right consistency. Cover with plastic and let rise for 30 minutes. Punch down and let rise for 1 hour. Shape into 6 loaves. Let rise until light. Bake at 325° for 30 minutes.

Anna Miller

Dutch Dinner Rolls

2 c. hot water
$^1/_2$ c. sugar
$^1/_4$ c. margarine
1 Tbsp. salt
2 Tbsp. yeast
$^1/_4$ c. warm water
1 tsp. sugar
2 eggs, beaten
7 c. flour

Combine 2 c. water, sugar, margarine, and salt. Cool to lukewarm. Combine yeast, $^1/_4$ c. water, and sugar. Let rise. Add yeast and eggs to first mixture. Add 4 c. flour. Beat well. Add 3 c. more flour. Let rise until double in size. Punch down. Let rise again and shape into rolls. Let rise and bake at 350° until golden brown. *Mary Esther Miller*

Dinner Rolls

2 c. milk, scalded
1 c. sugar
$^1/_2$ c. margarine
3 tsp. salt
4 eggs
4 Tbsp. yeast
2 c. warm water
flour

Combine milk, sugar, and margarine. Add remaining ingredients, using flour as needed. Do not make the dough too stiff. Very good. Yields 6 doz. dinner rolls or $4^1/_2$ doz. cinnamon rolls.

Dinner Rolls

1 Tbsp. yeast
$^1/_4$ c. warm water
$^1/_2$ Tbsp. sugar
$^1/_2$ c. milk
4 Tbsp. butter
$^1/_4$ c. sugar
$^1/_2$ tsp. salt
2 eggs
$^1/_2$ c. cold water
$^1/_2$ tsp. vanilla
2 c. donut mix
bread flour

Dissolve yeast in water. Add $^1/_2$ Tbsp. sugar. Scald milk. Add butter, sugar, and salt. Beat eggs. Add cold water, vanilla, and donut mix. Mix all together. Add bread flour until desired texture is reached.

Mrs. David A. Yoder

Quick & Easy Buns

4 Tbsp. yeast
1 tsp. sugar
warm water
4 eggs, beaten
1 c. sugar
2 tsp. salt
$^2/_3$ c. lard or oil
2 c. warm water
8 c. bread flour

Combine yeast, sugar, and warm water. Combine next five ingredients. Add yeast mixture. Beat in 4 c. flour. Add remaining flour and stir in. Let rise until double. Punch down twice. Roll out to $^1/_2$" thick on floured board. Cut with a 3" cutter. Let rise until almost double. Bake at 400°. Instead of cutting them out on a board, I just shape them with my hands and put them into a pan. Very good dinner rolls and buns.
Yields 5 dozen.

Ruby Kline

Melt-in-your-mouth Biscuits

cream
2 Tbsp. sugar
$^1/_2$ c. shortening
1 egg
$^1/_2$ tsp. cream of tartar
$^1/_2$ tsp. salt
4 tsp. baking powder
2 c. flour
$^2/_3$ c. milk

Combine cream, sugar, shortening, and egg. Add cream of tartar, salt, baking powder, and flour. Gradually add milk. Drop on cookie sheets and bake at 350°.

Mrs. Norman H. Mast

Butter Crescents

$^1/_2$ c. milk
$^1/_2$ c. butter, softened
$^1/_3$ c. sugar
$^1/_2$ tsp. salt
1 pkg. yeast
$^1/_2$ c. warm water
1 egg, lightly beaten
$3^1/_2$–4 c. bread flour

In saucepan, heat milk until bubbles appear at edges. Dissolve yeast in warm water. In a large bowl, cream butter, sugar, and salt. Beat yeast in with egg, and combine with milk, then add to sugar mixture and mix well. Gradually add flour and knead. Let rise until double, about 1 hour. Punch down. On a floured surface, divide dough in half. Cover and let rest for 10 minutes. Grease 2 baking sheets. Using a floured rolling pin, roll half of dough into a 12" circle. Cut into 6 wedges. Roll up each wedge, starting at wide end. Place on baking sheet and curve ends to form crescents. Cover loosely with a damp cloth. Let rise until almost double, about 30 minutes. Preheat oven to 400°. Brush dough with a large egg, beaten. Bake for 15 minutes or until golden. This is also good for vegetable pizza crust. Yields 2 crusts.

Mrs. David Miller

tid bits

Put alcohol and vinegar in warm water to clean windows in winter when they want to freeze.

Garlic Bubble Loaf

1 pkg. dry yeast
$^{1}/_{4}$ c. warm water
2 c. milk
2 Tbsp. sugar
1 Tbsp. shortening
2 tsp. salt
2 c. flour
$^{1}/_{2}$ c. butter
1 Tbsp. parsley flakes
2 tsp. garlic powder

Dissolve yeast in warm water. Let set for 5 minutes, then add milk, sugar, shortening, salt, and flour. Beat until smooth, then stir in enough flour to form a soft dough. Turn out onto a floured surface. Knead until smooth and elastic, about 6–8 minutes. Place in a greased bowl, turning once to grease top. Cover. Let rise until double in bulk. Melt butter. Add parsley flakes and garlic powder. When punched down, divide dough into 4 parts, then divide each part into 12 pieces. Roll into balls, dip into butter mixture, then place balls into 2 bread pans. Pour remaining butter mixture over dough. Let rise until double in bulk. Bake at 375° for 35–40 minutes. Cool. Remove. Serve warm. Very good.

Katie Hershberger

Bread Sticks

$^{1}/_{2}$ c. butter, melted
$^{1}/_{4}$ c. Parmesan cheese
$^{3}/_{4}$ Tbsp. garlic powder
$^{1}/_{2}$ Tbsp. seasoned salt
1 c. warm water
4 Tbsp. Wesson oil
1 pkg. yeast
1 Tbsp. sugar
$^{1}/_{4}$ tsp. salt
$2^{1}/_{2}$–3 c. flour

Combine butter, cheese, garlic powder, and seasoned salt. Set aside. Mix dough ingredients, then divide into 8 sections and place in strips on greased sheet cake pan. Spread with butter mixture. Bake at 350° for 15–20 minutes. Serve warm with heated pizza sauce. Delicious!

Mrs. Mahlon R. Yoder

Garlic Bread Sticks

Use regular bread dough and let rise. Shape into ¹/₂" X 7" long ropes. Do not let rise too long before baking. After baking, roll them in butter and sprinkle with garlic salt and Parmesan cheese.

Erma Mast

Very Good Corn Bread

1 c. cornmeal
2 c. biscuit mix
1 c. butter
1 c. half and half
¹/₂ tsp. baking soda
³/₄ c. sugar
¹/₂ tsp. salt
2 eggs, beaten slightly

Melt butter and mix with cream. Add to thoroughly mixed dry ingredients. Mix in eggs. Pour into a greased and floured 9 X 13 baking pan. Bake at 350° for 30 minutes.

Zucchini Bread

3 c. flour
1¹/₂ c. sugar
1 tsp. cinnamon
1 tsp. salt
³/₄ tsp. soda
2 c. unpeeled zucchini
1 c. nuts
1 c. raisins
3 eggs
1 c. vegetable oil

Bake at 325° for 1 hour.

Mrs. Jonathan Raber

tid bits

Dip broken shoelace tips in clear nail polish and allow to harden. The new tips will last a long time.

Pizza Hut Pizza Crust

2 pkgs. yeast
2 Tbsp. sugar
$^2/_3$ c. warm water
2 c. cold water
3 Tbsp. corn oil
$^1/_4$ tsp. garlic
$^1/_2$ tsp. oregano
$6^1/_2$–7 c. flour

Sprinkle yeast over warm water. Stir in sugar. Let set for 5 minutes or until bubbly. Combine remaining ingredients, adding only $^1/_2$ c. flour. Beat into a smooth batter. Add yeast, then remaining flour until dough is workable. Knead until smooth and elastic. Let rise until double. Punch down and shape to fit two 15" round pans that have been greased with $^1/_4$ c. oil (or less) and dusted with cornmeal. Do not push dough up the sides of the pan. Let rise about 20 minutes.

Mrs. Aden Yoder

Pizza Hut Crust

1 Tbsp. yeast
$1^1/_2$ Tbsp. sugar
1 c. warm water
$1^1/_2$ Tbsp. corn oil
$^1/_8$ tsp. garlic
$^1/_2$ tsp. salt
$^1/_4$ tsp. oregano
2–3 c. flour

Combine yeast, sugar, and water. Let set for 5 minutes. Add remaining ingredients. Mix and put in a large pizza pan. Top with your favorite sauce and toppings. Bake at 450° until lightly browned.

Mrs. Eddie E. Miller

Pizza Crust

$2^1/_2$ c. flour
2 Tbsp. sugar
1 tsp. salt
1 c. warm water
1 Tbsp. yeast
2 Tbsp. vegetable oil

Dissolve yeast in warm water. Add remaining ingredients and let set for 5 minutes. Press into lightly greased pizza pan. Let rise for about 30 minutes. Add your favorite pizza toppings and bake at 375° for 20–25 minutes or until crust is done.

Katie Mae Troyer

Soft Pretzels

2 1/2 c. water
3 Tbsp. yeast
1 tsp. salt
3/4 c. brown sugar
7–8 c. flour

Let dough rise until double. Shape into pretzels. Brush with beaten egg. Sprinkle with pretzel salt and bake at 425° until brown. Dip into butter. Serve plain or sprinkle with sugar and cinnamon. Or serve with sour cream and onion. They are also good dipped in caramel sauce.

Mrs. Dennis (Rosie) Yoder
Susie Kuhns
Clara Hershberger

Soft Pretzels

6 Tbsp. yeast
1 1/2 c. lukewarm water
1 1/2 c. brown sugar
2 tsp. salt
3 1/2 c. lukewarm water
14–16 c. Thesco flour

Dissolve yeast in 1 1/2 c. lukewarm water. Combine remaining ingredients in a large bowl. Mix like bread dough, then shape as pretzels, using 1/4 lb. dough and rolling out thin. Dip into soda water (2 Tbsp. soda to 1 c. water). Lay them on paper towels for a little while, and sprinkle with pretzel salt. Bake at 425°, then butter them as they come out of the oven. Yields about 35 lg. pretzels.

Miriam Mast
Katie Hershberger
Mrs. Vernon Schmucker

tid bits

Use lard to grease your bread pans and the bread will slide out more easily.

Banana Bread

1 c. sugar
2 eggs
$^1/_2$ c. shortening
3 ripe bananas
$^1/_2$ tsp. salt
1 tsp. soda
$^1/_2$ c. nuts
2 c. flour

Cream shortening, eggs, and sugar together. Stir in mashed bananas, then mix in remaining ingredients. Bake in greased loaf pans at 350° for 45 minutes or until done.

Mrs. Abe Miller

Banana Nut Bread

$^1/_2$ c. butter
1 c. sugar
2 eggs
3 ripe bananas
2 c. flour
1 tsp. soda
$^1/_4$ tsp. salt
$^1/_3$ c. sour cream
$^1/_2$ c. chopped nuts

Cream butter and sugar. Add sour cream, bananas, flour, soda, and salt. Mix together. Add eggs and nuts last. Mix. Bake in 2 greased loaf pans at 350° for 40 minutes.

Mrs. Atlee Mast

Pumpkin Nut Bread

3 c. sugar
1 c. oil
4 eggs
1 tsp. cinnamon
2 c. pumpkin
2 tsp. soda
$1^1/_2$ tsp. salt
$^2/_3$ c. water
$3^1/_2$ c. flour

Mix ingredients well and bake in loaf pans for about 1 hour. Yields 3 loaves.

Mrs. David E. Beachy

Pumpkin Bread

1 c. cooking oil
2 c. sugar
3 c. flour
1 tsp. nutmeg
$^1/_2$ tsp. cloves
$^1/_2$ tsp. ginger
2 tsp. cinnamon
1 tsp. allspice
2 tsp. soda
1 tsp. salt
2 c. pumpkin or 1 (16 oz.) can
4 eggs
nuts, optional

Bake in 3 loaf pans for 1 hour.

Mrs. Eli A. Mast

Best Cinnamon Rolls

2 pkgs. yeast
1 yellow or white cake mix
4 c. flour
3 eggs
$^1/_3$ c. oil
1 tsp. salt
melted butter
brown sugar
cinnamon

Dissolve yeast in $2^1/_2$ c. warm water for 3 minutes. Add cake mix, 1 c. flour, eggs, oil, and salt. Beat with beater until bubbles appear. Slowly add remaining flour. Stir with spoon, making a soft dough. Let rise until double in size. Roll out to about $^1/_4$" thick. Spread with melted butter, sugar, and cinnamon. Cut and let rise again. Bake at 350° for 20–30 minutes. Ice while still warm. Yields about 3 cake pans full.

Mrs. Ivan Hershberger

tid bits

Put frozen bread loaves into a clean paper bag and heat at 325° for 5 minutes to thaw completely.
—*Anna Miller*

Dick's Bundt Rolls

1/2 c. butter
1/2 c. maple syrup
3/4 c. brown sugar
1/2 c. nuts
2 tubes buttermilk biscuits

Melt butter and add remaining ingredients except biscuits. Mix well. Grease tube bundt pan. Place half of syrup mixture in bottom of pan. Place biscuits on end around tube pan. Pour remaining syrup over top of biscuits and bake at 350° for 30 minutes. Let set for 5 minutes. Remove from pan.

Pecan Coffee Ring

1/2 c. butter
1/2 c. maple syrup
2 pkgs. buttermilk biscuits
1/2 c. brown sugar
1/2 tsp. cinnamon
1/4 c. nuts

Heat butter and syrup until butter is melted. Pour half of mixture into a bundt cake pan. Mix cinnamon and sugar. Roll each biscuit in sugar, then place in pan. Pour remaining syrup over top. Bake at 350° for 25–30 minutes. Let cool in pan for 5 minutes, then put on a plate and sprinkle with nuts. Serve warm.

Mrs. David A. Yoder
Mrs. Philip L. Yoder

Cinnamon Rolls

6 c. water
6 Tbsp. yeast
6 Tbsp. sugar
2 Tbsp. vanilla
1 c. bread flour
21 c. doughnut mix

Roll with sugar and cinnamon. This dough can also be used for doughnuts.

Dorothy Yoder

Breakfast Rolls

1¼ c. butter
2 c. milk
3 Tbsp. yeast
2 Tbsp. sugar
1 c. warm water
4 eggs, beaten
2 c. mashed potatoes
1 c. sugar
2 Tbsp. salt
flour

Melt butter and add milk. Heat this until very warm. Combine yeast, sugar, and warm water. Combine eggs, mashed potatoes, sugar, salt, and flour. Mix all together. Be sure to pour the milk mixture into the bowl, then add some flour before adding the yeast mixture. (The milk may be too hot for the yeast.) Good luck and happy eating!

Anna Troyer

Soft Rolls

2 c. quick oats
4 c. boiling water
½ c. margarine
1⅓ c. brown sugar
2 tsp. salt
4 Tbsp. yeast
⅔ c. warm water
2 Tbsp. white sugar

Combine oats, brown sugar, and salt in a large bowl. Pour boiling water over this mixture. Add margarine. Mix yeast, white sugar, and ⅔ c. warm water together. When oat mixture is lukewarm, add the yeast mixture. Mix well. Add 10 c. bread flour, 1 c. at a time. Let rise once, then work out. Roll out and spread with soft butter, brown sugar, cinnamon, and nuts. Roll up, cut, and let rise. Bake at 325°. Ice with favorite icing.

Mrs. Albert M. L. Yoder

Bakery Rolls

2 Tbsp. yeast
1 c. warm water
2 c. scalded milk
1 c. white sugar
1 c. margarine
4 beaten eggs
2 c. mashed potatoes
2 tsp. salt
10 c. flour
Frosting:
1 c. butter, softened
5–6 Tbsp. water
6 c. powdered sugar
salt
1 Tbsp. maple flavoring

Soak yeast in warm water. Mix sugar, salt, and margarine with hot milk. Add potatoes, eggs, and yeast mixture. Add flour. Let rise once. Roll out and put melted butter and a mixture of white sugar, brown sugar, and cinnamon on top. Let rise until almost double. Bake at 350° for 15–20 minutes. *For frosting:* Beat butter and water until fluffy. Add remaining ingredients and beat well.

Mrs. Arlene Hershberger

Sour Cream Rolls

1 Tbsp. yeast
$1/4$ c. warm water
$1/4$ c. sugar
6 Tbsp. butter
1 tsp. salt
$1/2$ c. sour cream
2 eggs, beaten
$2^3/4$ c. flour
Glaze:
$1/4$ c. butter
$1/2$ c. sour cream
$3/4$ c. brown sugar

Knead like bread dough. Cover and let rise for 2 hours. Knead dough and divide into 2 parts. Roll each part into a 12" circle. Brush with melted butter. Top with a mixture of 1 c. brown sugar, 1 tsp. cinnamon, and nuts. Cut into 12 wedges. Roll from wide end to point. Put 24 rolls into a cake pan. Let rise. Bake at 350° for 25–30 minutes. *For glaze:* Bring to a slow boil. Pour over rolls as soon as out of oven.

Susie Keim

Jelly-Filled Rolls

2 Tbsp. yeast
$^1/_2$ Tbsp. sugar
$^1/_2$ c. warm water
2 c. warm water
$^1/_2$ c. melted Crisco
$^1/_2$ c. sugar
1 Tbsp. salt
2 eggs, beaten
6–7 c. Thesco flour

Dissolve yeast and $^1/_2$ Tbsp. sugar in $^1/_2$ c. warm water. Add remaining ingredients. Let rise once. Work down. Roll out like cinnamon rolls. Roll up, punch a hole in the middle, and fill with cream cheese (tube style) and your favorite pie filling. Bake at 350°–375° until lightly browned. Drizzle with icing.

Mrs. Alvin I. Yoder

Maple Nut Twist Rolls

$^3/_4$ c. milk
$^1/_4$ c. butter
1 Tbsp. yeast
$^1/_4$ c. lukewarm water
1 egg
1 tsp. maple flavoring
$^1/_2$ tsp. salt
3 Tbsp. sugar
3 c. flour
Filling:
$^1/_4$ c. butter, softened
$^1/_2$ c. brown sugar
$^1/_3$ c. nuts
1 tsp. cinnamon
Glaze:
1 c. powdered sugar
1 Tbsp. butter
1–2 tsp. milk
$^1/_2$ tsp. maple flavoring

Dissolve yeast in water. Heat milk and butter until scalding. Cool and add yeast. Beat egg, maple flavoring, salt, and sugar. Add flour. Cover and let rise for 1 hour. Divide into two equal parts. Roll out 1 part and put into a greased round pizza pan. Put filling ingredients on top. Roll out second part of dough and lay over filling. Use a greased pizza cutter and slice toward the middle, leaving 2" in the middle not cut. Continue cutting toward the middle, making 10–12 slices. Twist each slice 2 times. Let rise and bake at 350° for 20 minutes. Drizzle with glaze. Delicious!

Mary Esther Miller

Pineapple Cheese Braid

2 (¹/₄ oz.) pkgs. active dry yeast
1 c. warm water (110°–115°)
¹/₂ c. butter or margarine, softened
5 Tbsp. sugar
2 eggs
¹/₄ tsp. salt
4¹/₄–4¹/₂ c. all-purpose flour
Pineapple Filling:
1 (8 oz.) can crushed pineapple,
    undrained
¹/₂ c. sugar
3 Tbsp. cornstarch
Cream Cheese Filling:
16 oz. cream cheese, softened
¹/₃ c. sugar
1 Tbsp. lemon juice
¹/₂ tsp. vanilla extract
Icing:
1 c. powdered sugar
2–3 Tbsp. milk

In a mixing bowl, dissolve yeast in water. Let set for 5 minutes. Add butter, sugar, eggs, salt, and 2 c. flour. Beat on low speed for 3 minutes. Add enough remaining flour to form a soft dough. Turn onto a floured surface; knead until smooth and elastic, about 6–8 minutes. Let rise until double, about 45 minutes. Meanwhile, combine pineapple filling ingredients in a saucepan. Cook and stir until thickened. Cool. Combine cream cheese filling ingredients; mix well. Divide in half. On a floured surface, roll each portion into a 9 X 15 rectangle. Place on greased baking sheets. Spread the cream cheese filling lengthwise down center third of each rectangle. Spread the pineapple filling on top. On each long side, cut strips 1" wide and 3" long. Fold alternating strips at an angle across filling. Seal ends. Cover and let rise for 20 minutes. Bake at 350° for 25–30 minutes or until golden brown. Cool. If desired, combine icing and drizzle over braids. Any flavor filling may be used. Yields 2 braids.

Mrs. Lovina Schlabach

Overnight Danish Braids

1 c. margarine
5 c. all-purpose flour
$1/2$ tsp. salt
3 eggs
1 pkg. yeast
$3/4$ c. warm water
$1/2$ c. sugar
$1/4$ c. warm water
Filling:
1 c. butter, softened
1 c. brown sugar
1 Tbsp. cinnamon
1 c. chopped pecans
Glaze:
$1^1/2$ c. powered sugar
1–2 Tbsp. hot milk
3 tsp. melted margarine
$1/2$ tsp. salt

Cut margarine into flour and salt. Mix until it resembles cornmeal. Dissolve yeast in $1/4$ c. warm water. Add eggs, yeast mixture, $3/4$ c. warm water, and sugar. Mix by hand until dough is well mixed. Batter may be a little sticky. Refrigerate overnight. Cover for 5–6 hours. Bring dough to room temperature for 1 hour. Divide into 4 equal parts. Roll each part to 9 X 12 on a floured surface. Make filling, mixing well. Spread $1/2$ c. filling in 3" wide strip down the center of each rectangle of dough. With kitchen shears, cut sides toward center 3" long and 1" wide. Fold the strips over the filling, alternating from side to side. Place on a greased cookie sheet. Let rise until double. Bake at 350° for 20–25 minutes. Cool slightly. Top with glaze. These braids freeze beautifully and we like the caramel icing! Yields 4 braids.

Mrs. David J. Troyer
Ray Laura

Raspberry Creme Rolls

Use your favorite roll recipe. Roll out half of dough as for cinnamon rolls and spread with brown sugar and cinnamon. Roll up. Slice, then cut up into small pieces and put into a greased pan until bottom is covered. Spread softened cream cheese (in the tube) over the dough. Spread raspberry filling over cream cheese. Roll out remaining dough and roll and cut as before. Put over fillings. Let rise slightly, then bake at 350° until done. Glaze or frost as desired.

Mary Hostetler

Doughnuts

10 lbs. doughnut mix
14 c. water
6 oz. yeast
2 c. sugar
2¹/₂ lbs. bread flour

Let rise until double. Use about 12 lbs. Creamtex. Add 1 tsp. vinegar before oil is hot. After frying, glaze donuts. Yields 11–12 doz.

Mrs. Andy A. Troyer
Mrs. Mattie Miller

Fluffy Raised Doughnuts

2 c. water
1 pkg. yeast
¹/₂ c. Wesson oil
¹/₂ c. sugar
2 eggs, well beaten
2 tsp. salt
6 c. flour

Knead until smooth. Let rise until double. Roll out and let rise again. Fry in hot fat.

Mrs. Edward M. Hershberger

Snowball Doughnuts

2 eggs
1 tsp. vanilla
1 tsp. salt
1 c. milk
1 c. sugar
3 tsp. baking powder
4 c. flour
1 Tbsp. butter

Beat eggs until light. Add sugar, vanilla, and milk. Stir in flour, baking powder, and salt. Add melted butter. Drop by teaspoon into hot fat. Roll in white sugar or in powdered sugar.

Mrs. Mary Miller

tid bits

To cut rolls, use
a bread knife coated
with flour.

Breakfast

Sausage & Egg Casserole

1 lb. bulk pork sausage
6 eggs
2 c. milk
1 tsp. salt
1 tsp. ground mustard
6 slices white bread, $1/2$" cubes
1 c. shredded cheddar cheese

In a skillet, brown and crumble sausage; drain. In a large bowl, beat eggs. Add milk, salt, and mustard. Stir in bread cubes, cheese, and sausage. Pour into a greased 11 X 7 X 2 baking dish. Cover and refrigerate for 8 hours or overnight. Remove from refrigerator 30 minutes before baking. Bake, uncovered, at 350° for 40 minutes or until done. Yields 8–10 servings.

Mrs. Aden Burkholder

Ham & Cheese Breakfast Strata

12 slices white bread
1 lb. fully cooked ham, diced
2 c. shredded cheddar cheese
6 eggs
milk
2 tsp. Worcestershire sauce
1 tsp. ground mustard
$1/2$ tsp. salt
$1/4$ tsp. pepper
$1/4$ c. minced onion
$1/4$ c. minced green pepper
$1/4$ c. butter
1 c. crushed cornflakes

Arrange 6 slices of bread in the bottom of a greased 9 X 13 X 2 baking dish. Top with ham and cheese. Cover with remaining bread. In a bowl, beat eggs, milk, Worcestershire sauce, mustard, salt, and pepper. Stir in onion and green pepper. Pour over all. Cover and refrigerate overnight. Remove from refrigerator 30 minutes before baking. Pour butter over bread. Sprinkle wtih cornflakes. Bake, uncovered, at 350° for 50–60 minutes or until knife inserted in center comes out clean. Yields 8–10 servings.

Lizzie Raber

tid bits

Dry green celery or parsley leaves until crumbly. Put in oven on cookie sheets at 250° until dry. Store in glass jars. Use as seasoning in soups, etc.

Make-Ahead Breakfast Casserole

1 lb. sausage
2 slices bread, $1/2$" cubes
1 c. shredded cheddar cheese
1 tsp. dry mustard
6 eggs
2 c. milk
$1/2$ tsp. salt

Crumble sausage in skillet. Cook and drain. Spread bread cubes in buttered 8 X 12 X 2 baking dish. Top with sausage and cheese. Beat eggs, milk, and seasonings. Pour over cheese. Cover and refrigerate overnight. Bake at 350° for 30–40 minutes. Yields 6–8 servings.

Mrs. Wayne Yoder

Sausage Hash

1 lb. bulk sausage
1 med. onion, chopped
2 med. carrots, grated
3 c. diced, cooked potatoes
$1/2$ tsp. salt
$1/2$ tsp. pepper

In a skillet over medium heat, brown sausage. Add onion and carrots. Cook until tender. Stir in potatoes, salt, and pepper. Reduce heat. Cook and stir for 20 minutes.

Soufflé

8–10 slices bread, cubed
12 eggs
3 c. milk
1 tsp. salt
1 tsp. Lawry's seasoned salt
$1/2$ tsp. black pepper
$1/4$ c. margarine

Spread cubed bread in bottom of a 9 X 13 pan. Melt margarine in a saucepan and add your favorite meats. Add onions, green peppers, etc., if desired. Mix. Pour over bread. Spread with your favorite cheese, cut or shredded. Beat together eggs, milk, and seasonings. Pour over all. Let soak a little. Bake at 350° for 45–60 minutes. Very good!

Mrs. Andrew A. Troyer

Baked Breakfast Burritos

1 lb. bacon
8 fresh mushrooms, sliced
6 green onions, sliced
$^1/_3$ c. chopped green pepper
1 clove garlic or garlic powder
8 eggs
$^1/_4$ c. sour cream
$^3/_4$ c. shredded cheddar cheese or
    Monterey Jack cheese, divided
3 Tbsp. enchilada or taco sauce
1 Tbsp. butter
4 (9") flour tortillas

In skillet, cook bacon until crisp; drain. Reserve 1 Tbsp. drippings. Sauté mushrooms, onions, green peppers, and garlic in drippings. Set aside and keep warm. In a bowl, beat eggs and sour cream. Stir in $^1/_4$ c. cheese and enchilada sauce. In a skillet, melt butter and add egg mixture. Cook over low heat, stirring occasionally, until eggs are set. Remove from heat. Crumble bacon. Add to eggs with mushroom mixture. Spoon down center of tortillas. Roll up. Place seam side down in an 11 X 7 X 2 baking dish. Sprinkle with remaining cheese. Bake at 350° for 5 minutes or until cheese melts. Serve with sour cream and enchilada sauce, if desired.

Lizzie Raber

Esther's Swiss Scrambled Eggs

8 slices bacon
2 c. bread cubes (no crust)
$1^3/_4$ c. milk
8 eggs
$^3/_4$ tsp. salt
pepper
2 Tbsp. butter
$^1/_4$–$^1/_2$ lb. Swiss cheese slices

Fry bacon, crumble, and set aside. Combine bread cubes and milk. Let set for 5 minutes. Drain. Combine milk with eggs. Beat slightly. Add salt and pepper to taste. Melt butter and soft scramble the eggs. Add bread cubes and pour into a greased casserole. Sprinkle with seasoned salt. Top with Swiss cheese and buttered bread crumbs, lightly toasted. Sprinkle with bacon. Cover. Refrigerate overnight. Bake, covered, at 375° for 15–20 minutes or until cheese melts.

Mrs. Edwin N. (Ruth) Weaver

Winter Garden Scrambled Eggs

8 eggs
1 c. finely chopped ham
1/4 c. chopped red sweet pepper
1/4 c. chopped green sweet pepper
1/4 c. mushrooms
1/4 c. chopped onions
1/4 c. butter
1/4 tsp. garlic salt

Mix all ingredients. Melt butter in a large skillet. Add egg mixture. Cook over medium heat until eggs are completely set. May be topped with cheese if desired before serving.

Mrs. Wayne R. Weaver

Country-Style Scrambled Eggs

4 c. coarsely chopped potatoes
1 c. diced onions
1 c. diced green pepper
6 Tbsp. margarine or butter
12 eggs
4 Tbsp. milk
1/2 tsp. pepper
2 c. fully cooked ham, diced
2 c. shredded cheese

In a large skillet, sauté potatoes, onions, and green peppers in butter until tender, stirring often. Beat together eggs, milk, and pepper. Stir in ham. Pour over potato mixture. Cook without stirring until mixture begins to set on bottom and around sides. Using a large spatula, lift and fold the partially cooked mixture so the uncooked portion flows underneath. Continue cooking until done. Sprinkle with cheese.

Mary Hostetler

The Mess

1 pkg. frozen hash browns
1 lb. Li'l Smokies or ham, cut up
peppers, optional
onions, optional
1 doz. eggs, beaten
salt
pepper

Fry hash browns, meat, peppers, and onions in butter. When hash browns are done, add eggs. Fry until eggs are set. Serve with toast or pancakes. This is also delicious made over a campfire.

Mrs. John A. Miller

Bacon & Egg Sandwiches

1/2 c. sour cream
8 slices bread
8 bacon strips, fried, drained
2 hard-boiled eggs, sliced
4 green onions, chopped
4 slices American cheese
butter

Spread sour cream on one side of 4 slices of bread. Top with onions, cheese, eggs, and bacon. Top with remaining bread. Butter outsides of sandwiches. Cook in skillet over medium heat until golden brown on both sides.

Mrs. Myron Miller

Breakfast Pizza

frozen hash brown patties
1/2 c. chopped onion
6 slices bacon, fried
1 can mushrooms
10 slices American cheese
1 doz. eggs
1/2 c. water
1 pkg. mozzarella cheese

Arrange frozen hash browns on cookie sheet. Break bacon on top. Layer mushrooms and onions over hash browns, and top with American cheese. Hand-beat eggs and water. Season with salt and pepper and pour over hash browns. Sprinkle with mozzarella cheese. Bake at 350°.

Mrs. Aden M. Troyer

Breakfast Haystack

1 pkg. corn chips, crushed
6 pkgs. smoky links, cut up, heated
3 lg. pkg. french fries, heated
5 lbs. bacon, cut up, fried
3 doz. eggs, scrambled
1 loaf bread, cubed, toasted
3 qts. barbecue sauce
6 qts. cheese sauce

Yields 30 servings.

Erma Mast

Sausage Gravy

1 lb. seasoned bulk sausage
2 Tbsp. finely chopped onion
6 Tbsp. all-purpose flour
1 qt. milk
$1/_2$ tsp. parsley flakes
$1/_2$ tsp. nutmeg
$1/_4$ tsp. salt
Worcestershire sauce
hot pepper or black pepper

Brown sausage in shortening of your choice. Add onions, then flour and milk. Add seasonings. Very good.

Amanda Raber

Breakfast Stack

biscuits, crumbled
sausage gravy
scrambled eggs
ham, cubed
Tater-Tots
green peppers
diced tomatoes, optional
onions
Doritos, crushed
cheese sauce
Sausage Gravy:
2 lb. bulk sausage
$1/_4$ c. butter
$1^1/_4$ c. flour
2 qts. milk
salt
seasoned salt
black pepper

Layer in order given. Enjoy! *For gravy:* Cook sausage in butter until browned. Add flour and stir well. Gradually add $1^1/_2$ qts. milk. Continue to heat until it thickens. Add milk until right consistency. Yields about 3 quarts.

Mrs. Ivan Hershberger
Katie Hershberger

tjd bits

Wipe the inside walls, shelves, and door gasket of your refrigerator or freezer with a mixture of 1 Tbsp. baking soda and 1 qt. warm water. Rinse and wipe dry.

Sausage Gravy

2 lb. bulk sausage
$1/4$ c. butter or margarine
$1^1/4$ c. flour
2 qts. milk
salt
seasoned salt
black pepper

Cook sausage in butter until browned over medium heat. Add flour and stir in well. Gradually add $1^1/2$ qts. of the milk. Continue to heat and keep stirred. It will thicken as it cooks. Add more milk if necessary to make it right consistency. Continue to cook a while after right consistency is reached. Add seasonings according to your taste. Serve with biscuits or hash browns.

Mrs. Abe E. Mast
Mrs. Alvin I. Yoder
Mrs. Atlee M. Shetler

Hash Browns

3 c. finely shredded potatoes
2 eggs, well beaten
$1^1/2$ Tbsp. flour
$1/8$ tsp. baking powder
$1/2$–1 tsp. salt
$1/2$ tsp. grated onion

In mixing bowl, gently combine eggs and potatoes. Combine dry ingredients and onion. Stir into potato mixture. Drop by tablespoonful into hot oil. Brown lightly on both sides.

Miriam Mast

Pancakes

1 egg, beaten
$1/2$ tsp. salt
2 tsp. sugar
$1^1/4$ c. milk
$1/2$ tsp. soda
2 tsp. baking powder
$1^1/4$ c. bread flour
3 Tbsp. Mazola oil

Bake on hot griddle. No oil is needed if fried in shortening.

Mrs. Eli N. Hershberger

Pancakes

1 c. flour
1 egg
3/4 c. milk
2 Tbsp. vegetable oil
1 Tbsp. sugar
3 tsp. baking powder
1/2 tsp. salt

Mix with fork. Do not overbeat. Fry in oil on a hot skillet. Delicious served with Fluffy Syrup.

Mrs. Mose E. Beachy
Mrs. Roman E. Raber
Mrs. Levi (Susan) Troyer

Pancake Mix

10 c. flour
3 c. whole wheat flour
2 c. quick oats
3 c. crushed cornflakes
5 Tbsp. baking powder
1/4 c. sugar
3 Tbsp. soda
1 Tbsp. salt

Store in an airtight container. To use combine 1 c. mix, 1 beaten egg, 1 Tbsp. shortening, and milk to desired consistency. Bake on heated griddle.

Dorothy Yoder

Breakfast French Toast

2 Tbsp. Karo
1/2 c. margarine
1 c. brown sugar
12–16 slices bread
5 eggs
1 1/2 c. milk or buttermilk
vanilla
salt

Mix first 3 ingredients together in a saucepan. Bring to a boil, then pour into a 9 X 13 pan. Place slices of bread over syrup. Beat together eggs, milk, salt, and vanilla. Pour over bread and refrigerate overnight. The next morning, bake at 350° for 45 minutes. Cut into squares. Invert to serve.

Vanilla French Toast

2 eggs
$1/2$ c. milk
1 Tbsp. sugar
1 tsp. vanilla
pinch salt
6 slices day-old bread
maple syrup or cinnamon sugar

Beat eggs, milk, sugar, vanilla, and salt. Soak bread for 30 seconds on each side. Cook on greased griddle until golden brown on both sides and cooked through. Serve with syrup or cinnamon sugar.

Mrs. Jonas L. Miller

Angel Biscuits

2 Tbsp. dry yeast
$1/4$ c. warm water
2 c. warm buttermilk
5 c. all-purpose flour
$1/3$ c. sugar
1 Tbsp. baking powder
1 Tbsp. soda
1 tsp. salt
1 c. melted butter or margarine

Dissolve yeast in warm water. Let set for 5 minutes. Stir in buttermilk. Set aside. In a large bowl, combine flour, sugar, baking powder, soda, and salt. Cut in shortening with a pastry blender until mixture resembles coarse meal. Stir in buttermilk mixture. Mix well. Turn onto a lightly floured surface. Knead lightly 3–4 times. Roll to $1/2$" thick. Place on greased pan. Cut into sized desired. Cover and let rise in a warm place for $1^1/2$ hours. Bake at 450° for 8–10 minutes. Yields $2^1/2$ dozen biscuits.

Amanda Wengerd

Melt-in-your-mouth Biscuits

2 c. flour
4 tsp. baking powder
$1/2$ tsp. cream of tartar
$1/2$ tsp. salt
2 Tbsp. sugar
$1/2$ c. shortening
1 egg
$2/3$ c. milk

Sift dry ingredients together and cut in shortening until mixture resembles coarse meal. Pour milk in slowly. Add egg and stir well. Drop dough on a cookie sheet. Bake at 450° for 10–15 minutes.

Mrs. Aden A. Yoder
Mae Mast

Buttermilk Biscuits

Mrs. Henry C. Yoder

2 c. flour
1/2 c. buttermilk
1 tsp. salt
1/2 tsp. soda
1 tsp. baking powder
3 Tbsp. shortening

Baking Powder Biscuits

4 c. flour
8 tsp. baking powder
2 tsp. salt
8 Tbsp. shortening
2 c. milk

Mix flour, baking powder, and salt. Cut in shortening and add milk. Knead lightly and roll out to desired thickness, preferably about 3/4" thick. Cut and put on cookie sheets, almost touching each other. Spread melted butter over biscuits. Bake at 450° until lightly browned.

Mrs. Andrew A. Troyer

Breakfast Oatmeal Muffins

1 c. all-purpose flour
1 c. brown sugar
1 tsp. baking powder
1 tsp. baking soda
1/2 c. vegetable oil
2 eggs, lightly beaten
1 c. oatmeal
1 c. raisins
1 tsp. vanilla

In a large bowl, combine flour, brown sugar, baking powder, and soda. In another bowl, combine oil, eggs, oatmeal, raisins, and vanilla. Add to dry ingredients and stir just until moistened (the batter will be thin). Spoon into 12 greased muffin cups. Bake at 350° for 18 minutes or until muffins test done. Yields 1 dozen.

Erma Mast

Blueberry Cream Muffins

4 eggs
2 c. sugar
1 c. vegetable oil
1 tsp. vanilla
4 c. all-purpose flour
1 tsp. salt
1 tsp. baking soda
2 tsp. baking powder
2 c. sour cream
2 c. fresh blueberries

In a mixing bowl, beat eggs. Gradually add sugar. While beating, slowly pour in oil. Add vanilla. Combine dry ingredients. Add alternately with the sour cream to the egg mixture. Gently fold in blueberries. Spoon into greased muffin tins. Bake at 400° for 20 minutes. Yields 24 muffins.

Erma Mast

Cornmeal Muffins

1 c. all-purpose flour
1 c. yellow cornmeal
$1/3$ c. sugar
1 Tbsp. baking powder
1 tsp. salt
2 Tbsp. finely chopped onion
1 c. cream-style corn
$1/2$ c. mayonnaise
3 Tbsp. vegetable oil
1 egg

In a large mixing bowl, combine dry ingredients. Make a well in the center and add all remaining ingredients. Stir just until mixed. Spoon into 12 greased muffin tins. Bake at 400° for 20 minutes. Yields 12 muffins.

Amanda Mast

Feather-Light Muffins

$1/3$ c. shortening
$1/2$ c. sugar
1 egg
$1^1/2$ c. cake flour
$1^1/2$ tsp. baking powder
$1/2$ tsp. salt
$1/4$ tsp. ground nutmeg
$1/2$ c. milk
Topping:
$1/2$ c. sugar
1 tsp. ground cinnamon
$1/2$ c. butter or margarine, melted

In a mixing bowl, cream shortening, sugar, and egg. Combine dry ingredients. Add to creamed mixture alternately with milk. Fill greased muffin tins $2/3$ full. Bake at 325° for 3–4 minutes. Meanwhile, combine sugar and cinnamon in a small bowl. Roll warm muffins in melted butter, then in sugar mixture. Serve warm. Yields 8–10 muffins.

Erma Mast

Pumpkin Apple Streusel Muffins

2 1/2 c. flour
2 c. sugar
1 Tbsp. pumpkin pie spice
1 tsp. baking soda
1/2 tsp. salt
2 eggs
3/4 c. cooked pumpkin
1/2 c. vegetable oil
2 c. peeled, chopped apples
Streusel Topping:
2 Tbsp. flour
1/4 c. sugar
1/2 tsp. cinnamon
2 tsp. butter, softened

In a large bowl, combine flour, sugar, spice, soda, and salt. In another bowl, beat eggs, pumpkin, and oil. Add to dry ingredients and stir until moistened. Stir in apples. Fill greased muffin pans about 3/4 full. Combine topping ingredients and sprinkle on top. Bake at 350° for 30–40 minutes. Yields 36 muffins.

Mrs. Jerry Erb

Oatmeal Apple Raisin Muffins

1 egg
3/4 c. milk
1 c. raisins
1 c. chopped apple
1/2 c. oil
1 c. all-purpose flour
1 c. quick oats
1/3 c. sugar
3 tsp. baking powder
1 tsp. salt
1 tsp. nutmeg
2 tsp. cinnamon

Beat egg. Stir in remaining ingredients, mixing just to moisten. Pour into 12 greased muffin cups until 3/4 full. Bake at 400° for 15–20 minutes. Serve cool or piping hot with butter.

Erma Mast

Oatmeal Muffins

1 c. buttermilk
1 c. quick oatmeal
$1/2$ c. light brown sugar
1 c. sifted flour
$1/2$ tsp. salt
$1/2$ tsp. baking soda
2 tsp. baking powder
1 egg, beaten
$1/4$ c. melted shortening

Combine buttermilk, oatmeal, and sugar. Let set for 10 minutes. Sift flour with salt, baking soda, and baking powder. Add beaten egg to oatmeal mixture, then add melted shortening. Mix well. Stir in flour mixture, using only enough strokes to moisten all ingredients. Do not beat. Fill 12 greased muffin cups. Bake at 375° for about 25 minutes. Yields 12 muffins.

Cheese Rolls

8 oz. cream cheese
$1/2$ c. white sugar
1 egg yolk
18 slices white bread
1 c. melted margarine
1 tsp. cinnamon

Mix cream cheese, $1/4$ c. sugar, and egg yolk. Cut crusts off bread and roll each slice flat with rolling pin. Spread cheese mixture over slices. Roll up each slice and cut in half. Dip in melted margarine, then roll in remaining sugar and cinnamon. Chill for at least 2 hours. Bake at 400° for 10–15 minutes. Serve warm. These can be made ahead of time and frozen until ready to use. This makes a good appetizer when serving brunch.

Mrs. David E. Beachy
Mrs. Robert Mast

Breakfast Cereal

10 c. oatmeal
4 c. wheat germ
2 c. coconut
1 c. brown sugar
2 tsp. salt
2 c. melted butter or margarine

Mix well and toast at 250° until coconut is turning brown. When cooled, add 2 c. small chocolate chips or raisins, if desired.

Mrs. Roman Hershberger

Homemade Granola Cereal

8 c. quick oats
1 tsp. salt
1 c. brown sugar
1 1/2 tsp. baking soda
1 c. maple syrup
2 c. coconut
1 c. whole wheat flour
1 c. melted butter
22 graham crackers, crushed
1/2 c. chopped nuts
1/2 c. chocolate chips

Combine oats, salt, sugar, soda, maple syrup, coconut, flour, and butter. Put on cookie sheets and toast in oven until nicely browned, about 1 hour at 250°. Add crackers and nuts for the last 15 minutes of baking time. While still warm but not hot, add chocolate chips. This is also good as a topping for fruit or ice cream.

Mrs. Atlee Mast
Mrs. David M. Miller
Mrs. Abe E. Mast

Grapenuts

Dorothy Yoder

1 c. brown sugar
6 c. whole wheat flour
1 c. cane molasses
1/2 Tbsp. salt
1/2 Tbsp. soda
1/2 Tbsp. vanilla
1/2 Tbsp. maple flavoring
1/2 c. margarine or butter
3 c. buttermilk

Cereal

8 c. whole wheat flour
8 c. quick oats
2–3 c. coconut
2 tsp. soda
4 c. brown sugar
2 c. margarine

Mix all ingredients except margarine. Melt margarine and pour over other ingredients. Mix well. Bake at 250° for 45 minutes.

Mrs. David J. Troyer

Breakfast Fruit

3 lg. cooking apples, peeled,
    thickly sliced
$^1/_2$ c. pitted prunes
$^3/_4$ c. raisins
1 orange, peeled, sectioned
3 c. plus 3 Tbsp. water
$^1/_2$ c. sugar
$^1/_2$ tsp. ground cinnamon
2 Tbsp. cornstarch

In a saucepan, combine apples, prunes, raisins, orange, and 3 c. water. Bring to a boil. Reduce heat and simmer for 10 minutes. Stir in cinnamon and sugar. Combine cornstarch and remaining water. Stir into saucepan. Bring to a boil, stirring constantly. Cook for 2 minutes. Very good.

Mrs. Henry Mast

Fluffy Syrup

1 c. butter, softened
$^1/_2$ c. pancake syrup
1 egg
1$^1/_2$ c. powdered sugar

Beat all together for several minutes. Serve on pancakes, waffles, zucchini bread, etc.

Mrs. Levi (Susan) Troyer

Homemade Pancake Syrup

1 c. sugar
1 c. brown sugar
1$^3/_4$ c. water

Cook for 3 minutes, then simmer for 3 minutes. Thicken with a small amount of Mira-Clear. Add maple flavor and a pinch of salt. Delicious.

Fannie Weaver

tid bits

The bags inside cereal boxes can be cut to put between cookies when storing them in Tupperware. It saves on wax paper. I also use it to cover my bowl when I have dough rising. Sometimes coffee cake dough stick to the cloth. This paper can just be thrown away. It needs to be torn open at one end of the seams so it's big enough to cover.

—*Mrs. Atlee Hershberger*

Main Dishes

Grilled Chicken Breasts

1/2 bottle Italian dressing
8 boneless, skinless chicken breasts
2 tsp. seasoned meat tenderizer
1 tsp. paprika

Sprinkle seasoning over chicken and add dressing. Marinate for 6 hours or overnight. Grill about 4 minutes on each side, depending on thickness of breasts. Do not overcook.

Mrs. David A. Yoder

Delicious Baked Chicken

6 pcs. chicken
2 c. Ritz crackers, crushed
1/3 c. Parmesan cheese
1/2 Tbsp. seasoning salt
pepper
pinch garlic salt

Mix dry ingredients together. Brown butter in skillet and roll chicken in browned butter, then in cracker mixture. Put on baking sheet or a 9 X 13 pan and bake at 350° for 1 1/2– 1 3/4 hours.

Mrs. Neva J. Hershberger

Oven Barbecued Chicken

3–4 lbs. chicken pieces
1/3 c. chopped onions
3 Tbsp. butter
3/4 c. ketchup
1/3 c. vinegar
3 Tbsp. brown sugar
1/2 c. water
2 tsp. prepared mustard
1 Tbsp. Worcestershire sauce
1/4 tsp. salt
1/2 tsp. black pepper

Fry chicken and place in a baking dish. Sauté onions in butter until tender. Stir in remaining ingredients. Simmer, uncovered, for 15 minutes. Pour over chicken. Bake at 350° for 1 hour or until chicken is done.

Mrs. John E. Troyer

Chicken

25 lbs. chicken pieces
eggs, well beaten
4 c. flour
4 c. crushed soda crackers
3 Tbsp. salt
1 Tbsp. paprika
5 tsp. garlic salt
6 tsp. Accent
2 Tbsp. sugar
6 Tbsp. Lawry's seasoned salt
3 tsp. black pepper
$^1/_2$ c. butter
$^1/_2$–1 c. water

Combine flour, crushed crackers, salt, paprika, garlic salt, Accent, sugar, Lawry's seasoned salt, and black pepper. Dip chicken pieces in eggs, then in flour mixture. Fry in butter and enough oil to cover chicken until golden brown. Put foil into bottom of a large roaster, shiny side up. Fill with chicken. Add water. Put foil on top, shiny side down. Cut a few slits in top foil. Bake at 350° for 2$^1/_2$ hours or until tender. The crumb mixture can be made a week ahead of time, if needed. This works with any kind of meat, especially fish.

Mrs. Atlee C. Miller

Quick Chicken Stir-Fry

2 Tbsp. oil
3 boneless, skinless chicken breasts, halved
1 clove garlic, minced
1 c. red pepper strips
$^1/_4$ c. diced onion
1 c. broccoli florets
1 c. carrot slices
$^1/_2$ c. Miracle Whip
1 Tbsp. soy sauce
$^1/_2$ tsp. ground ginger

Heat oil in skillet. Cut chicken into strips and put into skillet with garlic. Stir-fry until chicken is tender. Add vegetables. Stir-fry until vegetables are tender. Reduce heat to medium and stir in Miracle Whip, soy sauce, and ginger. Simmer for 1 minute. Serve over rice. Yields 4 servings.

Mrs. Owen Yoder

tid bits

When an old recipe asks for butter the size of an egg, use 4 Tbsp.

Sweet 'N' Sour Chicken

3 Tbsp. brown sugar
3 Tbsp. vinegar
4 Tbsp. catsup
3 Tbsp. soy sauce
1 Tbsp. cornstarch
$^{1}/_{2}$ tsp. mustard
1 c. water
juice from 1 med. can pineapple
1 green pepper, diced
1 red pepper, diced
1 chopped onion
cooking oil
pineapple chunks
1 lb. boneless, skinless chicken, diced

Combine sugar, vinegar, catsup, soy sauce, mustard, cornstarch, pineapple juice, and water in a saucepan. Cook until thick. Stir-fry chicken in cooking oil in skillet over medium heat until done. Add peppers and onion. Stir-fry until tender. Add pineapple and sauce. Simmer for 10 minutes over low heat. Serve with rice or chow mein noodles.

Mrs. Myron Miller

Kentucky Fried Chicken

1 c. flour
1 egg
milk
salt
1 tsp. baking powder
seasoning, if desired

Cook 3–4 pounds chicken until tender, then drain. Dip in sauce, then roll in crushed saltines. Deep fat fry until crispy brown.

Mrs. Harry M. Miller

Chicken Nuggets

chicken breast, bite-sized pieces
1 c. flour
1 c. milk
1 egg

Make a batter with flour, milk, and egg. Dip chicken in batter, then roll in finely crushed crackers and deep fry. Serve with barbecue sauce.

Mrs. Junior (Dora) Miller

Turkey or Chicken Nuggets

1/3 c. flour
1/4 tsp. salt
1 1/2 tsp. vinegar
1 egg
1/4 tsp. soda
1/3 c. water
1/2 lb. breast meat, cubed

Combine flour, salt, vinegar, egg, soda, and water. Dip chicken in batter. Sprinkle with salt. Deep fat fry until golden brown. Use any kind of corn or vegetable oil.

Ada Nisley

Chicken Potpie

2 cans cream of chicken soup
2 (9 oz.) pkgs. frozen mixed vegetables, thawed
2 c. diced chicken
1 c. milk
2 eggs
2 c. Bisquick baking mix

Preheat oven to 400°. Mix soup, chicken, and vegetables. Put into a 9 X 13 pan. Mix milk, eggs, and Bisquick. Pour over chicken mixture. Bake for 30 minutes or longer until brown. If you have no Bisquick, use your own biscuit recipe and add a little more milk.

Mrs. Eli S. Miller

Country Chicken & Biscuits

2 1/2 c. diced chicken
1 1/2 c. Velveeta cheese
1–2 cans cream of chicken soup
10 oz. frozen mixed vegetables, cooked
2 c. cubed potatoes, cooked
salt
seasoned salt
oven-ready biscuits

Mix and bake at 350° for 20 minutes. Arrange biscuits on top. Leave uncovered and return to oven and bake 20 minutes longer or until biscuits are done.

Katie Hershberger

Chicken Rice Casserole

1 c. seasoned rice
2 1/2 c. chicken broth
1 can cream of mushroom soup
2 Tbsp. chopped onion, optional
2 c. diced chicken
2 c. celery or celery soup
Velveeta cheese

Cook rice in broth for 20 minutes. Mix with next four ingredients. Top with cheese. Bake at 350° for 30 minutes. Add crushed cornflakes mixed with butter. Bake, uncovered, for 15 minutes longer.

Mrs. Dan J.A. Yoder
Verna Yoder

Chicken Spaghetti

1 green pepper, diced
1 c. diced celery
1 med. onion, diced
1 c. chicken, cooked, boned
1 sm. jar pimientos
1 can mushrooms
1 lb. spaghetti
1 can cream of mushroom soup
1 can cream of chicken soup
1 lb. Velveeta cheese

Sauté pepper, celery, and onion in butter. Melt cheese with soups. Add sautéed vegetables. Cook spaghetti in chicken broth and water until tender. Drain. Mix together and bake in a greased pan. Top with grated cheddar cheese. Bake for 30–35 minutes.

Mary Hostetler

Chicken Supreme Casserole

2 c. cooked chicken
2 c. uncooked macaroni
2 cans cream of chicken soup
2 c. milk
1/2 med. onion, chopped, optional
1/2 tsp. salt
1/4 tsp. pepper
3 Tbsp. butter
1 c. grated Velveeta cheese

Mix all together. Refrigerate overnight. Bake for 1 1/2 hours at 350°.

Mrs. John E. Troyer

Dressing & Noodle Casserole

1 loaf bread, cubed, toasted
2 c. diced potatoes, cooked
1 c. chopped carrots, cooked
¹/₂ c. chopped celery, cooked
6 eggs, well beaten
2 c. chicken broth
2 c. milk
2 c. cooked, diced chicken
1 Tbsp. chicken base
pepper

Beat eggs. Add liquids, vegetables, salt, pepper, seasoning, and chicken. Stir in bread cubes. Fry in butter until done. Put dressing in bottom of roaster. Cover with Velveeta cheese. Cook 2 (8 oz.) pkgs. noodles in salt water. Put on top of dressing. Make 1 qt. chicken gravy and pour over noodles. Cover with cheese. Bake at 350° for 1 hour. One batch makes a Stanley roaster full. One and a half batches make a Lifetime roaster full.

Mrs. Arlene Hershberger

Potluck Chicken Casserole

4 c. cubed, cooked chicken
1 can cream of chicken soup
¹/₂ c. sour cream
1 c. crushed Ritz crackers
2 Tbsp. butter
1 tsp. celery salt

Mix chicken, soup, and sour cream. Put into a casserole. Bake for 30–35 minutes. Combine remaining ingredients. Sprinkle over chicken for the last 10 minutes of baking time. Bake uncovered.

Mrs. Roman E. Raber

Knepp

2 c. flour
3¹/₂ tsp. baking powder
¹/₂ tsp. salt
1 egg, beaten
2 Tbsp. butter, melted
¹/₃–¹/₂ c. milk

Drop batter by spoonful into boiling broth. Cover tightly and cook for 12–15 minutes. Do not lift cover until ready to serve. This is very good with ham broth!

Mrs. Andrew A. Troyer

Breaded Pork Chops

½ c. milk
1 egg, lightly beaten
6 pork chops
1½ c. crushed soda crackers

In a bowl, combine milk and egg. Dip pork chops into egg mixture, then coat with cracker crumbs. Put ½" oil into skillet. Fry pork chops until golden brown, about 8 minutes.

Mrs. Ivan Hershberger

Country Pork Ribs

pork ribs
1 c. catsup
4 Tbsp. vinegar
2 Tbsp. brown sugar
3 Tbsp. Worcestershire sauce
½ c. water
2 Tbsp. prepared mustard
1 tsp. dry onion or chopped onion

Cook pork ribs until almost tender. Drain and trim off excess fat. Put into a large casserole. Combine remaining ingredients. Heat and pour over ribs. Bake, covered, for 1 hour. Delicious.

Mrs. Reuben Mast

Spaghetti & Ham Casserole

½ c. margarine
¾ c. flour
2 c. chicken broth
2 c. evaporated milk
2½ c. milk
1½ c. Velveeta cheese
⅓ c. Parmesan cheese
2 Tbsp. mustard
3 Tbsp. ReaLemon
1 c. mayonnaise
1 sm. onion, chopped
salt to taste

Brown margarine and flour in saucepan. Add remaining ingredients. Pour this over 1½ lbs. cooked spaghetti and 2 lbs. diced ham. Add some chopped parsley for color and extra flavor. Bake at 375° for 1 hour. This can be prepared the day before serving.

Mrs. Mose (Elsie) Troyer

Underground Ham Casserole

4 c. diced ham
4 Tbsp. butter
$1/2$ c. onions
1 Tbsp. Worcestershire sauce
2 cans cream of mushroom soup
1–2 c. Velveeta cheese
1 c. milk
4 qt. mashed potatoes
1 pt. sour cream
fried, crumbled bacon, optional

Combine ham, butter, onions, and Worcestershire sauce. Heat until onions are soft. Put in bottom of roaster. In saucepan, heat soup, milk and cheese until melted. Place over top of ham. Mash potatoes and add sour cream. Do not add salt. Put potatoes on top of ham mixture. Add cheese on top. Bake for 45 minutes if baked right away, longer if prepared the day before.

Mrs. Roy N. Miller
Mary Esther Miller

Baked Rice & Sausage

2 lbs. bulk sausage
4 ribs celery, thinly sliced
1 onion, chopped
1 lg. green pepper, chopped
$1^1/2$ env. ($3/4$ c.) dry chicken
   noodle soup mix
$4^1/2$ c. water
1 can cream of chicken soup
1 c. uncooked rice
1 c. bread crumbs
4 Tbsp. butter or margarine

In a large skillet, cook sausage, celery, onion, and pepper over medium heat until meat is no longer pink and vegetables are tender. Drain. In a large saucepan, bring water to a boil; add dry soup mix. Reduce heat and simmer, uncovered, until noodles are tender. Stir in canned soup, rice, and sausage mixture. Mix well. Put into a greased 9 X 13 baking dish. Cover and bake at 350° for 40 minutes. Toss bread crumbs and butter. Sprinkle over rice mixture. Bake, uncovered, for 10–15 minutes or until rice is tender. Let set for 10 minutes before serving.

Mrs. Leroy (Barbara) Erb

Sweet & Sour Sausage & Rice

12 oz. uncooked sausage links,
   cut into bite-sized pieces
1 c. sugar
3 Tbsp. cornstarch
1 c. water
$1/2$ c. vinegar
$1/2$ c. ketchup
1 (8 oz.) can crushed pineapple,
   drained
hot cooked rice

In skillet, cook sausage until no longer pink. Set aside. Combine sugar, cornstarch, water, vinegar, and ketchup. Bring to a boil. Reduce heat and cook for 2 minutes or until thickened. Add pineapple and sausage. Heat through. Serve over rice. Yields 4 servings.

Susie Ellen Yoder

Barbecued Sausage

2 lbs. sausage links or patties
2 Tbsp. butter
$1/2$ c. catsup
2 Tbsp. mustard
2 Tbsp. brown sugar
1 tsp. Worcestershire sauce

Brown sausage in butter. Combine remaining ingredients. Arrange sausage in a baking dish. Brush sauce liberally on each piece. Cover and bake at 350° for 1 hour. Yields 8–10 servings.

Mrs. Jerry Erb

Cheesy Biscuit Casserole

$1^1/2$ lb. hamburger
2 cans cream of mushroom soup
16 oz. cream cheese
1 tsp. salt
$1/2$ c. chopped onion
$1/4$ c. catsup

Brown hamburger and onions. Add remaining ingredients. Bake in a 9 X 13 pan at 375° for 10 minutes. Mix 4 c. Bisquick, $1^1/4$ c. milk, and 1 c. shredded cheddar cheese with a fork. Spread on top of hamburger mixture and bake at 450° for 8–10 minutes or until golden brown. Experiment with different cheese!

Esta & Vesta Yoder

Ground Beef Casserole

1 can oven-ready biscuits
1 1/2 lb. hamburger
1/4 c. milk
1 tsp. salt
1/2 c. chopped onions
8 oz. cream cheese
1 can cream of mushroom soup
1/4 c. ketchup

Brown meat and onion. Combine cheese, soup, milk, salt, and ketchup. Pour into a casserole. Bake at 375° for 10 minutes. Put biscuits on top and bake for 15–20 minutes longer until biscuits are brown.

Mrs. Mahlon R. Yoder
Barbara Hershberger

One-Dish Oven Meal

sliced raw potatoes
1 lb. hamburger
sliced raw carrots
sliced onions
Velveeta cheese

Put into casserole in order listed. Cover with 1 can cream of mushroom soup and 1/2 c. milk. Bake in a covered dish at 350° for 1–1 1/2 hours.

Mrs. R.E. Weaver

Raw Vegetable Casserole

In a roaster or baking dish, put a thick layer of fresh cabbage. Add a layer of thickly sliced potatoes. Top with onions and carrots. Season with salt and pepper. Add more layers until pan is full. Other vegetables can be used, but use only cabbage on the bottom. Over top, put a layer of raw meat, preferably hamburger. Cover tightly with lid or foil. Bake at 375° for 1 1/2–2 hours. Top with cheese slices before serving.

Mrs. Henry A. Yoder

tid bits

Use baking soda to clean your oven, stove top, kitchen counters, and stainless steel.

Tater-Tot Casserole

1 lb. hamburger
4 c. mixed vegetables
1 can cream of mushroom soup
8 slices Velveeta cheese
3 c. Tater-Tots

Fry hamburger in skillet. Drain. Put meat in a casserole. Add mixed vegetables. Add cream of mushroom soup. Top with Velveeta cheese. Last, add Tater-Tots. Bake at 350° for 45–60 minutes.

Mrs. Monroe Yoder

Seven-Layer Casserole

1 lb. hamburger
2 c. potatoes, sliced
2 c. carrots, sliced
1 onion
1 c. chopped celery
1 can kidney beans
1 pt. green beans
1 can cream of mushroom soup
Velveeta cheese

Fry hamburger with salt and pepper. Put into casserole in order given. Bake at 350° for 1 hour.

Mrs. Monroe Yoder

Cheeseburger Pie

1 lb. ground beef
1 c. chopped onion
$1/2$ tsp. salt
1 c. shredded cheddar cheese
$1/2$ c. Bisquick
1 c. milk
2 eggs

Brown beef and onion, then drain grease. Stir in salt. Spread in greased pie plate. Sprinkle with cheese. Stir remaining ingredients together. Put on top of beef and cheese. Bake for 25 minutes or until knife comes out clean.

Mrs. Ivan A. Miller

Impossible Cheeseburger Pie

1 lb. ground beef or sausage
$^1/_2$ tsp. salt
3 eggs
1 c. pizza sauce
$^1/_2$ c. chopped onion
$^1/_4$ tsp. pepper
$^3/_4$ c. Bisquick
1$^1/_2$ c. milk
1 c. shredded cheese

Brown meat and onions together. Add salt and pepper and spread in cake pan. Beat milk, eggs, and Bisquick until smooth. Pour over meat and bake at 400° for 25–30 minutes. Top with pizza sauce and cheese. Bake until inserted knife comes out clean.

Mrs. Monroe Yoder

Impossible Cheeseburger Pie

1 lb. ground beef
1 c. chopped onion
$^1/_2$ tsp. salt
1 c. shredded cheddar cheese
1 c. milk
$^1/_2$ c. Bisquick
2 eggs

Brown beef and onions. Drain. Stir in salt. Spread in a greased 9" plate. Sprinkle with cheese. Stir remaining ingredients with forks until blended. Pour into plate. Bake for 25 minutes or until knife inserted in center comes out clean. Yields 8 servings.

Mrs. David A. Yoder

Cheeseburger Bake

1 lb. hamburger
$^1/_2$ c. chopped onion
1 can cheddar cheese soup
1 c. frozen mixed vegetables
$^1/_4$ c. milk
2 c. Bisquick
$^3/_4$ c. water
1 c. shredded cheese

Heat oven to 350°. Grease a 9 X 13 baking dish. Fry hamburger and onion until brown. Drain. Stir in soup, vegetables, and milk. Stir Bisquick and water until moistened. Spread batter in pan, then meat and vegetables. Sprinkle with cheese. Bake for 30 minutes or until done.

Mrs. David A. Yoder

Shepherd's Pie Deluxe

First Layer:
2¹/₂ c. milk
2¹/₂ c. water
¹/₂ c. margarine
1 tsp. salt
4 c. Hungry Jack potato flakes or
  your own mashed potatoes
Second Layer:
1¹/₂ lb. hamburger
1 can cream of mushroom soup
1 pkg. onion soup mix
Third Layer:
1 (16–20 oz.) pkg. mixed vegetables,
  cooked, drained
Fourth Layer:
Velveeta cheese
1 lg. can crushed French-fried onions

Bring milk, water, margarine, and salt to a boil. Add potato flakes. Stir until smooth. Put in bottom of a buttered casserole dish. Brown hamburger. Add soup and onion soup mix. Bring to a boil. Pour over potatoes. Cook vegetables. Drain and layer on top of hamburger. Place cheese slices on top of vegetables. Sprinkle crushed onions on top of cheese.

Mrs. Roy J. Wengerd

Spaghetti Bake

8–10 oz. spaghetti, broken,
  cooked, drained
1–2 c. shredded mozzarella cheese
1¹/₂ lb. ground beef,
  browned, drained
1 (4 oz.) can mushroom stems and
  pieces, drained
1 jar Ragu pizza quick sauce
¹/₃ c. grated Parmesan
pepperoni, optional

Put spaghetti in the bottom of a 9 X 13 pan. Cover with mozzarella cheese. Combine ground beef, mushrooms, and pizza sauce. Pour over cheese. Sprinkle with Parmesan cheese and top with pepperoni. Bake at 375° for 30 minutes. This is easy and fast.

Mrs. Allen Jay Beechy

Salsa Macaroni & Cheese

1 lb. ground beef
1½ c. salsa
1¾ c. water
2 c. uncooked macaroni
6–8 slices Velveeta cheese

Brown meat in large skillet. Drain. Stir in salsa and water. Bring to a boil. Stir in macaroni. Cover and reduce heat. Simmer for 10 minutes or until macaroni is tender. Add cheese. Stir until melted.

Mrs. Leroy A. Miller

No-Fuss Lasagna

1½ lb. hamburger, browned, salted
2 tsp. oregano
3 c. pizza sauce
2½ c. water
12 uncooked lasagna noodles
4 oz. cream cheese
¾ tsp. garlic powder
¼ c. milk
½ c. onion
1 c. mozzarella cheese

Combine hamburger, oregano, and 2½ c. pizza sauce. Layer noodles and meat mixture in a baking dish, beginning and ending with 4 noodles. Pour water over all. Spread with remaining pizza sauce. Cover thckly with foil and bake at 350° for 1½ hours or until noodles are tender. Mix cream cheese, garlic powder, milk, and onions. Spread over top. Sprinkle with cheese. Return to oven to melt cheese. May add a can of refried beans or chili beans to the hamburger mixture. May substitute 1 cup sour cream for cream cheese and milk.

Mrs. Mary Miller
Mrs. Atlee Hershberger

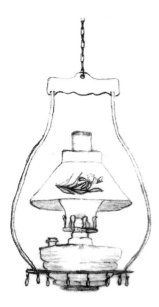

Bachelor Stew

2 potatoes, diced
1/2 c. celery
1 c. tomato soup
1 lb. lean hamburger
1 med. onion, chopped
1 can pork and beans
salt
pepper

Put potatoes, onion, and celery in bottom of casserole. Sprinkle with salt and pepper. Put beans on top, then tomato soup. Cover with raw hamburger. Bake at 350° for 2 hours.

Mrs. Ben N. Weaver

Stuffed Peppers

4 med. green peppers
2 c. browned hamburger
3/4 c. cooked rice
1/2 tsp. salt
1 egg, slightly beaten
2 Tbsp. minced onions
1 can cream of tomato soup

Remove tops and seeds from peppers. Steam shells for 5 minutes. Combine remaining ingredients, using only half of soup. Mix well. Fill peppers with mixture. Place in shallow baking pan. Bake at 375° for 30 minutes. Remove from oven and pour remaining soup over peppers and sprinkle with cheese. Return to oven and bake for 15 minutes.

Mrs. Ben N. Weaver

Husband's Delight

8 oz. cream cheese, softened
2 c. sour cream or 1 c. milk
1 sm. onion, chopped
1 1/2 lbs. ground beef
2 Tbsp. butter
16 oz. pizza sauce
1/2 tsp. Worcestershire sauce
10 oz. noodles
salt
pepper
Velveeta cheese

Mix cream cheese, sour cream, and onion. Brown meat in butter. Add pizza sauce, salt, pepper, and Worcestershire sauce. Cook noodles. In a 2-qt. casserole dish, layer cooked noodles, beef mixture, and sour cream mixture. Top with cheese. Bake at 350°.

Mrs. Marion Miller

Swedish Meatballs

1 qt. hamburger
1 qt. bulk sausage
1 tsp. salt
1 c. cracker crumbs
1 c. milk
Sauce:
4 c. catsup
$^1/_2$ c. vinegar
2 c. brown sugar
1 Tbsp. Worcestershire sauce
1 Tbsp. mustard
1 Tbsp. butter

Mix hamburger, sausage, salt, cracker crumbs, and milk. Shape into balls and fry. Mix sauce ingredients and pour over meatballs in a baking dish. Bake at 350° for 1 hour.

Mrs. Sylvanus Raber

Barbecued Meatballs

3 lbs. ground beef
1 can evaporated milk
1 c. oatmeal
1 c. cracker crumbs
2 eggs
$^1/_2$ c. chopped onions
$^1/_2$ tsp. garlic powder
2 tsp. salt
$^1/_2$ Tbsp. pepper
2 tsp. chili powder
Sauce:
2 c. catsup
1 c. brown sugar
$^1/_2$ Tbsp. liquid smoke
$^1/_2$ Tbsp. garlic powder
$^1/_4$ c. chopped onion

Combine meatball ingredients. This mixture will be soft. Shape into walnut-sized balls. Place in a single layer on wax paper-lined cookie sheet. Freeze until solid, then put into freezer bags until ready to use. Combine all sauce ingredients and stir until sugar is dissolved. Place frozen meatballs into a baking dish. Pour sauce over top. Bake at 350° for 1$^1/_2$ hours.

Mrs. Jerry Miller
Mrs. Wayne R. Weaver

tid bits

Skin-So-Soft will remove marks from floor, bookbags, glass, etc.

—*Mandy Troyer*

Meatballs

9 lbs. hamburger
6 c. oatmeal
6 eggs
1 can evaporated milk
6 tsp. salt
1 tsp. pepper
garlic powder
Sauce:
6 c. ketchup
2 c. brown sugar
6 Tbsp. Worcestershire sauce
barbecue sauce

Combine meatball ingredients and shape into balls. Mix sauce ingredients and spread over meatballs. Bake at 350°–375° for 1 hour, uncovered. When I make these for our family, I put some shredded cheese inside each meatball. Delicious!

Mrs. John A. Miller

Vegetable Meatballs

1 lb. hamburger
³/₄ c. grated potatoes
³/₄ c. grated carrots
1 sm. onion
salt
pepper
1 can cream of mushroom soup
¹/₂ c. water

Combine hamburger, potatoes, carrots, onion, salt, and pepper. Shape into small balls, then brown in oil. Put into a baking dish. Mix soup and water and pour over meatballs. Bake at 350°–400° for 30 minutes.

Clara Miller

Pizza Meat Loaf

2 lbs. hamburger
2 eggs
³/₄ c. tomato juice
³/₄ c. oatmeal
¹/₄ c. chopped onion
2 tsp. salt
¹/₄ tsp. pepper
1¹/₂ c. pizza sauce
1 c. mozzarella cheese

Combine all ingredients except pizza sauce and cheese. Mix thoroughly. Pack firmly in loaf pan. Bake at 350° for 45 minutes. Remove from oven and pour pizza sauce on top. Spread with cheese. Return to oven for 15 minutes or until done.

Mrs. Mahlon R. Yoder

Meat Loaf

3/4 c. oatmeal
2 eggs, beaten
1 c. milk
1/4 c. chopped onion
salt
pepper
1 1/2–2 lbs. hamburger
Sauce:
1/2 c. brown sugar
1 1/2 tsp. mustard
1 Tbsp. Worcestershire sauce
1/4 c. catsup

Mix well and bake. Top with sauce.

Mrs. David E. Beachy

Mock Ham Loaf

1 lb. hot dogs
2 lbs. ground beef
2 c. cracker crumbs
2 eggs
Glaze:
1 1/2 c. brown sugar
1 tsp. dry mustard
2 c. water
1 tsp. salt
2 tsp. vinegar
pepper
liquid smoke

Beat eggs and cracker crumbs. Grind up hot dogs and add to egg mixture with the ground beef. Add 1/2 c. syrup to mixture. Shape into a loaf. Heat syrup before pouring over loaf. Bake for 1 1/2 hours, basting with syrup every 15 minutes.

Mrs. Mary Miller
Mrs. David M. Miller

Salisbury Steaks

1 lb. hamburger
4 tsp. diced onion, optional
4 tsp. Worcestershire sauce
8 Tbsp. bread crumbs
4 eggs
1 tsp. salt
1 tsp. pepper

Knead all ingredients together until bread crumbs soak up liquid. Shape into desired size, like steaks. Fry until brown. Make a gravy with drippings and pour over steaks. Good with mashed potatoes. If you wish, bread crumbs may be browned slightly in butter before adding.

Mrs. Marion Miller

Upside-Down Pizza

2 lbs. hamburger or fresh sausage
2 c. pizza sauce
pepperoni
green peppers
mushrooms
2 c. sour cream
mozzarella cheese
crescent rolls

Brown meat. Add salt and pepper to taste. Add pizza sauce. Put in bottom of casserole pan. Layer with pepperoni, green peppers, and mushrooms. Bake at 350° for 30 minutes. Remove from oven and spread with sour cream. Put cheese on top of that. Top with crescent rolls. Bake until rolls are done.

Mrs. Andrew A. Troyer

Pizza Casserole

Crust:
1¹/₃ c. flour
2 tsp. baking powder
²/₃ tsp. salt
¹/₂ c. milk (scant)
¹/₄ c. Wesson oil
Filling:
2 lbs. hamburger
onions, optional
¹/₂ c. uncooked spaghetti
pizza sauce
1 c. sour cream
3 Tbsp. salad dressing (scant)
3 c. grated cheese

Mix dough ingredients and put in the bottom of a 9 X 13 pan. Fry hamburger with onions and put on top of dough. Cook spaghetti and drain. Put on top of hamburger. Spread pizza sauce on top. Mix sour cream, salad dressing, and cheese. Spread over top. Bake at 350°, uncovered, until crust is done. Yields 7–8 servings.

Susie Kuhns

Pizza Casserole Crust

1¹/₂ c. flour
2 tsp. baking powder
²/₃ tsp. salt
¹/₄ c. vegetable oil
¹/₂ c. milk

Press into bottom of a 9 X 13 pan. Put pizza casserole on top and bake. This may also be used with a vegetable casserole.

Mattie Yoder

Pizza Casserole

2 lbs. hamburger
1/2 c. green pepper
1 can cream of mushroom soup
2 c. pizza sauce
1 can mushrooms, undrained
1/4 tsp. garlic powder
1/4 tsp. oregano
1/4 c. Parmesan cheese
8 oz. noodles

Brown meat. Add salt, pepper, and onions to taste. Cook noodles for 3–5 minutes. Drain. Place noodles in bottom of baking dish. Add meat mixture and remaining ingredients. Top with pepperoni and mozzarella cheese. Bake at 350° for 30 minutes.

Mrs. Mahlon R. Yoder

Rice Pizza

2 c. cooked rice
2 Tbsp. melted butter
1 egg, beaten
1 qt. hamburger
2 c. pizza sauce
1/2 c. onion
1/2 tsp. salt
1/4 tsp. oregano
cheese
mushrooms

Combine rice, butter, and egg. Line the bottom of a 12" pizza pan with the rice mixture, pressing it with the back of a tablespoon. Make a rim around the edge about 1/4" high. Bake at 350° for 10 minutes. Arrange meat in rice crust. Mix sauce and onions. Spoon over meat. Top with cheese and return to oven until cheese is melted.

Ada Nisley

Bubble Up Pizza

3 cans biscuits, quartered
16 oz. pizza sauce
2 c. shredded cheese
pepperoni
chopped peppers
1/2 onion, chopped
1 can cream of mushroom soup
sausage and hamburger

Layer in a baking dish, saving some cheese for the top. Bake at 350° for 30–40 minutes.

Mrs. Aden Yoder
Mrs. Mose A. Miller
Mrs. Levi (Susan) Troyer

BLT Pizza

Prepare pizza crust and put in pan. Spoon a layer of pizza sauce on top. Sprinkle with mozzarella cheese and plenty of fried, crumbled bacon. Bake until done. Immediately after removing it from the oven, spread with mayonnaise. Top with shredded lettuce and diced tomatoes.

Mrs. Eddie E. Miller

Zucchini Pizza

3 c. peeled, diced zucchini
$^1/_2$ c. Parmesan cheese
$^1/_2$ tsp. salt
$^1/_2$ c. oil
$^1/_2$ c. chopped green pepper
$^1/_4$ tsp. garlic powder
1 c. chopped pepperoni
1 c. Bisquick
$^1/_2$ Tbsp. oregano
4 eggs, beaten
$^1/_2$ Tbsp. onion
2 Tbsp. parsley

Combine everything except eggs and oil. Beat eggs. Add oil. Stir into mixture. Pour into a 9 X 13 pan. Bake at 350° for 30–35 minutes.

Mrs. Wayne R. Weaver

Pan Pizza

$1^1/_4$ c. Thesco flour
$^1/_2$ tsp. salt
$^1/_2$ tsp. sugar
$^1/_2$ c. water
$^1/_2$ Tbsp. yeast
1 Tbsp. oil

Mix and let rise slightly. Put into a large iron pan and put on toppings. Let rise for 30 minutes. Bake at 375° for 35 minutes.

Mrs. Delbert Miller

Taco Pizza

1 lb. ground beef
1 pkg. taco seasoning
1 c. water
2 (12") prebaked Italian
   bread shell crusts
3/4 c. salsa
2 c. coarsely crushed tortilla chips
2 c. shredded cheddar cheese
2 med. tomatoes, chopped
1 c. shredded lettuce

In a saucepan, cook beef over med. heat until no longer pink. Drain. Add taco seasoning and water. Bring to a boil. Reduce heat and simmer, uncovered, for 10 minutes. Set aside. Place crusts on ungreased pizza pans. Combine beans and salsa. Spread over crusts. Top with beef mixture, chips, and cheese. Bake at 350° for 13–16 minutes or until cheese is melted. Sprinkle with tomatoes and lettuce. Yields 2 pizzas.

Mrs. Atlee (Lizzie) Raber

Easy Taco Skillet Meal

1 lb. hamburger
2 c. tomato juice
1 c. uncooked rice
1 c. shredded cheddar cheese
3/4 c. water
2 Tbsp. brown sugar
1 pkg. taco seasoning

Brown hamburger. Add tomato juice, water, seasonings, and rice. Simmer for 20 minutes or until rice is tender, stirring several times. Top with cheese. Serve with shredded lettuce, onions, sour cream, and salsa.

Clara Miller

Taco Quiche

2 lbs. ground beef
1/2 pkg. taco seasoning
4 eggs
3/4 c. milk
1 1/4 c. biscuit baking mix
pepper
1/2 c. sour cream
3 c. chopped lettuce
1/4 c. green onion
2 c. shredded cheddar cheese

In a skillet brown beef. Drain. Add taco seasoning. Spoon meat into a greased 9 X 13 baking dish. In a bowl, beat eggs and milk. Add biscuit mix. Pour over meat. Bake, uncovered, at 400° for 20–25 minutes or until golden brown. Spread sour cream on top. Top with lettuce, onion, and cheese.

Taco Bake

Dough:
2 c. flour
3 tsp. baking powder
1 tsp. salt
4 Tbsp. shortening
³/₄ c. milk
Filling:
2 lbs. hamburger
1 sm. onion
1 pkg. taco seasoning
1 can kidney beans, drained
¹/₃ c. brown sugar
1 tomato
1 green pepper
¹/₂ c. sour cream
¹/₃ c. salad dressing
cheddar cheese

Mix dough ingredients together. Spread into a 9 X 13 pan. Fry hamburger, onion, and taco seasoning. Add beans and brown sugar. Spread on top of dough. Chop tomato and green pepper. Put on top of hamburger mixture. Mix sour cream and salad dressing together. Spread over all. Top with cheese. Bake at 350° for 35 minutes or until done.

Mrs. Atlee Hershberger

Mush Taco

mashed potatoes
hamburger, browned
lettuce, chopped
tomatoes, chopped
shredded cheddar cheese
cheese sauce
Doritos, crushed
taco sauce

Add salt, pepper, and taco seasoning to hamburger. Make cheese sauce with cheddar cheese soup, milk, and Velveeta cheese. Layer ingredients in order listed.

Mrs. Allen Jay Beechy

Taco Shells

1¹/₂ c. cold water
1 c. flour
¹/₂ c. cornmeal
¹/₄ tsp. salt
1 egg

Mix all together with whisk. Fry like pancakes. Pour ¹/₄ c. dough in pan. Rotate and tilt pan to make a nice round ring. Serve with hamburger, lettuce, onions, cheese, tomatoes, and taco sauce or salsa. Wrap and serve.

Mrs. Myron J. Miller

Favorite Mexican Lasagna

1 box lasagna noodles
1 lb. lean ground beef
1 can refried beans
2 tsp. dried oregano
1 tsp. ground cumin
$^3/_4$ tsp. garlic powder
$^3/_4$ c. finely sliced green onions
1 can sliced black olives, optional
$2^1/_2$ c. lukewarm water
$2^1/_2$ c. medium salsa
4 c. sour cream
2 c. shredded mozzarella cheese

Combine beef, seasonings, and beans. Put a single layer of noodles in a deep casserole. Spread half of beef mixture over noodles. Top with another single layer of noodles and remaining beef mixture. Again top with a single layer of noodles. Combine water and salsa. Pour over everything. Cover tightly. Bake at 350° for $1^1/_2$ hours or until tender. Mix sour cream, onions, olives, and shredded mozzarella cheese. Just before serving, spread over top. Return to oven for 10 minutes or until cheese is melted.

Esta & Vesta Yoder

Mexican Chicken Roll-Ups

$2^1/_2$ c. cooked, diced chicken
$^1/_2$ c. sour cream
$1^1/_2$ tsp. taco seasoning
$^1/_2$ can cream of mushroom soup
1 c. cheddar cheese
1 sm. onion
$^1/_2$ c. salsa
10 (7") flour tortillas
Topping:
1 c. sour cream
$^1/_2$ can cream of mushroom soup
$1^1/_2$ tsp. taco seasoning

Combine ingredients and place $^1/_3$ cup filling in each tortilla. Roll up and place seam side down in a 9 X 13 pan. Pour topping over tortillas. Bake at 350° for 30 minutes. Sprinkle $^1/_2$ cup cheddar cheese over topping.

Mrs. Alvin I. Yoder

Cheesy Enchiladas

Cheese Sauce:
$^1/_2$ c. margarine
4 Tbsp. flour
3 c. milk
8 oz. Velveeta cheese
1 c. sour cream
1 can nacho cheese soup, optional
Meat Mixture:
2 lbs. hamburger, browned
1 med. onion
2 Tbsp. flour
1 tsp. salt
1 c. pizza sauce
$^1/_2$ tsp. oregano
10–12 flour tortillas
2 c. grated cheese

Place meat mixture and grated cheese in tortillas. Roll up and place in a 9 X 13 greased pan. Pour cheese sauce over tortillas. Bake at 350° for 20–30 minutes.

Mrs. Ivan Hershberger

Enchiladas

1 pkg. flour tortillas
$^3/_4$ c. chopped onion
$^3/_4$ c. chopped mushrooms, optional
4 c. Colby or cheddar cheese
1 green pepper, optional
1 lb. hamburger
1 pkg. taco seasoning
1 can refried beans
Sauce:
2 cans cream of mushroom soup
2 c. sour cream
1 sm. can green chilies, optional

Brown hamburger and onions. Add remaining ingredients and heat. Put in tortillas and wrap up. Put half of soup and sour cream mixture in bottom of pan. Lay enchiladas on top. Put remaining soup mixture on top of enchiladas. Cover with shredded cheese. Bake at 350° for 20–30 minutes until cheese is melted. Serve with shredded lettuce and cut up tomato or with salsa and taco sauce. Note: Use only 1 can soup and 1 c. sour cream if you don't want it too saucy.

Mrs. David J. Troyer

Chicken Enchiladas

3 c. diced chicken
$1/2$ c. salsa
$1/2$ c. sour cream
chopped onion, optional
flour tortillas
Topping:
1 can cream of chicken soup
$1/2$ can milk
Velveeta cheese slices
mozzarella, cheddar, or Swiss cheese

Combine chicken, salsa, and sour cream. Wrap in tortillas and put into a baking pan, seam side down. Heat cream of chicken soup, milk, and Velveeta cheese until cheese is melted. Pour over tortillas. Top with shredded cheese. Bake at 350° for 20–30 minutes.

Mrs. Levi (Susan) Troyer

Burritos

Filling:
2 lbs. hamburger, browned
1 (16 oz.) can refried beans
2 pkgs. taco seasoning
Sauce:
2 cans cream of mushroom soup
2 c. sour cream

Mix filling ingredients and fill 10 tortillas. Mix sauce ingredients. Spread half in bottom of baking dish. Place burritos on top, then pour remaining sauce over top. Sprinkle with cheese. Bake at 325° for 1 hour.

Mrs. Roy M. Kuhns

Wet Burrito Casserole

1 lb. hamburger
onion
1 c. salsa
1 green pepper
$1/2$ pkg. taco seasoning
1 can cream of mushroom soup
$1^1/2$ c. sour cream

Fry hamburger, onion, and green pepper together. Add taco seasoning and salsa. Combine soup and sour cream. Pour half of soup mixture into a 9 X 13 pan. Fill each tortilla with 1 Tbsp. meat mixture. Roll up and place in pan side by side. Top with remaining soup mixture. Bake at 350° for 20 minutes. Add 1 c. taco-flavored cheese and 2 c. cheddar cheese. Bake for 10 minutes more. Serve with lettuce, tomatoes, and sour cream.

Mrs. Arlene Hershberger
Mrs. Alvin H. Hershberger

Frankfurter Bake

2 lbs. frankfurters
16 oz. noodles
2 1/2 c. cheese
2 c. milk
1/2 c. butter
1 tsp. salt
1/2 c. brown sugar
1/2 c. salad dressing
2 Tbsp. mustard
4 Tbsp. flour

In a large kettle, cook noodles until soft. Drain noodles and return to kettle. Stir in cheese, milk, butter, and salt until well mixed. Pour into a greased roaster. Combine frankfurters with remaining ingredients and spoon evenly over noodles. Bake at 375° for 25 minutes or until hot and bubbly.

Mrs. David J. Troyer
Mrs. Andy A. Troyer

My Casserole

1 1/2 qts. noodles
1 qt. frozen peas, thawed
1 lb. frankfurters, 1 1/4" slices
1 med. onion, chopped, cooked
4 stems celery, cooked
Sauce:
1 qt. milk
6 Tbsp. flour
1 lb. Velveeta cheese

Cook noodles, but not too soft. Combine with other ingredients. For sauce, bring milk to a boil. Combine flour with enough milk to make a paste. Add to hot milk. Add Velveeta cheese. Pour over noodle mixture and mix. This casserole freezes well. It can be made one day to bake on the next. Bake at 275° for 1 1/4 hours. Top with buttered bread crumbs before serving. Yields 5–6 quarts.

Mrs. David Yoder

Tuna Zucchini Burgers

1 (6 oz.) can tuna, drained
1 c. grated zucchini
1 egg
1/2 c. fine cracker crumbs
1 tsp. salt
1/4 tsp. pepper
1 Tbsp. mustard

Combine all ingredients and form patties. Fry to taste. For variety, add Parmesan cheese or bake in a loaf pan instead of frying.

Mrs. Mary Miller

Pizza Burgers

3 lbs. hamburger, browned, drained
2 c. pizza sauce or tomato soup
1 sm. onion, chopped
chopped pepper, optional
1 tsp. salt
1/2 tsp. pepper
1 Tbsp. oregano
pepperoni slices
mozzarella or Velveeta cheese

Mix first 7 ingredients and spread on sandwich bun halves. Next, put pepperoni slices on, and top with a slice of cheese. Bake at 350° until cheese has melted. Yields 2–3 dozen.

Mrs. Ben J. Troyer
Mrs. Dennis (Rosie) Yoder
Mrs. Atlee Hershberger

Grilled Pineapple Burgers

2 lbs. ground beef
3 Tbsp. Italian salad dressing
1 tsp. salt
1/2 tsp. pepper
1 (15 1/4 oz.) can pineapple slices, drained
8 slices bacon
3/4 c. barbecue sauce
1/4 c. brown sugar
1/4 c. honey
1 Tbsp. lemon juice

Mix ground beef, Italian dressing, salt, and pepper. Shape into 8 patties. Press a pineapple slice into each patty. Wrap each patty with a bacon slice, securing bacon with a toothpick. Mix barbecue sauce, sugar, honey, and lemon juice. Place patties in a covered dish. Pour barbecue mixture on top. Refrigerate for 2 hours or overnight. Grill patties, basting with barbecue sauce as you grill.

Mrs. Roy E. Mast

BBQ Hamburgers

Mrs. Edward M. Hershberger

2 lb. hamburger
1 onion
2 Tbsp. brown sugar
1 pkg. crackers
2 Tbsp. mustard
1 tsp. Worcestershire sauce
1 tsp. salt
1 egg

Stuffed Burgers

Stuffing:
4 slices bacon, fried, crumbled
1/4 c. chopped onion
1 (4 oz.) can mushrooms, finely diced
Burgers:
1 lb. ground beef
1 lb. bulk sausage
1/4 c. Parmesan cheese
1/2 tsp. black pepper
1/4 tsp. garlic powder
2 Tbsp. steak sauce

Divide into 16 burgers. Divide stuffing onto 8 burgers and put remaining 8 burgers on top. Press edges to seal. Put on grill. Baste with your favorite barbecue sauce.

Mrs. Andrew A. Troyer

Hamburgers to Grill

5 lbs. hamburger
1/2 c. onions
2 slices bread
1 c. water
2 tsp. salt
1/2 tsp. pepper
1 Tbsp. soy sauce
diced peppers

Soak bread in water. Mix all ingredients. Put on grill. Top with barbecue sauce. Serve with salsa.

Mrs. Roman E. Raber

Barbecue Sandwiches

1 1/2 lbs. ground beef
1/2 c. water
3 Tbsp. chopped onion
3 Tbsp. brown sugar
2 Tbsp. barbecue sauce
2 Tbsp. vinegar
1 1/2 c. ketchup
pepper
3/4 c. rolled oats

Mix all together except oats. Cook until meat is done. Add oats and cook a little more. Serve on bread or buns.

Mrs. Eli N. Hershberger

Barbecued Beef Sandwiches

1/2 c. ketchup
2 tsp. mustard
2 Tbsp. brown sugar
2 Tbsp. vinegar
2 tsp. Worcestershire sauce

Mix with 1 qt. chunk meat.

Barbecued Ham Sandwiches

1/2 c. catsup
1/2 c. Open Pit barbecue sauce
1/2 c. water
1/4 c. vinegar
3 Tbsp. brown sugar
1 Tbsp. Worcestershire sauce
4 lb. chipped chopped ham

Simmer for 5 minutes. Bake at 300°
for 1 hour.

Mrs. David A. Yoder

Bluegill Parmesan

1/4 c. butter, melted
1/2 dry bread crumbs
1/3 c. grated Parmesan cheese
2 Tbsp. fresh parsley or
　1 tsp. dried parsley
1 tsp. salt
1/2 tsp. paprika
1/4 tsp. pepper
1 lb. fresh or frozen perch or
　bluegill fillets, thawed

Place butter in a shallow dish.
Combine bread crumbs, cheese, and
seasonings. Dip fillets in butter, then
coat with crumb mixture. Place a
single layer in a tinfoil-covered,
greased pan. Bake, uncovered, at
350° for 20 minutes. Turn, then bake
for 10 minutes more.

Mary Esther Miller

Rice & Broccoli Melt

1 (16 oz.) pkg. frozen broccoli,
   thawed, drained
3 Tbsp. chopped onions
1 clove minced garlic
1 Tbsp. vegetable oil
2 c. cooked hot rice
$^1/_3$ c. mayonnaise
2 Tbsp. soy sauce
$^1/_2$ c. shredded cheddar cheese
$^3/_4$ c. French-fried onions

Preheat oven to 350°. Mix broccoli, onions, garlic, oil, rice, mayonnaise, and soy sauce. Put into a $1^1/_2$-qt. casserole dish. Top with cheese and sprinkle with French-fried onions. Cover and bake for 25 minutes or until cheese has melted.

Mrs. Owen Yoder

Dressing

14 eggs
4 loaves bread, cubed, toasted
$2^1/_2$ qts. chicken
2 qts. chicken broth
2 Tbsp. salt
6 c. milk
4 c. celery
4 c. carrots
1 Tbsp. seasoned salt

In a large bowl, beat eggs and add other ingredients. Fry in butter. Can fry until about done, then cool and put into containers and freeze. Yields 80 servings.

Mrs. Aden Chupp

Dressing

2 qts. potatoes, cubed
1 qt. carrots, cubed
1 qt. celery, chopped
1 sm. onion
15 eggs
$1^1/_2$ qt. chicken broth
5 Tbsp. chicken base
3 Tbsp. Lawry's seasoned salt
2 Tbsp. black pepper
$^3/_4$ gal. milk
$1^1/_2$ qt. cooked, boned chicken
4 (20 oz.) loaves bread, cubed

Cook potatoes, carrots, celery, and onion until soft. Drain. Beat together eggs, broth, chicken base, Lawry's, black pepper, and milk. Add cooled vegetables and chicken. Toast bread cubes in butter. Add to dressing. Bake or fry in butter. This can be mixed and frozen in small containers according to your family size, before baking or frying. Yields 75 servings.

Mrs. Paul E. Miller

Amish Dressing

1 loaf bread, cubed, toasted
6 eggs, beaten
2$^1/_2$ c. milk
2 c. canned carrot/celery mix
2 c. chicken bits and broth
2 tsp. finely chopped onions
2 tsp. chicken base
1 Tbsp. parsley
salt
pepper

Fry in butter until browned or bake at 325° for 1 hour and 45 minutes.

Mrs. Andrew A. Troyer

Homemade Noodles

2 c. egg yolks
2 whole eggs
1 c. water (scant)
1$^1/_2$ tsp. salt
flour

Beat eggs, water, and salt together. Add flour gradually and beat with egg beater until too thick, then add more flour and work with hands until dough is very firm. Put small bunches of dough through noodle maker to desired thickness. Lay out to dry a little, then put through noodle maker again to cut to desired width. Lay out until completely dry. Store.

Mrs. Andrew A. Troyer

Potatoes Delight

4 lg. baking potatoes
1 c. broccoli stems
$^1/_2$ c. chopped fresh mushrooms
$^1/_4$ c. grated carrot
$^1/_4$ c. sliced green onions
$^1/_4$ c. shredded red cabbage
1$^1/_2$ c. diced, fully cooked ham
$^1/_4$ c. butter
sour cream, optional

Bake potatoes in oven until done. In a skillet, sauté the next six ingredients in butter for 5 minutes or until vegetables are tender. Serve over hot potatoes. Top with sour cream, if desired. Yields 4 servings.

Mrs. Lovina Schlabach

Parmesan Potato Round-Up

1/2 c. butter, melted
1/4 c. flour
1/4 c. Parmesan cheese
salt
pepper
Lawry's seasoned salt
6 med. potatoes, each sliced
    into 4 rounds

Pour butter into a 10 X 15 baking pan. In plastic bag, combine flour, cheese, salt, and seasonings. Shake a few potato slices at a time. Place potatoes in baking dish. Bake at 375° for 30 minutes. Serve with sour cream.

Mrs. Mahlon R. Yoder
Barbara Hershberger

Creamy Potato Sticks

1/4 c. all-purpose flour
1/2 tsp. salt
1 1/2 c. milk
1 can cream of celery soup
1/2 lb. processed American cheese
5–6 lg. baking potatoes, peeled
1 c. onion, chopped
paprika

In a saucepan, combine flour and salt. Gradually whisk in milk until smooth. Bring to a boil. Cook and stir for 2 minutes. Remove from heat. Whisk in soup and cheese until smooth. Set aside. Cut potatoes into 4" X 1/2" X 1/2" sticks. Place in a greased 9 X 13 baking dish. Sprinkle with onions. Top with cheese sauce. Bake, uncovered, at 350° for 55–60 minutes or until potatoes are tender. Sprinkle with paprika.

Cheesy Potatoes

1 1/2 lb. sour cream
8 oz. cream cheese
1/2 c. butter
Velveeta cheese, cubed
salt, optional
10–12 lbs. potatoes, peeled, cooked,
    and cubed or shredded

Combine all ingredients except potatoes. Pour over potatoes and mix. Pour into baking dish and bake, uncovered, at 350° for 1 hour.

Mrs. Fred A. Raber

Potluck Potatoes

2 lbs. cooked potatoes
4 Tbsp. butter
2 c. sour cream
1/4 tsp. pepper
1/2 c. chopped onions
1 can cream of mushroom soup
2 c. Velveeta cheese
2 c. crushed corn flakes

Heat butter and cheese in skillet until melted. Pour over potatoes and mix. Add sour cream, onions, and soup. Mix corn flakes with 1/4 c. butter. Put these on top of potatoes and bake at 350° for 45 minutes.

Mrs. Jonathan Raber

Scalloped Potatoes

5 lbs. potatoes, cooked, diced
1–3 lbs. ham, cubed
1 sm. onion
Sauce:
2/3 c. butter
2/3 c. flour
1/2 tsp. Worcestershire sauce
1/4 tsp. pepper
1 Tbsp. salt
1 can cream of mushroom soup
1 qt. milk
1/4–1/2 lb. Velveeta cheese

Prepare sauce like a white sauce, then add cheese and let it melt.

Mrs. Susan Miller

Holiday Mashed Potatoes

12 med. potatoes
8 oz. cream cheese
1/4 c. butter
1/2 c. sour cream
2 eggs, beaten
1/2 c. milk
1 tsp. salt
pepper
1/4 c. chopped onions, optional
baking powder, optional

Cook and mash potatoes. Add cream cheese in small bits to hot potatoes. Add butter and sour cream. Mix well. Combine milk and eggs. Add and mix well. Add salt, pepper, and onions. Beat until light and fluffy. Place in a 9" round casserole and refrigerate several hours or overnight. Bake at 350° for 45 minutes.

Mrs. Henry Mast

Cheesy Potato Patties

2 c. leftover mashed potatoes
1 egg, beaten
1 Tbsp. flour

Shape into thin patties. Put chopped onions and cheddar cheese on each. Top with another patty and seal edges. Brown in butter on both sides.

Mrs. Roman E. Raber

Ranch Potato Patties

4 c. leftover mashed potatoes
$1/4$ c. flour
2 eggs, beaten
1 tsp. seasoned salt
$1/4$ tsp. onion powder
$1^1/2$ Tbsp. Ranch dressing mix

Drop on a greased cookie sheet. Bake at 400° for 8–12 minutes. About half through baking time, sprinkle top with cheddar cheese and paprika.

Mrs. Roman E. Raber

Stuffed Baked Potatoes

2 lg. baking potatoes
2 Tbsp. butter
$2/3$ c. cheddar cheese
1 Tbsp. chives, optional
salt
pepper
3 bacon slices, fried, crumbled
$1/2$ c. sour cream

Bake potatoes until tender and skins are crisp, about $1^1/4$ hours. Cut potatoes in half lengthwise and scoop out centers in a bowl. Add butter and mash until smooth. Fold in cheese, sour cream, chives, salt, pepper, and bacon. Mound mixture in potato shells and bake for 15 minutes more.

Mrs. Mary Miller

Crusty Baked Potatoes

6 med. potatoes
4 Tbsp. melted butter
$1/2$ c. cracker crumbs
1 tsp. salt
seasoned salt

Wash potatoes and dry. Roll in melted butter, then in crumbs. Place in a greased pan and bake at 350° for 1 hour.

Mrs. David M. Miller

Twice-Baked Potatoes

6 lg. baking potatoes
$^1/_2$ c. butter, softened
$^3/_4$–1 c. milk or cream
3 Tbsp. crumbled, fried bacon
1 Tbsp. minced onion
1 Tbsp. snipped chives
$^1/_2$ tsp. salt
pepper
1$^1/_2$ c. shredded cheddar cheese,
　divided
paprika

Bake potatoes at 400° for 60 minutes or until soft. Cut a lengthwise slice from the top of the potatoes. Scoop out the pulp and place in a bowl. Mash potatoes and butter. Blend in milk or cream, bacon, onion, chives, salt, pepper, and 1 c. cheese. Refill potato shell. Top with remaining cheese and sprinkle with paprika. Bake at 375° for 25–30 minutes or until heated through. Yields 6 servings.

Katie Yoder

Cornmeal Mush

3 c. cornmeal
$^1/_2$ c. pastry flour
1$^1/_2$ c. milk
2 qt. boiling water
1 tsp. salt

Bring water to a boil. Mix cornmeal, flour, salt, and milk to make a paste. Remove water from heat. Slowly add paste. Stir well. Cook on low heat for 30 minutes. Pour into Pyrex bread pans to mold. When cold, slice and fry on greased griddle. Serve with maple syrup or apple butter.

Mrs. David A. Yoder
Mrs. Andrew A. Troyer

Calico Beans to Can

3 lbs. bacon, fried
3 lbs. hamburger, fried
1–2 lg. onions
5 pts. butter beans or lima beans
5 pts. kidney beans
5 qts. pork and beans
Sauce:
6 c. brown sugar
3 c. ketcup
12 Tbsp. vinegar

Drain all beans slightly. Mix all top ingredients together in a large bowl. Add the bacon grease. Salt to taste. Mix sauce and add. Cold pack for 2 hours. Very good. Yields about 30 pints.

Mrs. Ivan Hershberger

Baked Beans

1 (32 oz.) can pork and beans
1 (16 oz.) can kidney beans
1 (16 oz.) can butter beans
1 sm. onion, chopped
1 lb. bacon, fried, crumbled
$^1/_4$ c. bacon drippings
1 c. catsup
1 c. brown sugar
1 Tbsp. prepared mustard

Mix all together and stir gently. Bake in a casserole dish at 350° for 50–60 minutes. We love to top these beans with crushed corn chips and sour cream. And for something different and tasty, add 1 (15$^1/_2$ oz.) can pineapple tidbits before baking. Delicious! Yields 8 servings.

Mrs. Abe A. Yoder

Baked Beans

1 (32 oz.) can pork and beans
1 (16 oz.) can kidney beans, drained
1 (16 oz.) can butter beans, drained
1 sm. onion, chopped
1 lb. bacon, fried, crumbled
$^1/_4$ c. bacon drippings
1 c. catsup
1 c. brown sugar
1 Tbsp. prepared mustard
1 (15 oz.) can pineapple tidbits

Mix all together and stir gently. Bake in a casserole dish at 350° for 50–60 minutes.

Mrs. Alvin I. Yoder

Three-Bean Casserole

1 can kidney beans
1 can lima or butter beans
3 cans pork and beans
1 c. catsup
$^1/_2$ lb. bacon, cut up
2 sm. onions, chopped
1 c. brown sugar
1 tsp. mustard

Brown bacon. Drain most of drippings. Add onions and cook for a while. Add brown sugar, catsup, and mustard; mix. Pour all beans together without draining them. Pour bacon mixture over them and bake at 350° for 1 hour. Can be prepared the day before for baking the next day. Leftovers freeze well.

Mrs. Levi (Susan) Troyer

Lima Beans

1/2 lb. bacon
2 onions, chopped
3 reg. cans Seaside lima beans
2 cans tomato soup
1 lb. hamburger
1 c. brown sugar

Fry bacon, onions, and hamburger together. Drain grease. Add remaining ingredients. Bake at 325° for 1 1/2 hours.

Mrs. Atlee Hershberger

Baked Zucchini

6 c. sliced zucchini
1/4 c. chopped onion
1 can cream of chicken soup
1 c. sour cream
1 c. shredded carrots
6 pcs. bread
1/2 c. melted butter
chicken seasoning

In saucepan, cook sliced zucchini, onions, and carrots for 5 minutes. Drain well. Combine soup and sour cream. Fold in vegetables. Cube bread and toss with melted butter and chicken seasoning. Spread half of this in a pan and spoon vegetable mixture on top. Sprinkle remaining bread on top.

Mrs. John B. Beachy

Zucchini Fritters

2 c. peeled, grated zucchini
2 med. carrots, grated
4 Tbsp. chopped onion
1 c. flour
salt
pepper
1 tsp. seasoned salt

Mix all together. Batter will be very stiff. Brown butter in a large skillet. Drop batter by tablespoons. Flatten to form patties. Brown until crisp. Serve immediately. Good served with salad dressing.

Mrs. Wayne R. Weaver
Mrs. R.E. Weaver

Scalloped Corn

1 can creamed corn
2 Tbsp. flour
2 Tbsp. sugar
2 eggs, slightly beaten
$^1/_2$ pkg. Ritz crackers
$^1/_4$ c. butter

Combine corn, flour, sugar, and eggs. Pour into a pan. Mix crackers and butter. Pour over top. Bake at 350° for 25 minutes. For 4 batches, bake 45 minutes.

Susie Kuhns

Green Bean Casserole

4 Tbsp. butter, melted
4 Tbsp. flour
$^1/_4$ tsp. salt
2 tsp. sugar
2 Tbsp. chopped onion
1 c. sour cream
2 qts. green beans, cooked or canned
Swiss cheese, grated
2 Tbsp. butter, melted
2 c. crushed corn flakes

Combine butter, flour, salt, sugar, and onion. Sauté until browned. Stir together sour cream and green beans and blend with above mixture. In a casserole dish, alternate layers of green beans and cheese, ending with cheese. Combine butter and corn flakes. Put on top of casserole. Bake at 350° for 25 minutes or until heated through.

Mrs. John B. Beachy

Barbecued Green Beans

10 slices bacon
$^1/_4$ c. chopped onions
$^3/_4$ c. catsup
$^1/_2$ c. brown sugar
3 tsp. Worcestershire sauce
$^3/_4$ Tbsp. salt
4 c. green beans

Fry bacon, then break into pieces. Sauté onions in bacon drippings. Combine catsup, brown sugar, Worcestershire sauce, and salt. Add onions and bacon pieces. Pour over green beans and mix lightly. Bake in a 1-qt. covered casserole dish at 300° for 35–40 minutes or until heated through. Yields 4–6 servings.

Mrs. Jerry Erb

Sweet and Sauerkraut

Melt 2 Tbsp. butter in a 9" frying pan. Chop and sauté as much onion and green pepper as desired. Add 2–3 Tbsp. brown sugar. Drain 1 qt. homemade sauerkraut. Heat and serve with sausage, corned beef, or ribs.

Barbara Coblentz

Chicken Gravy

Big Batch:
6 egg yolks
2³/₄ c. flour
1 c. cornstarch
6 qt. chicken broth
Small Batch:
2 egg yolks
¹/₂ c. flour
2 Tbsp. cornstarch
1 qt. broth

Add water to make a thick dough. Put 1 batch in a 13-qt. mixing bowl. Strain before putting in bowl. Heat chicken broth. Add 2 Tbsp. chicken base to large batch, and salt as needed. Slowly add the broth to the dough, beating constantly with wire whip. Some water may be added if it's too thick. Do not bring to a boil again, and do not cover tightly. This is very smooth and good.

Amanda Mast

Dandelion Gravy

1 Tbsp. butter, melted
3 Tbsp. flour
milk
3 hard-boiled eggs, chopped
1 tsp. vinegar
1 tsp. salt
1 sm. onion
2 Tbsp. sugar
¹/₂ c. dandelion leaves,
    washed, chopped

Combine flour and butter. Add enough milk to make a thin gravy and bring to a boil. Add eggs, vinegar, salt, onion, and sugar. Just before serving, add dandelion leaves.

Mrs. Aden Chupp

Beef Jerky

3/4 c. soy sauce
3/4 c. Worcestershire sauce
1/2 bottle liquid smoke
2 tsp. seasoned salt
2/3 tsp. onion salt
2/3 tsp. fine black pepper

Layer beef strips in a glass cake pan. Sprinkle lightly with lemon pepper, then cover with juices. Repeat layers until pan is full. Bake at 125°–140° for 4–6 hours. Do not store in airtight container.

Mary Esther Miller

Deer Jerky

1 1/2 tsp. coarse pepper
2 Tbsp. liquid smoke
1 Tbsp. salt
1/2 tsp. garlic powder
1 Tbsp. onion powder
1/4 c. soy sauce
1/4 c. Worcestershire sauce

Cut meat into 1/4"–3/8" strips. Marinate meat in mixture for 24 hours. Thread onto toothpicks and hang in oven on low heat with door cracked for 8–10 hours.

Erma Mast

Salt Brine for Turkey

1 c. Tender Quick
1 1/2 c. sugar cure
2 tsp. sugar cure spice
2 Tbsp. liquid smoke
1 1/2–2 gal. cold water

Mix all together. Marinate meat for 24–48 hours, then roast or cook. Can be used for deer, hogs, etc.

Mattie Yoder

Chicken Crumbs for Boneless White Chicken

2 1/2 lb. Bisquick
1 1/4 lb. wheat flour
1 1/4 lb. white flour
1 1/2 c. Lawry's seasoned salt
2 Tbsp. black pepper
1 1/4 Tbsp. salt
1 Tbsp. paprika

For chicken with the bone, use 2 c. Lawry's seasoned salt.

Mrs. Aden Chupp

Soups & Salads

Favorite Chili Soup

6 lbs. hamburger
salt
pepper
2 lg. onions
1 c. flour
1 gal. kidney beans, chili beans,
    or pork and beans
2 c. ketchup
4 c. brown sugar
1 pkg. chili seasoning
5 qt. tomato juice
2 qt. water
3 Tbsp. salt
2 tsp. chili powder

Fry meat with salt, pepper, and onions. Add flour and mix well. Put the rest of the ingredients in a large canner. Bring to a boil. Add meat mixture. Bring to a boil again. Cold pack for 2 hours. Yields 14 qts.

Mrs. Mahlon R. Yoder

Chili Soup

15 oz. tomato puree
26 oz. tomato soup
2 c. ketchup
6 lbs. hamburger
1 1/2 c. white sugar
1 1/2 Tbsp. dry mustard
1 1/2 Tbsp. chili powder
5 qts. tomato juice
7 oz. tomato paste
1 1/2 qts. kidney beans
1 onion
1 1/2 c. brown sugar
4 Tbsp. flour
1/2 tsp. catsup spice

Brown hamburger. Season with onion, seasoned salt, salt, and pepper. Combine all ingredients, adding hamburger and kidney beans last. Bring to a boil and simmer to let flavor go through about 10 minutes. Cold pack for 2 hours. Yields 12 quarts.

Katie Mae Troyer

Chili Soup to Can

8 lbs. hamburger
3 1/2 c. chopped onion
4 c. brown sugar
2 c. flour
1 1/4 c. clear jel
3/4 c. chili powder
1/3 c. salt
1/2 c. seasoned salt

Fry hamburger and onion together. Put into a large stainless steel canner. Add 2 qts. water. Stir. Combine remaining ingredients and add to meat. Stir well. Add 2 qts. tomato juice and stir. Add 15 more qts. tomato juice and 12 (16 oz.) cans kidney beans or pork and beans. Mix well. Put into jars and cold pack for 2 hours or pressure cook for 1 hour at 10 lbs. pressure. This is very good! Yields 28 quarts.

Mrs. Wayne J. Miller
Mrs. John E. Troyer
Mrs. David J. Troyer

Esther's White Chili

28 oz. chicken broth
48 oz. Great Northern beans
1 Tbsp. olive oil
2 c. finely chopped onion
2 Tbsp. minced garlic
1 1/2 lbs. chicken breast pieces
1 tsp. cumin
2 tsp. oregano
cayenne pepper

Heat broth and beans together. Sauté onion and garlic in oil. Add to beans. Add chicken. Add spices. For thicker chili, add another can of beans that has been blended. Serve soup with a dollop of sour cream on each serving.

Mrs. Edwin N. (Ruth) Weaver

Ham & Potato Soup

6 qts. chopped potatoes
1 1/2 c. butter
5 Tbsp. flour (heaping)
1 onion, chopped fine
6 qts. cubed ham
1 1/2 gal. milk
4 lbs. Velveeta cheese

Cover potatoes with water and cook for 2 minutes. Do not drain. Brown butter in skillet. Add remaining ingredients. This fills a 4-gal. canner. Do not boil. Use salt sparingly.

Mrs. Abe E. Mast
Mrs. Raymond D. (Edna) Miller

Taco Soup

2 lbs. hamburger
2 pkgs. taco seasoning
1 sm. onion, chopped
2 qts. tomato juice
3/4 c. sugar
2 cans pork and beans
1 qt. corn
crushed taco chips
cheddar cheese, grated
sour cream
lettuce

Brown hamburger and onion. Add tomato juice, sugar, corn, beans, and taco seasoning. Bring to a boil, then simmer for 15–30 minutes. Serve over crushed chips. Sprinkle cheese over top and add sour cream and lettuce.

Mrs. Ben J. Troyer
Mrs. Levi (Susan) Troyer
Mrs. Jerry Miller

Taco Soup

1 lb. hamburger, browned, seasoned
    or canned hamburger crumbles
1 qt. water
1 qt. pizza sauce
1 can hot chili beans, optional
1 pkg. taco seasoning

Simmer for 15 minutes. Serve with cheddar cheese, sour cream, and nacho chips instead of crackers.

Mrs. Myron Miller

Cream of Tomato Soup

1 c. butter
8 tsp. salt
2 2/3 Tbsp. chopped onion
4 qts. tomato juice
1 1/2 c. flour
1 1/2 c. white sugar
1 tsp. pepper

Sauté onion in butter. Combine flour, sugar, salt, and pepper. Add to butter and onion. Cook until smooth and bubbly, stirring constantly. Remove from heat. Gradually stir in tomato juice. Bring to a boil, stirring constantly. Cook for 1 minute. Cold pack for 1 hour.

Mrs. Mahlon R. Yoder

Captain's Soup

1 pkg. mixed vegetables
4 c. tomato soup
2 c. milk
¹/₂ lb. Velveeta cheese
1¹/₂ lb. diced ham

Cook vegetables until tender. Add remaining ingredients. Salt to taste.

Mrs. Ivan Hershberger

Hearty Ham Soup

1 c. diced potatoes
1 c. diced carrots
¹/₄ c. chopped onions
¹/₂ c. diced celery
1¹/₂ c. chopped ham
1¹/₂ tsp. chicken base
¹/₄ c. butter
1 qt. milk
American or Velveeta cheese

In a saucepan, cook potatoes, celery, carrots, onions, butter, and chicken base in enough water to cover vegetables until tender. Add ham and milk. Bring to a boil, then thicken with cornstarch and water as desired. Add cheese.

Mary Hostetler
Mrs. David M. Miller

Chunky Cheese Soup

2 c. water
2 c. peeled, diced potatoes
¹/₂ c. diced carrots
¹/₂ c. chopped celery
¹/₄ c. chopped onions
¹/₂–1 tsp. salt
¹/₄ tsp. pepper
1 c. cubed ham
¹/₄ c. butter or margarine
¹/₄ c. flour
2 c. milk
1 c. Velveeta cheese

In a saucepan, combine the first 7 ingredients. Bring to a boil. Reduce heat; cover and simmer until the vegetables are tender. Add ham. In another saucepan, melt the butter. Stir in flour until smooth. Gradually add milk. Bring to a boil. Cook and stir for 2 minutes or until thickened. Stir in cheese until melted. Add to soup. For different flavors, add 1 c. cooked ground beef or bulk sausage, or 1 lb. bacon, cooked and crumbled. Delicious!

Mrs. Norman Mast

Esther's Potato Cheese Soup

6 c. chopped potatoes
1 c. chopped celery
1 c. carrots
$1/2$ c. onions
2 tsp. parsley
1 tsp. salt
pepper
2 chicken bouillon cubes
2 c. water
3 c. milk
4 Tbsp. flour
1 lb. Velveeta cheese

Combine first 9 ingredients in a large pot. Simmer at medium heat for 20 minutes. Blend milk and flour. Add it to potatoes. Cook until thick. Add Velveeta cheese. Cook until melted.

Mrs. Edwin N. (Ruth) Weaver

Golden Cream Soup

3 c. chopped potatoes
1 c. water
$1/2$ c. celery
$1/2$ c. carrots
$1/4$ c. onions
1 tsp. parsley
2 Tbsp. chicken base
$1/2$ tsp. salt
$1^1/2$ c. milk
2 Tbsp. flour
$1/2$ lb. Velveeta cheese

In large saucepan, cook all except milk, flour, and cheese for 15–20 minutes. Gradually add milk and flour. Cook until thickened, then add cheese.

Mrs. Felty J. Erb

Hearty Chicken & Rice Soup

$1^1/2$ c. chicken broth
3 c. cold water
$1/2$ c. uncooked rice
$1/2$ c. celery
$1/2$ c. carrots
$1^1/2$ c. cooked, diced chicken
$3/4$ lb. Velveeta cheese

Combine first 5 ingredients. Cover and bring to a boil. Simmer for 25 minutes. Add chicken. Last, add cheese. Stir until melted. Delicious!

Mrs. Norman H. Mast

Cheeseburger Soup

4 lbs. hamburger, fried
1^1/$_2$ c. chopped onions
2 lg. cans chicken broth
3 c. celery, cut up
3 c. carrots, cut up
9 c. potatoes, cut up
3 tsp. salt
1^1/$_2$ tsp. pepper
White Sauce:
1 c. butter
1^3/$_4$ c. flour
6 c. milk
6 c. Velveeta cheese

Bring top ingredients to a boil in a 12-qt. saucepan. Let cook just until potatoes are tender. Add 1 qt. water to vegetables. Make white sauce by combining butter and flour. Slowly add milk. Cook until thick. Add cheese. Stir until melted, then add white sauce into boiling soup. This can be frozen.

Mrs. Aden B. Miller

Cheeseburger Soup

^{1}/$_2$ lb. ground beef
^{3}/$_4$ c. chopped onion
^{3}/$_4$ c. shredded carrots
^{3}/$_4$ c. diced celery
1 tsp. dried parsley flakes
4 Tbsp. butter, divided
3 c. chicken broth
4 c. peeled, diced potatoes
^{1}/$_4$ c. all-purpose flour
8 oz. Velveeta cheese
1^1/$_2$ c. milk
^{3}/$_4$ tsp. salt
^{1}/$_4$–^{1}/$_2$ tsp. pepper
^{1}/$_4$ c. sour cream

In a 3-qt. saucepan brown beef. Drain and set aside. In the same saucepan, sauté onions, celery, carrots, and parsley in 1 Tbsp. butter until vegetables are tender, about 10 minutes. Add broth, potatoes, and beef. Bring to a boil. Reduce heat. Cover and simmer for 10–12 minutes or until potatoes are tender. Meanwhile, in a small skillet, melt remaining butter. Add flour. Cook and stir for 3–5 minutes or until bubbly. Add to soup. Bring to a boil. Cook and stir for 2 minutes. Reduce heat to low. Add cheese, milk, salt, and pepper. Cook and stir until cheese melts. Remove from heat. Blend in sour cream. Yields 2^1/$_4$ qts.

Mrs. Levi (Susan) Troyer
Mrs. Junior A. Troyer

Chunky Beef Soup

2 1/2 gal. water
1 1/4 c. beef soup mix
2 lg. cans College Inn beef broth
4 qts. tomato juice
2 c. brown sugar
1/4 c. salt (scant)
3 c. butter, browned
2 lg. onions, diced
5 c. Perma-Flo
4 qts. diced carrots
3 qts. frozen peas
1 qt. dry navy beans, cooked
10 lbs. hamburger
1 lb. fried bacon, crumbled
4 qts. potatoes, diced

Combine water, soup mix, broth, tomato juice, brown sugar, and salt. Fry onions in butter. Add to liquid. Heat and thicken with Perma-Flo. Cook and salt vegetables separately. Brown meat and season with salt and pepper. Add meat and vegetables to liquid. Cold pack for 2 hours.

Mrs. Aden W. Chupp

Carrot Beef Soup

1 1/2 lbs. ground beef
1 lg. onion, chopped
1 Tbsp. sugar
2 cans cream of celery soup
1 garlic clove, minced
1 qt. tomato juice
1 bay leaf
2 c. grated carrots

In a skillet, brown beef, garlic, and onion until beef is no longer pink and the onion is tender. Drain and set aside. Meanwhile, combine remaining ingredients in a saucepan. Bring to a boil. Reduce heat. Simmer for 15 minutes. Add beef mixture and continue to simmer for 1 hour. Yields 6–8 servings.

Barbara Coblentz

Cream of Chicken Soup

1/4 c. butter or margarine
5 Tbsp. flour
3 tsp. chicken soup base
3 c. boiling water
1 c. chicken broth (half chicken bits)
1 c. rich milk

Melt butter in saucepan. Blend in flour. Gradually add the boiling water with soup base added. Stir until smooth. Add broth and bring to a boil until it thickens slightly. Stir in milk. Add salt if you wish.

Mrs. Eli Burkholder

Cheese Chicken Chowder Soup

6 c. College Inn chicken broth
2 cans chicken
4 c. milk
20 oz. mixed vegetables
2 tsp. chicken soup base
1 lb. Velveeta cheese
4 Tbsp. butter
1 sm. onion
2 Tbsp. flour (rounded)
salt
pepper
seasoned salt

Cook vegetables in broth. Add soup base and chicken. In skillet, brown butter, onion, and flour. Add milk slowly. Blend and add to soup. Simmer until thickened, then add cheese and simmer until cheese is melted.

Mrs. John A. Miller

Chicken Soup for Church

1 gal. diced carrots
1 gal. diced potatoes
2 qts. diced celery
8 qts. diced chicken
5 lbs. fine Inn Maid noodles
2 lbs. chicken seasoning
2 c. butter, browned

This is enough for 2 canners. I fill 2 canners half full of water. Divide noodles between the canners and bring to a boil. Let set for about 30 minutes, then divide remaining ingredients and add. Brown butter and add. I use some salt instead of so much chicken seasoning.

Mrs. R.E. Weaver

Broccoli Cheese Soup

3/4 c. chopped onions
2 Tbsp. margarine
6 c. chicken broth
6 chicken bouillon cubes
8 oz. fine noodles
2 (10 oz.) pkgs. frozen
    chopped broccoli
6 c. milk
8 c. Velveeta cheese, cubed

Sauté onions in margarine. Add broth and bouillon cubes. Bring to a boil. Add noodles and cook until noodles are almost done. Add broccoli and cook for 5–10 minutes. Add milk and Velveeta cheese. Enjoy!

Mrs. Susan Miller

Spaghetti Soup

¹/₂ bu. tomatoes
4 lbs. hamburger
3 lbs. spaghetti
2 lbs. navy beans
2 pkgs. ABC macaroni
4 onions
2 c. butter
¹/₂ c. sugar

Soak beans overnight, then cook until very soft. Cook spaghetti. Fry hamburger and onions. Cold pack for 2 hours. Add water to serve. I used 3 qts. beef broth and some beef soup base and not so much tomato juice.

Mrs. R.E. Weaver

Tasty Tomatoes

¹/₄ c. chopped celery
2 Tbsp. chopped onion
1 c. salad dressing
cheddar cheese

Mix first 3 ingredients. Spoon over sliced tomatoes. Sprinkle with cheese.

Mrs. Atlee Mast

Cabbage

1 lg. head cabbage, shredded
1 c. celery
1 red or green pepper
1 sm. onion
1 tsp. celery seed
2 c. sugar
¹/₂ c. vinegar
1 tsp. mustard seed
1 tsp. salt

Miriam Mast

tid bits

To keep vegetables colorful, add a pinch of baking soda to cooking water.

Creamy Cole Slaw

1 tsp. mustard seed
1 tsp. celery seed
$^{1}/_{2}$ tsp. salt
2 Tbsp. vinegar
2 Tbsp. minced onion
3 Tbsp. sugar
2 Tbsp. mayonnaise (heaping)
1 c. sour cream
6 c. shredded cabbage

Mix an hour before serving to blend flavors.

Mrs. Susan Miller

Better Than Potato Salad

4 c. cooked rice
2 c. cooked macaroni
2 c. uncooked rice
1 c. uncooked macaroni
4 hard-boiled eggs, chopped
$^{1}/_{4}$ c. minced onion
$^{1}/_{2}$ c. carrot, cut fine
Dressing:
1$^{1}/_{2}$ c. salad dressing
3 Tbsp. prepared mustard
1 Tbsp. salt
$^{1}/_{4}$ c. sugar
2 Tbsp. vinegar

In a large bowl, combine macaroni, rice, eggs, onion, and carrots. Mix dressing ingredients. Pour over rice mixture and toss. Can be made the day before serving.

Mrs. David M. Miller

tid bits

If soup tastes very salty, a raw piece of potato placed in the pot will absorb the salt.

Potato Salad

12 c. cooked, cubed potatoes
12 eggs, hard-boiled
1 1/2 c. chopped celery
1 c. diced, cooked carrots
1 chopped onion, optional
Dressing:
3 c. Miracle Whip
6 Tbsp. mustard
1/4 c. vinegar
3 c. sugar
4 tsp. salt
pepper
seasoned salt
celery seed

Mix all together. This makes a Fix 'n' Mix bowl almost full. This is better when made the day before serving.

Mrs. Mosie Yoder

Broccoli Salad

1 bundle broccoli, cut fine
1 head cauliflower, cut fine
1 lb. bacon, fried, crumbled
2 c. shredded cheddar cheese
1 sm. onion, optional
Dressing:
3/4 c. sour cream
1/2 c. sugar
3/4 c. mayonnaise
1/4 tsp. salt

Combine dressing ingredients and mix well. Pour over broccoli mixture. This can be made a day ahead.

Mrs. John E. Troyer
Mrs. Mahlon R. Yoder
Mrs. Monroe Yoder

Broccoli & Cauliflower Salad

1 lg. bunch broccoli
1 lg. head cauliflower
1 lb. bacon, fried, crumbled
1 sm. onion
2 c. shredded cheddar cheese
Dressing:
1 c. Miracle Whip
1 c. sour cream
1/2 tsp. salt
1/2 c. sugar

Mrs. Paul J. Hostetler

Overnight Salad

1 head lettuce
1 head cauliflower
6 hard-boiled eggs, chopped fine
10 oz. frozen peas, thawed
$^1/_2$ c. shredded carrots
1 lb. bacon, fried, crumbled
Dressing:
2 c. salad dressing
$^1/_2$ c. sugar

Arrange in layers in order given. Mix dressing and spread on top. Let set 8 hours or overnight. Toss before serving and top with cheddar cheese.

Esta & Vesta Yoder

Pasta Salad

1$^1/_2$ lb. spiral pasta, cooked
8 oz. diced ham
shredded cheddar cheese
$^1/_2$ c. chopped tomatoes
1 sm. onion
1 green pepper
3 c. salad dressing
$^1/_4$ c. mustard
$^3/_4$ c. salad oil
$^1/_2$ c. vinegar
1$^1/_2$ c. sugar
1 Tbsp. onion salt
$^1/_2$ Tbsp. celery seed
$^1/_2$ tsp. salt

Mix all together and let set overnight.

Mrs. John B. Beachy

Vegetable Pizza Crust

$^1/_4$ c. margarine
$^1/_4$ c. boiling water
2 Tbsp. sugar
1 pkg. yeast
$^1/_4$ c. very warm water
1 egg, beaten
1$^1/_2$ c. all-purpose flour
1 tsp. salt

Combine margarine, boiling water, and sugar in a large bowl. Stir until dissolved. Cool to lukewarm. Sprinkle yeast over very warm water. Let set several minutes, then stir until dissolved. Add yeast to first mixture. Add egg, flour, and salt. Mix well. Cool. Let rise once. Pour on well-greased pan. Spread evenly. Bake at 325°.

Mrs. Roy J. Wengerd

Vegetable Pizza

Crust:
2 c. flour
3 tsp. baking powder
$^1/_2$ tsp. salt
$^1/_2$ tsp. cream of tartar
$^1/_2$ c. cold margarine
$^3/_4$ c. milk
Filling:
8 oz. cream cheese
8 oz. sour cream
$^1/_2$ c. Miracle Whip
1 pkg. Hidden Valley Ranch
    salad dressing mix
1 Tbsp. white sugar

For crust: Mix dry ingredients, then cut in margarine. Mix in milk only until blended. Do not overmix. Roll or pat out in a greased cake or pizza pan. Bake at 450° for 10 minutes. Cool. For filling: Mix all ingredients and put on cooled crust. Top with assorted vegetables, chopped fine. Refrigerate.

Mrs. Wayne J. Miller

Vegetable Pizza

2 tubes crescent rolls
8 oz. cream cheese, softened
1 c. mayonnaise
1 pkg. dry buttermilk dressing mix
    or Hidden Valley Ranch dressing
    mix
1 c. finely chopped broccoli
1 c. finely chopped tomatoes
1 c. finely chopped cauliflower
$^1/_2$ c. finely chopped peppers
$^1/_2$ c. finely chopped carrots
$^1/_2$ c. finely chopped onions
4 oz. shredded cheddar cheese
$^1/_4$ c. bacon bits

Unroll crescent rolls and spread in a single layer in a greased 10 X 15 jelly-roll pan. Press seams to seal. Bake at 375° for 8–10 minutes. Beat together cream cheese, mayonnaise, and dressing mix. Spread over cooled crust. Arrange vegetables on top of cream cheese mixture. Gently press in. Sprinkle cheese and bacon bits on top. Chill. Cut into squares to serve.

Dora Schlabach
Mrs. David Miller
Mrs. Abe E. Mast

Dressing for Lettuce

1 c. salad dressing
$^3/_4$ c. sour cream
$^1/_2$ c. sugar
1 tsp. salt

This is enough for 1 head lettuce.

Mrs. Nelson L. Miller

Lettuce Dressing

1 1/2 c. sugar
1 1/2 c. vegetable oil
1/2 c. plus 1 Tbsp. salad dressing
3/4 c. chopped onions
1/4 c. water
1/4 tsp. black pepper
2 Tbsp. mustard
3/8 c. vinegar
1 tsp. salt
1 tsp. celery seed

Combine sugar and oil. Mix well.
Add remaining ingredients and mix
well.

Mrs. Myron J. Miller

Dressing for Lettuce Salad

1 qt. Miracle Whip
4 c. sugar
1/2 bottle Catalina dressing
1 c. sweet and sour dressing
2 Tbsp. mustard
1 tsp. salt
3 cans evaporated milk

Mix all together. This keeps well in
refrigerator.

Katie Hershberger

Sweet & Sour Dressing

2 c. salad dressing
1 c. sugar
1/2 c. oil
1/8 c. vinegar
1/8 c. mustard
1/2 tsp. celery seed

Serve with tossed salad. This is also
very good with cabbage.

Mrs. Sylvanus Raber
Mrs. R.E. Weaver

French Dressing

4 c. Wesson oil
4 c. sugar
1 1/2 c. vinegar
1 1/2 c. catsup
4 tsp. salt

Mix well. Serve over tossed salad.

Mrs. Aden B. Miller

Chef Adler Dressing

3 c. salad dressing
1/4 c. mustard
3/4 c. oil
1/2 c. vinegar
1 1/2 c. sugar
1 tsp. onion salt
1 tsp. celery seed
1/2 tsp. salt

Mix all together, adding oil last.

Mrs. Felty J. Erb

Sweet Relish

9 c. cucumbers
2 peppers
4 onions
4 tsp. salt
4 c. sugar
1 tsp. turmeric
2 c. vinegar
2 tsp. celery seed
2 tsp. mustard seed

Grind cucumbers, peppers, and onions together. Add salt and cover with cold water. Let set at least 30 minutes. Drain and add remaining ingredients. Bring to a rolling boil. Put into glass jars and seal. This is very good on hot dogs.

Mrs. Andy M.A. Troyer

tid bits

Browning butter brings out the flavor. Only half as much butter is needed when browning it before adding to vegetables.

—*Anna Miller*

Cakes

Angel Food Cake

2 c. egg whites
1¹/₂ tsp. cream of tartar
1¹/₃ c. sugar
¹/₂ c. sugar
1¹/₃ c. plus 2 Tbsp. cake flour
¹/₂ tsp. salt
2 tsp. vanilla

Beat egg whites and cream of tartar until peaks form. Slowly add 1¹/₃ c. sugar. Combine ¹/₂ c. sugar, flour, salt, and vanilla. Add to egg whites. For different flavors, add maple flavor or ¹/₃ c. of your favorite Jell-O. When using Jell-O, use ¹/₃ c. less sugar.

Mrs. Norman Mast

Angel Cream Cake

Part 1:
1¹/₂ c. egg whites
¹/₂ tsp. salt
1¹/₂ c. sugar
1 tsp. lemon flavoring
1 tsp. cream of tartar
²/₃ c. flour
Part 2:
egg yolks
¹/₂ tsp. lemon flavoring
¹/₂ c. flour
Filling:
³/₄ c. sugar
3 egg yolks
¹/₄ c. flour
1¹/₄ c. milk
¹/₂ Tbsp. gelatin
2 Tbsp. cold water
1 c. Rich's whipped topping
2 tsp. vanilla

Part 1: Beat egg whites until frothy, then add salt and cream of tartar. Beat until stiff. Fold in sugar and lemon flavoring. *Part 2:* Beat yolks until slightly thick, then add ¹/₄ of the white mixture. Add flavoring. Fold flour into first mixture. Fold flour into second mixture. Pour both mixtures in layers into a tube pan. Swirl slightly with a spoon. *For filling:* Cook sugar, yolks, flour, and milk together. Soak gelatin in cold water. Add to hot mixture. Cool. Whip topping and add vanilla. Add to gelatin mixture. Chill slightly. Spread filling over cake and fill the center of cake. Keep refrigerated or in a cool place. I sometimes slice the cake and pour filling over top. Do not use lemon extract. I use Blair lemon flavoring. Very delicious.

Mrs. Ben D. Miller

Layered Toffee Cake

2 c. Rich's topping
1/2 c. caramel or butterscotch
   ice cream topping
1/2 tsp. vanilla
1 angel food cake
3–4 Heath candy bars

Beat topping until it begins to thicken. Gradually add ice cream topping and vanilla. Beat until soft peaks form. Cut cake horizontally in half. Place bottom layer on a serving plate. Spread with cream mixture and sprinkle with candy bars. Place top layer on cake. Frost top and sides with remaining cream mixture and sprinkle with candy bars. Delicious!

Mrs. Atlee M. Shetler

Custard Chiffon Cake

7 egg yolks, slightly beaten
3/4 c. scalding hot milk
2 c. sifted Gold Medal flour
1 1/2 c. sugar
3 tsp. baking powder
1 tsp. salt
1/2 c. Wesson oil
2 tsp. vanilla
1 c. egg whites
1 tsp. cream of tartar

Blend hot milk with egg yolks. Cool. Sift flour, sugar, baking powder, and salt together. Make a well and add oil and vanilla. Add cooled milk mixture. Beat with spoon until smooth. In a large mixing bowl, beat cream of tartar and egg whites until very stiff peaks form. Do not underbeat. Egg whites are stiff enough when a dry rubber scraper drawn through batter leaves a clean path. Pour first mixture gradually over egg whites, gently folding with a rubber scraper just until blended. Do not stir. Pour into ungreased tube pan and bake at 325° for 55 minutes. Increase heat to 350° and bake 10–15 minutes longer. Tip: Milk must be very hot when poured over egg yolks.

Mrs. Emma Hershberger

Chiffon Cake

2¼ c. sifted cake flour
1½ c. sugar
3 tsp. baking powder
1 tsp. salt
½ c. Wesson oil
5 egg yolks, unbeaten
¾ c. cold water
2 tsp. vanilla
1 c. egg whites
½ tsp. cream of tartar

Sift flour, sugar, baking powder, and salt into a bowl. Make a well. Add oil, egg yolks, water, and vanilla. Beat with a spoon. Beat egg whites and cream of tartar in a large mixing bowl until they form very stiff peaks. Use a dry rubber scraper drawn through them until it leaves a clean path. Pour egg yolk mixture slowly over beaten egg whites, folding just until blended. Do not stir. Pour into ungreased tube pan. Bake at 325° for 55 minutes.

Mrs. Marion Miller

Yellow Cake

3 c. flour
2 c. sugar
1 c. milk
1 c. sour cream
2 tsp. vanilla
2 tsp. baking soda
2 eggs
1 tsp. salt

Cream sugar and sour cream. Add eggs, soda, salt, and vanilla. Sift flour and add alternately with milk. Bake at 350°.

Mrs. Mary Miller

Moist White Cake

¾ c. shortening
2 c. white sugar
3 c. cake flour
1¼ c. cold water
pinch salt
1 tsp. vanilla
4 egg whites
3 tsp. baking powder

Cream shortening and sugar. Add flour and water alternately, then add salt and vanilla. Beat egg whites. When almost stiff enough, add baking powder and continue beating. Fold into batter. Bake at 350° for 30 minutes. Be sure to use cake flour. This is a recipe used for weddings. Yields 2 (9") layers or 1 (9 X 13) cake.

Mrs. Albert (Ada) Yoder

White Cake

1/2 c. shortening
1 c. sugar
1 c. cold water
2 c. pastry or cake flour
2 tsp. baking powder
3 egg whites, beaten stiff
1 tsp. vanilla

Cream shortening and sugar until very light. Add water very slowly and beat constantly. Stir in flour and baking powder which has been sifted twice. Add vanilla and egg whites. Bake for 20–25 minutes.

Mrs. H.C.Y.

Pastel Marble Cake

2 1/4 c. cake flour
1 1/2 c. sugar
1/4 c. shortening
1/4 c. butter, softened
1 c. buttermilk
1 1/2 tsp. baking powder
1 tsp. salt
1/2 tsp. baking soda
1 tsp. vanilla
2 eggs
red and green food coloring

Heat oven to 350°. Combine and mix all ingredients except food coloring. Blend well. Divide batter into 3 equal parts. Tint 1/3 pink with 2–3 drops red food coloring. Tint 1/3 green with 2–3 drops green food coloring. Drop 3 mixtures alternately by spoonfuls into pan. Bake for 40–45 minutes. Cool.

Mrs. Aden W. Chupp

Lemon Lime Cake

1 pkg. lime Jell-O
3/4 c. boiling water
1/2 c. cold water
1 lemon cake mix
Topping:
1 sm. carton Cool Whip
1 pkg. instant lemon pudding
1–1 1/2 c. milk

Bake cake as directed. Dissolve Jell-O in boiling water. Add cold water and set aside. Poke holes through warm cake with a fork, spacing holes 1" apart. Slowly pour Jell-O mixture into holes. Refrigerate. *For topping:* Blend instant pudding with milk. Add Cool Whip. Frost cake. Keep refrigerated.

Mrs. Mosie Yoder

Jell-O Cake

1 white cake mix
3/4 c. boiling water
1 (3 oz.) pkg. orange Jell-O
Topping:
1 pkg. instant vanilla pudding
2 1/2 c. milk
1 tsp. vanilla
4 oz. Cool Whip

Bake cake in 9 X 13 pan as directed. Dissolve Jell-O in boiling water. Cool to room temperature. After cake has cooled for 20–25 minutes, poke holes in cake with a fork or toothpick, spacing holes 1/2" apart. Slowly pour dissolved Jell-O into holes. Refrigerate. *For topping:* Mix all ingredients. Spread over cake. Refrigerate.

Rachel Yoder

Pudding Cake

1 yellow or white cake mix
1 pkg. butterscotch instant pudding
1 pkg. vanilla instant pudding
1 c. water
1 c. cooking oil
4 eggs
Crumbs:
1 c. sugar
1/2 c. nuts
1 tsp. cinnamon

Combine ingredients and mix well. Beat for 1 minute. Mix crumbs. Pour half of batter into a 9 X 13 pan. Top with half of crumbs. Repeat. Bake at 350° for 35 minutes.

Katie B. Yoder

Butterscotch Cake

1 yellow cake mix
1 (3 oz.) pkg. butterscotch
   instant pudding
1 c. nuts
1 c. butterscotch chips
1/2 c. sugar

Mix cake according to instructions, then add instant pudding mix. Pour into greased loaf pan. Top with nuts, butterscotch chips, and sugar. Bake at 350° until cake is done.

Mrs. Mahlon R. Yoder

Buttermilk Cake

5 c. flour
2 c. sugar
1 c. shortening or lard
1¼ c. buttermilk
1 tsp. vanilla
pinch salt
1 tsp. soda
1 tsp. baking powder

Mix dry ingredients. Add shortening and mix until crumbly. Reserve 1 c. crumbs to put on top. Add buttermilk and vanilla to remaining crumbs. Bake at 350° for 30–40 minutes.

Mrs. Dan Mast

Buttermilk Spice Cake

2 c. plus 2 Tbsp. flour
1 c. sugar
1 tsp. baking powder
¾ tsp. soda
1 tsp. salt
¾ tsp. cloves
¾ tsp. cinnamon
¾ c. brown sugar
½ c. shortening
1 c. buttermilk
3 eggs

Mix all dry ingredients first. Add eggs last. Bake at 350°.

Sarah Raber

Choice Spice Cake

1½ c. sugar
½ c. butter and lard
3 egg yolks
1 c. sour milk or buttermilk
¾ tsp. nutmeg
pinch salt
2 tsp. baking powder
1 tsp. soda
3 c. flour
3 egg whites, beaten

Cream sugar and butter to a cream. Add egg yolks and beat well. Add milk, nutmeg, salt, baking powder, soda, and flour. Add the egg whites.

Mrs. H.C.Y.

Crumb Spice Cake

3 c. flour
1 c. lard or shortening
2 c. brown sugar
spice
2 eggs
1 tsp. soda
1 c. buttermilk

Mix shortening, sugar, flour, and spice. Mix and reserve 1 cup for the top. Add buttermilk, soda, and eggs. Bake.

Mrs. Henry C. Yoder

Old-Fashioned Ginger Cake

2$^{1}/_{2}$ c. flour
$^{1}/_{2}$ c. sugar
1 tsp. soda
1 tsp. baking powder
$^{3}/_{4}$ tsp. salt
1$^{1}/_{4}$ tsp. cinnamon
$^{3}/_{4}$ tsp. cloves
$^{1}/_{4}$ tsp. nutmeg
1 tsp. ginger
$^{1}/_{2}$ c. shortening
1 c. boiling water
$^{3}/_{4}$ c. molasses
1 egg, beaten

Dissolve soda in boiling water. Cream together shortening and sugar. Add egg, molasses, and water. Add all dry ingredients. Bake at 350° for 35 minutes or until done. Top with whipped cream before serving.

Esta & Vesta Yoder

Amish Cake

$^{1}/_{2}$ c. margarine
2 c. brown sugar
2 c. buttermilk
2 tsp. soda
2 tsp. vanilla
3 c. flour
Topping:
6 Tbsp. butter, melted
4 Tbsp. milk
1 c. brown sugar
$^{3}/_{4}$ c. nuts

Cream together margarine and brown sugar. Add buttermilk, soda, vanilla, and flour. Bake. When done, pour topping on top. Return to oven until bubbly, about 1 minute.

Mrs. Eli A. Mast

Coconut Cream Cake

1 white cake mix with pudding
1 can Eagle Brand milk
1 (8.5 oz.) can cream of coconut
1 carton Cool Whip
1 can flaked coconut

Bake cake as directed on box. While cake is hot, punch holes in cake. Pour Eagle Brand milk and cream of coconut over top. Cool. Spread with Cool Whip and top with flaked coconut. This is moist and delicious!

Mandy Troyer

Rave Reviews Coconut Cake

1 yellow cake mix
1 pkg. instant vanilla pudding
1^1/$_3$ c. water
4 eggs
2 c. coconut
^{1}/$_4$ c. oil

Mix in order given. Bake in a 9 X 13 pan at 350°.

Mrs. Raymond Wengerd

Oatmeal Cake

1^1/$_2$ c. boiling water
1 c. rolled oats
^{1}/$_2$ c. margarine
1^1/$_2$ c. flour
1 tsp. soda
1 tsp. cinnamon
1 c. nuts
2 eggs
1 c. white sugar
1 c. brown sugar
1 tsp. vanilla
^{1}/$_2$ tsp. salt
Frosting:
8 oz. cream cheese, softened
^{1}/$_2$ c. butter or margarine,
   room temperature
1 tsp. vanilla
1^3/$_4$ c. powdered sugar

Pour water over oats and margarine. Let set for 20 minutes. Beat eggs with sugars, vanilla, and salt. Add remaining ingredients. Bake at 375° for 45 minutes.

Mrs. Monroe Yoder

Delicious Oatmeal Cake

1¼ c. boiling water
1 c. quick oats
½ c. shortening
1 c. brown sugar
1 c. white sugar
2 eggs
1½ c. flour
1 tsp. nutmeg
1 tsp. cinnamon
1 tsp. soda
½ tsp. salt
1 tsp. vanilla
Topping:
⅔ c. brown sugar
1 c. nuts
1 c. coconut
6 Tbsp. melted butter
¼ c. cream
1 tsp. vanilla

Pour boiling water over oats. Let set for 20 minutes. Cream shortening and sugars. Add eggs one at a time. Blend in oatmeal mixture. Add dry ingredients. Bake at 325°. While cake is still hot, mix topping and pour over cake. Broil until browned.

Mrs Eli N. Hershberger
Mrs. Andrew A. Troyer

Peanut Crunch Cake

1 yellow cake mix
1 c. peanut butter
½ c. brown sugar
1 c. water
3 eggs
¼ c. vegetable oil
¾ c. chocolate chips, divided
¾ c. peanut butter chips, divided
½ c. chopped peanuts

In a mixing bowl, beat cake mix, peanut butter, and brown sugar until crumbly. Set aside ½ cup. Add water, eggs, and oil to remaining crumb mixture. Blend on low until moist. Beat on high for 2 minutes. Stir in ¼ c. each of chocolate and peanut butter chips. Pour into a greased 9 X 13 baking pan. Combine peanuts with reserved crumb mixture and remaining chips. Sprinkle on top. Bake at 350° for 40–45 minutes.

Mrs. Abe E. Mast

Butterscotch Chocolate Cake

1 chocolate cake mix
1 (17 oz.) jar butterscotch
   ice cream topping
8 oz. frozen whipped
   topping, thawed
3 Butterfinger candy bars,
   coarsely crushed

Prepare and bake cake according to package directions, using a greased 9 X 13 pan. Cool for 30 minutes. Using the end of a wooden spoon, poke 12 holes in warm cake. Pour topping over cake. Cool completely. Spread with whipped topping and sprinkle with crushed candy bars. Refrigerate at least 2 hours before serving.

Mrs. Roy E. Mast

Chocolate Chip Cream Cheese Cake

1 chocolate cake mix
Cream Cheese Mixture:
8 oz. cream cheese, room temp.
$^1/_2$ c. sugar
2 eggs, beaten
$^1/_2$ chocolate chips
Topping:
2 c. milk
2 pkgs. instant vanilla pudding
16 oz. Cool Whip

Mix chocolate cake according to package directions. Pour into a sheet cake pan. Mix cream cheese, sugar, eggs, and chocolate chips. Dab by teaspoon on top of cake. Bake at 350° until done. Cool. Mix topping ingredients. Spread over cooled cake.

Mrs. Edwin N. (Ruth) Weaver

Texas Sheet Cake

1 c. butter
4 Tbsp. cocoa
2 c. flour
$^1/_2$ tsp. salt
2 eggs
$^1/_2$ c. sour cream
1 c. water
2 c. sugar
1 tsp. vanilla
1 tsp. soda

Melt butter in saucepan. Add water and cocoa. Bring to boil. Add remaining ingredients, stirring lightly. Pour into a greased, floured oblong cookie sheet. Bake at 350° for 15–20 minutes.

Lovelight Chocolate Chiffon Cake

1³/₄ c. sifted flour
1 c. sugar
³/₄ tsp. soda
1 tsp. salt
¹/₃ c. cooking oil
1 c. buttermilk, divided
2 egg yolks
2 squares chocolate, melted
2 egg whites
¹/₂ c. sugar

Sift together flour, sugar, soda, and salt into a bowl. Add oil and ¹/₂ c. buttermilk and beat well. Add egg yolks, remaining buttermilk, and chocolate. Beat for 1 minute. Beat egg whites and sugar until stiff. Fold into batter. Bake at 350°. I put this into a sheet pan and make bars. When done baking, I put small marshmallows on top and return to oven for a few minutes. When cool, frost. Very good.

Biena Schlabach

Four-Layer Chocolate Cake

1 chocolate cake mix
Filling:
8 oz. cream cheese, softened
²/₃ c. brown sugar
1 tsp. vanilla extract
¹/₈ tsp. salt
2 c. whipping cream, whipped

Mix and bake cake according to package directions, using 2 (9") round or square cake pans. Cool in pans for 15 minutes. Remove from pans and cool completely on a wire rack. Mix together cream cheese, sugar, vanilla, and salt. Fold in whipping cream. Split each cake into 2 horizontal layers. Place one on a serving plate. Spread with a fourth of the cream mixture. Sprinkle with 1 Tbsp. grated chocolate. Repeat with each layer. Cover and refrigerate for 8 hours or overnight.

Mrs. Atlee C. Miller

Upside-Down Chocolate Cake

³/₄ c. sugar
1¹/₄ c. flour
2 tsp. baking powder
¹/₄ tsp. salt
1 square chocolate or cocoa
2 Tbsp. butter
1 Tbsp. vanilla
¹/₂ c. milk
¹/₂ c. nuts
Fudge:
2 tsp. cocoa
¹/₂ c. brown sugar
1 c. boiling water

Mix all cake ingredients except nuts.
Mix fudge. Pour batter into pan. Pour
fudge on top. Or put fudge in first.
Top with nuts. Bake at 350° for 1
hour. Very good with ice cream.

Mrs. Aden Burkholder

Chocolate Dream Cake

1 chocolate cake mix
Cream Cheese Layer:
Cool Whip
¹/₂ c. powdered sugar
8 oz. cream cheese
Jam Layer:
1 c. sugar
1 qt. strawberries
2–4 Tbsp. clear jel
1 qt. water
1 pkg. strawberry Kool-Aid

Mix cake as directed on package.
Bake and cool. Mix Cool Whip,
cream cheese, and powdered sugar.
Set aside. *For jam layer:* Heat water to
boiling, then add Kool-Aid and
sugar. Mix clear jel with water to use
as thickening. Add strawberries.
Cool. Spread cream cheese layer on
cake. Spread jam layer on top. Top
with Cool Whip.

Mrs. Albert Barkman

Moist Miracle Whip Cake

2 c. flour
1 c. sugar
2 tsp. soda
4 Tbsp. cocoa
¹/₂ tsp. salt
1 tsp. vanilla
1 c. Miracle Whip
1 c. cold water

Bake at 350°.

Mrs. Mahlon R. Yoder

Turtle Cake

1 chocolate cake mix
$^1/_2$ c. butter
1 can sweetened condensed milk
16 caramels
nuts, optional
chocolate chips, optional

Mix cake according to package directions. Pour half of batter into a greased 9 X 13 pan. Bake at 350° until done. Over low heat, melt caramels, milk, and butter together. Remove cake from oven. Pour mixture over cake. Top with remaining batter and return to oven until cake is finished. Sprinkle with nuts or chocolate chips. Very good served with ice cream while cake is still warm.

Mrs. Junior Troyer
Mrs. Mose (Elsie) Troyer

Zucchini Cake

3 eggs
1 c. vegetable oil
3 tsp. vanilla
3 c. flour
1 c. nuts
1 c. brown sugar
1 c. white sugar
1 tsp. baking powder
1 tsp. soda
3 tsp. cinnamon
1 tsp. salt
2 c. raw grated zucchini
Topping:
$^1/_2$ c. butter
$^1/_2$ c. buttermilk
$^3/_4$ c. sugar

Beat eggs and oil. Add sugar and vanilla. Add dry ingredients. Mix well. Add nuts and zucchini. Bake at 350° for 35–40 minutes or until done. Bring topping ingredients to a boil. Punch holes in top of cake with a fork. Pour topping over cake. Serve warm with milk and fresh peaches. Very good.

Mrs. Roman E. Raber

Carrot Cake

4 eggs
1 c. vegetable oil
2 c. flour
2 c. brown sugar
2 tsp. soda
1 tsp. salt
2 tsp. cinnamon
4 c. grated carrots
$^1/_2$ c. chopped nuts
Frosting:
2 Tbsp. butter, softened
3 oz. cream cheese
2 c. powdered sugar
1 tsp. vanilla

Stir dry ingredients together and sift. Set aside. In large mixing bowl, beat eggs until frothy. Slowly beat in oil. Gradually add flour mixture, beating until smooth. Mix in carrots and nuts. Bake at 350° for 25–30 minutes.

Pineapple Cake

2 eggs
2 c. sugar
2 Tbsp. vegetable oil
2 c. flour
2 tsp. soda
1 tsp. salt
$2^1/_4$ c. crushed pineapple with juice
1 tsp. vanilla
$^1/_2$ c. chopped nuts, optional
Frosting:
8 oz. cream cheese, softened
$^1/_2$ c. butter, softened
1 tsp. vanilla
$1^3/_4$ c. powdered sugar

Mix all ingredients and bake at 300° for 35 minutes or longer. Spread frosting on cooled cake.
Mrs. David Miller

tid bits

Laundry won't freeze onto clotheslines if you add vinegar to the water used to wet the rag for cleaning the lines.

Quick Pineapple Cake

1 yellow cake mix
3 eggs
$^1/_4$ c. oil
1 c. pineapple juice
1 (20 oz.) can crushed pineapple
$^1/_2$ c. brown sugar
$^1/_4$ c. butter

Drain 1 c. juice from pineapple. Put in bowl with eggs, oil, and cake mix. Beat by hand. Melt butter in deep dish pizza pan. Sprinkle brown sugar over butter. Pour pineapple over sugar. Pour cake batter over this. Bake at 350° for 45 minutes or until done. Invert on pizza pan while still warm. Serve with ice cream. Delicious!

Mrs. Melvin Mast

Delicious Cake

1 Duncan Hines yellow cake mix
4 eggs
$^1/_2$ c. salad oil
1 can mandarin oranges, undrained
Topping:
1 lg. carton Cool Whip
1 can crushed pineapple, undrained
2 pkgs. instant vanilla pudding

Mix well and bake until done. When cake is completely cooled, add topping.

Susie Kuhns

Quick Banana Cake

1 yellow cake mix
1 pkg. instant vanilla pudding
4 eggs
$^1/_2$ c. oil
1 c. water
2 bananas, mashed
Cream Cheese Frosting:
$^1/_2$ c. Crisco
8 oz. cream cheese
3 c. powdered sugar
1 tsp. vanilla
$^3/_4$–1 c. Rich's topping, whipped

Bake at 350° for 30–40 minutes. Stir frosting ingredients until creamy. Store in refrigerator.

Mrs. Eddie E. Miller

Maple Nut Twist Cake

3/4 c. milk
1/4 c. butter
1 Tbsp. yeast
1 egg
1/2 tsp. salt
3 Tbsp. sugar
1 tsp. maple flavoring
3 c. Thesco flour
Filling:
1/4 c. butter
1/2 c. brown sugar
1 tsp. cinnamon
1 tsp. maple flavoring
1/3 c. nuts
Glaze:
1 c. powdered sugar
1 Tbsp. butter
1–2 tsp. milk
1/2 tsp. maple flavoring

Heat milk and butter until very warm. Mix yeast with enough water to dissolve. Beat together egg, salt, sugar, and flavoring. Add flour. Mix all together. Let set until double. Work out and put in pizza pan. Put filling on top and let set for 15 minutes. Cut into 16 pieces and twist 4 times. Bake at 350° for 13–15 minutes.

Mrs. Alvin H. Hershberger

Raspberry Creme-Filled Coffee Cake

3 lbs. donut mix
3 c. lukewarm water
2 Tbsp. sugar
pinch salt
2 Tbsp. yeast
cream cheese filling (in tube)
raspberry pie filling

Mix together first 5 ingredients like bread dough, kneading until not too sticky. You may need to add 1/2 c. flour. Cover and let rise until double in size. Knead down, then roll out on a floured surface. Spread margarine, cinnamon, and brown sugar over this. Roll up in a long roll. Chop up fine and put pieces in a greased coffee cake pan until bottom is covered. Spread cream cheese filling over top. Spread pie filling on top. Cover with remaining dough pieces and let rise. Bake at 350° for 30 minutes. Drizzle with icing.

Mrs. Ivan A. Miller
Verna Yoder

Berry Coffee Cake

1 c. sugar
1 c. butter, softened
2 eggs
1 tsp. baking powder
1 tsp. baking soda
$^1/_2$ tsp. salt
1 tsp. almond extract
1 c. sour cream
2 c. all-purpose flour
1 (16 oz.) can berry sauce
$^1/_2$ c. nuts
Glaze:
$^1/_3$ c. powdered sugar
$^1/_2$ tsp. vanilla
5 tsp. warm water

Put batter, nuts, and sauce in layers in a cake pan. You may also make your own fruit sauce. Bake at 350° for 55–60 minutes.

Mrs. Aden Burkholder

Cherry Coffee Cake

1 c. butter
$1^1/_2$ c. sugar
4 eggs
1 tsp. vanilla
3 c. flour
$1^1/_2$ tsp. baking powder
$^1/_4$ tsp. salt
1 can cherry pie filling
Glaze:
$1^1/_2$ c. powdered sugar
2 Tbsp. melted butter
milk

Cream butter and sugar. Add beaten eggs and vanilla. Sift and add dry ingredients. Spread $^2/_3$ of dough in a greased jellyroll pan. Cover with cherry pie filling. Spoon remaining dough over top. Bake at 350° for 35 minutes or until done. Drizzle with glaze while warm.

Mrs. David A. Yoder

A half teaspoon vinegar beaten into boiled frosting will keep it from being brittle or breaking when cut.

Walnut Wonder Coffee Cake

3 c. flour
1½ tsp. baking powder
1½ tsp. soda
½ tsp. salt
1½ c. sour milk
1 c. margarine
1½ c. sugar
3 eggs, beaten
1½ tsp. vanilla
Topping:
⅓ c. brown sugar
¼ c. white sugar
1 tsp. cinnamon
1 c. chopped nuts
Filling:
2 eggs, beaten
2 c. powdered sugar
1½ c. Crisco
vanilla

Sift dry ingredients together. Cream margarine with sugar. Stir in eggs and vanilla. Alternately add sour milk with dry ingredients. Divide batter in 2 cookie sheets and bake at 350°.

Clara Hershberger
Mrs. Henry J.C. Yoder
Barbara Hershberger

Apple Coffee Cake

2 c. sugar
3 c. flour
¼ tsp. salt
2 tsp. soda
1 c. shortening
2 eggs, beaten
1 c. milk
2 tsp. vanilla
4 chopped apples
Topping:
4 Tbsp. melted butter
1 c. brown sugar
4 Tbsp. flour
2 tsp. cinnamon
1 c. chopped nuts

Mix sugar, flour, salt, and soda. Add shortening and make crumbs. Add eggs, milk, and vanilla. Mix. Add apples. Mix topping ingredients and sprinkle over batter. Bake at 350° for 45 minutes. This makes a large cake. Use a half batch for a small cake pan.

Mrs. Mose E. Beachy

Fresh Apple Cake

¹/₂ c. margarine
1 c. brown sugar
1 egg
1¹/₂ c. flour
1 tsp. cinnamon
1 tsp. soda
¹/₄ tsp. salt
2 c. peeled, chopped or
   shredded apples
Topping:
¹/₄ c. brown sugar
1 Tbsp. melted butter or margarine
¹/₄ c. chopped nuts

Cream together margarine and sugar. Add egg. Sift together flour, cinnamon, soda, and salt. Add to creamed mixture. Fold in apples. Pour into a greased 9 X 9 pan. Mix topping ingredients and sprinkle on top. Bake at 350° for 30–35 minutes or until done.

Mrs. Roman Hershberger

Apple Sour Cream Cake

¹/₂ c. chopped nuts
1 tsp. cinnamon
¹/₂ c. sugar
¹/₂ c. butter
1 c. sugar
2 c. flour
1 c. sour cream
2 eggs
1 tsp. baking powder
1 tsp. baking soda
1 tsp. vanilla
1¹/₂–2 c. finely shredded apples
Caramel Glaze:
³/₄ c. sugar
¹/₂ c. corn syrup
¹/₄ c. butter
pinch salt
1 c. cream
1 tsp. vanilla

Combine nuts, cinnamon, and ¹/₂ c. sugar. Set aside. Cream butter and sugar. Add eggs and remaining ingredients. Grease pan and spread half of batter in pan. Sprinkle with half of nut mixture, then apples, then remaining nut mixture. Pour remaining batter over top. Bake at 350°. *For glaze:* Mix all together except vanilla. Cook in saucepan over low heat, stirring constantly to soft ball or a thick, smooth consistency. Remove from heat and add vanilla. Add cinnamonor apple pie spice, if desired.

Mrs. Jonas L. Miller

Sour Cream Coffee Cake

1/2 c. margarine, softened
1 c. sugar
2 eggs
1 c. sour cream
1 tsp. vanilla
2 c. flour
1 tsp. baking powder
1 tsp. soda
1 tsp. salt
Topping:
1/4 c. butter
2 tsp. cinnamon
1/3 c. brown sugar
1/2 c. chopped nuts

Cream butter and sugar. Add eggs, sour cream, and vanilla. Combine flour, baking powder, soda and salt. Add to creamed mixture and beat well. Pour half of batter in a greased 9 X 13 pan. Sprinkle with half of topping. Repeat. Bake at 325° for 40 minutes or until done.

Susie Keim

Good Morning Coffee Cake

1 1/2 c. sifted flour
2 tsp. baking powder
1/2 tsp. salt
1/2 c. sugar
1/4 c. lard
1 egg, beaten
1/2 c. milk
1 tsp. vanilla
Topping:
1/2 c. brown sugar
2 Tbsp. flour
1/8 tsp. salt
1 tsp. cinnamon
3 Tbsp. butter
1/2 c. chopped pecans
1/2 c. chocolate chips

Sift together flour, sugar, baking powder, and salt. Cut in lard. Stir in egg, milk, and vanilla. Spread half of batter in pan. Cover with half of topping mixture. Repeat. Bake at 375° for 25–30 minutes. *For topping:* Combine sugar, flour, cinnamon, and salt. Cut in butter until mixture is fine crumbs. Add chocolate chips and pecans.

Mrs. Henry J.C. Yoder
Mrs. Eli D.S. Yoder

Finnish Coffee Cake

1 1/4 c. white sugar
1 c. vegetable oil
2 eggs
1 tsp. vanilla
1 c. milk
2 c. flour
1/2 tsp. salt
1/2 tsp. soda
1/2 tsp. baking powder
4 Tbsp. brown sugar
1 Tbsp. cinnamon
Glaze:
2 c. powdered sugar
4 tsp. vanilla
hot water for right consistency

Beat together sugar, oil, eggs, vanilla, and milk. Add flour, salt, baking powder, and soda. Mix well. Pour half of batter in greased 9 X 13 pan. Combine brown sugar and cinnamon. Sprinkle half of mixture over batter. Repeat. Bake at 350°. When done, poke holes in cake and drizzle glaze over top.

Mrs. Mahlon R. Yoder

Conversation Coffee Cake

1 Tbsp. yeast
1/4 c. warm water
3/4 c. milk, heated
3 Tbsp. butter
3/4 tsp. salt
1 egg, beaten
2 Tbsp. sugar
3 c. all-purpose flour
Sugar Mixture:
3/4 c. white sugar
1/4 c. brown sugar
3 tsp. cinnamon
3 tsp. nuts

Dissolve yeast in warm water. Heat milk. Add butter, salt, egg, and sugar. Let mixture cool. Add yeast and stir. Add flour and knead. Let rise about 30 minutes. Put foil, dull side up, on a large pizza pan. Roll a small piece of dough, about the size of a walnut, into a rope about 6" long. Dip in 1/2 c. melted butter. Roll in sugar mixture. Starting in center of pan, make a roll. Repeat, adding onto the roll in the center to make a large roll. Let rise until oven is hot. Bake at 350° for 15–20 minutes. Glaze when cool.

Mrs. Delbert Miller

The Most Wanted Coffee Cake in the World

1 c. butter
2 c. sugar
2 eggs
1 c. sour cream
2 c. sifted flour
1 tsp. baking powder
1/4 tsp. salt
1 1/2 tsp. vanilla
Topping:
1/2 c. chopped nuts
1/4 c. brown sugar
1 1/2 tsp. vanilla

Cream butter and sugar. Add eggs, sour cream, and vanilla. Continue beating. Add flour, baking powder, and salt. Grease and flour a bundt pan. Put a third of the batter in pan. Sprinkle half of the topping over top. Add more batter, then remaining topping. Add last of batter. Bake at 350° for 50–60 minutes. Let cool for 15 minutes, then turn onto plate.

Mrs. Edwin N. (Ruth) Weaver

Pumpkin Coffee Cake

1/2 c. butter-flavored shortening
1 c. sugar
1 c. pumpkin
2 eggs, beaten
2 c. flour
2 tsp. baking powder
1/2 tsp. soda
1/2 tsp. salt
1 tsp. cinnamon
1/4 tsp. ginger
1/4 tsp. nutmeg
1 tsp. vanilla
Streusel:
1/4 c. brown sugar
1/4 c. white sugar
1/4 c. flour
1/4 c. quick oats
3 Tbsp. butter
nuts
cinnamon
Glaze:
1/2 c. powdered sugar
1 1/2 tsp. powdered sugar
vanilla

Pour half of batter into a 9" round pan. Add 1/2 c. applesauce and half of streusel. Pour remaining batter on top and then streusel. Bake at 350° for 50–55 minutes.

Mrs. Aden Yoder

Coffee Cake

1/2 c. sugar
1 1/4 tsp. salt
1/2 c. margarine
3/4 c. milk
1 1/2 Tbsp. yeast
1/2 c. warm water
2 eggs, beaten
4 c. flour
Crumbs:
3/4 c. flour
1/2 c. brown sugar
1/4 c. margarine
cinnamon
Filling:
4 2/3 c. powdered sugar
1/2 tsp. salt
2 egg whites, beaten
4 Tbsp. water
1/2 c. sugar
1 c. Crisco
2 tsp. vanilla

Dissolve yeast in warm water. Heat first 4 ingredients to lukewarm. Add eggs and yeast. Add flour to make a sticky dough. Let rise for 1 hour. Put in foil pans. Top with crumbs and let rise until double. Bake at 325°. Cool. Cut in half horizontally and fill. *For filling:* Combine powdered sugar, salt, and egg whites. Set aside. Cook water and sugar for 1 minute. Add to first mixture. Add Crisco and vanilla. Beat well.

Mrs. Abe Miller
Dorothy Yoder

Jellyroll

4 egg yolks, room temp.
1/4 tsp. salt
4 Tbsp. boiling water
1 c. sugar
1 c. flour
2 tsp. baking powder
4 egg whites, room temp.
Filling:
7 Tbsp. flour
2/3 c. brown sugar
1 1/3 c. hot water
5 Tbsp. butter

Beat egg yolks, salt, and boiling water together. Gradually add sugar, flour, and baking powder. Beat egg whites and fold in last. Bake at 350° for 25 minutes. *For filling:* Cook hot water, flour, and sugar together. Add butter and cool.

Prize-Winning Jellyroll

¹/₂ c. all-purpose flour
¹/₃ c. cocoa
¹/₂ tsp. baking soda
¹/₂ tsp. salt
4 eggs, separated
³/₄ c. sugar
1 tsp. vanilla

Sift flour, cocoa, soda, and salt. Set aside. Beat egg whites until soft peaks form. Gradually add sugar, continuing to beat until stiff peaks form. Beat egg yolks at high speed until thick and foamy. Blend in vanilla. Fold gently into egg whites. Fold in dry ingredients gently but thoroughly. Put waxed paper into a jellyroll pan. Pour batter into pan. Spread evenly. Bake at 400° for 12 minutes. Loosen edges and turn hot cake onto towel dusted with powdered sugar. Roll up cake with towel from wide end. Cool completely. Unroll and spread with your favorite filling. For a yellow roll, use ¹/₃ c. flour instead of cocoa. Variation: I like to used whipped topping mixed with 8 oz. cream cheese for filling. Fill jellyroll and refrigerate until filling is solid.

Mrs. Ivan Hershberger

Johnny Cake

¹/₂ c. sugar
¹/₂ c. lard
2 eggs
4 tsp. baking powder
1¹/₂ c. milk
2 c. flour
2 c. corn flour

Bake at 325°. Serve warm with milk and fruit.

Mrs. Andrew A. Troyer

Short Cake

Mrs. H.C.Y.

2¹/₄ c. flour
1 c. sweet milk
³/₄ c. sugar
3 tsp. baking powder
¹/₄ c. butter
1 egg
pinch salt

Christmas Fruit Cake

2 c. flour
2 tsp. baking powder
¹/₂ tsp. salt
1 lb. candied pineapple, coarsely cut
1 lb. whole candied cherries
1¹/₂ lb. pitted dates, coarsely cut
4 eggs
1 c. sugar
2 lbs. pecan pieces
pecan halves
additional candied cherries
light corn syrup

Sift flour, baking powder, and salt into a large bowl. Add pineapple, cherries, and dates. Mix well with hands to coat each piece of fruit with flour. Beat eggs until light and gradually beat in sugar. Add to fruit and mix well with hands. Mix in pecan pieces. Grease and line with brown paper two 9 X 5 X 3 loaf pans. Add mixture and press down firmly with fingers. Decorate top with rows of cherries and pecan halves. Bake at 275° for 1¹/₂ hours. Let cake set in pan for 5 minutes. Take brown paper off. Turn top side up and brush with corn syrup. When cold, wrap well and store in a cool place. Enjoy! This is better than candy.

Biena Schlabach

Better Cake Mixes

³/₄ c. flour
1 tsp. baking powder
¹/₂ c. sugar
¹/₃ c. water
1 egg
1 Tbsp. vegetable oil

Stir flour, baking powder, and sugar into dry cake mix. Prepare mix as directed on package, also adding remaining ingredients.

Mrs. Fannie Mae Barkman
Mrs. Mary Miller
Mattie Yoder

Zucchini Cupcakes

3 eggs
1 1/2 c. sugar
1/2 c. vegetable oil
1/2 c. orange juice
1 tsp. almond extract
2 1/2 c. all-purpose flour
2 tsp. cinnamon
2 tsp. baking powder
1 tsp. soda
1 tsp. salt
1/2 tsp. cloves
1 1/2 c. shredded zucchini

In a mixing bowl, beat eggs, sugar, oil, orange juice, and extract. Combine dry ingredients. Add to egg mixture and mix well. Add zucchini. Fill muffin cups 2/3 full. Bake at 350° for 20–25 minutes. Good with caramel frosting.

Mrs. Aden B. Miller

Surprise Cupcakes

1 chocolate cake mix
8 oz. cream cheese
1/3 c. sugar
1 egg, beaten
salt

Mix cake mix according to package directions. Fill cupcake papers 2/3 full. Blend rest of ingredients. Drop 1 tsp. of mixture on top of each cupcake. Bake at 350° for 20 minutes. Yields 24 cupcakes.

Mrs. Jerry Erb

Yummy Cupcakes

2 c. sugar
3 c. flour
1/2 c. cocoa
2/3 c. oil
2 tsp. vanilla
2 tsp. soda
2 Tbsp. vinegar
2 c. water
Filling:
8 oz. cream cheese
1 egg
1/2 c. sugar
1/4 tsp. salt
12 oz. chocolate chips

Combine first 8 ingredients and mix thoroughly. Mix filling ingredients and blend well. Fill cupcake papers half full of batter and top with 1 Tbsp. filling. Bake at 350° for 15–20 minutes.

Seven-Minute Frosting

2 egg whites, unbeaten
1 1/2 c. sugar
5 Tbsp. cold water
1/4 tsp. cream of tartar
1 tsp. vanilla

Combine egg whites, sugar, water, and cream of tartar in top of double boiler. Place in rapidly boiling water and beat constantly with rotary beater until mixture holds a peak. This requires 7 minutes. Remove from heat. Add vanilla and beat until thick enough to spread on cake.

Mrs. Reuben Mast

Creamy Vanilla Frosting

2 Tbsp. water
1/4 c. sugar
1/4 tsp. salt
1/2 c. margarine
1 tsp. vanilla
1 egg, beaten
powdered sugar

In a saucepan, combine water, sugar, and salt. Cook for 1 minute. Add margarine. Cool. Add vanilla and egg. Add powdered sugar.

Mrs. Raymond Wengerd

Maple Frosting

1/2 c. maple syrup
1 Tbsp. butter
2 c. powdered sugar

Bring syrup to a boil for 1 minute. Remove from heat and stir in butter. Add powdered sugar. Continue stirring until spreadable. Frosting will thicken as it cools.

Mrs. Dan E. Mast

Jellyroll Filling

1 c. sugar
2 Tbsp. cornstarch
2 Tbsp. clear jel
1/2 c. red Jell-O
3 c. hot water

Cook. Cool. Spread

Mrs. Mose E. Beachy

Quick Caramel Frosting

1 c. brown sugar
1/4 c. milk
1/2 c. butter
1 3/4–2 c. powdered sugar

Melt butter. Add brown sugar and cook over low heat for 2 minutes, stirring constantly. Slowly add milk and continue stirring until mixture comes to boil again. Remove from heat and add powdered sugar.

Mrs. Emma Hershberger
Mrs. David A. Yoder
Mandy Troyer

Wedding Cake Icing

1/2 c. shortening
1/2 c. butter
1 tsp. vanilla
4 c. powdered sugar
2 Tbsp. milk

Cream butter and shortening. Add vanilla. Add sugar, 1 c. at a time, beating well. When all sugar has been added, icing will appear dry. Add milk and beat until light and fluffy. Cover with a damp cloth until ready to use.

Mrs. Philip L. Yoder

German Chocolate Cake Frosting

2 egg yolks
2/3 c. brown sugar
2/3 c. canned milk
1/3 c. margarine
1/2 tsp. vanilla
1 1/3 c. coconut
1 c. nuts

Beat all together in saucepan and cook until thick. Spread immediately on cake.

Amanda Raber

Chocolate Frosting

¹/₄ c. melted Crisco
¹/₄ tsp. salt
1¹/₂ tsp. vanilla
¹/₂ c. cocoa
¹/₃ c. milk
3¹/₂ c. powdered sugar

Combine Crisco, cocoa, and salt. Add milk and vanilla. Stir in sugar in 3 parts. Mix until smooth and creamy. Add more sugar to thicken or milk to thin, if needed for good spreading consistency. This frosts a 9 X 13 cake.

Mrs. Aden A. Raber

"Perfectly Chocolate" Frosting

¹/₂ c. butter or margarine
¹/₂ c. cocoa
3 c. powdered sugar
¹/₃ c. milk
1 tsp. vanilla

Melt butter, stir in cocoa, and alternately add powdered sugar and milk, beating on medium speed until spreadable. Add more milk, if needed. Yields 2 cups.

Mrs. Mose E. Beachy

Baking Powder

2 Tbsp. cream of tartar
1 Tbsp. soda
1 Tbsp. cornstarch

Sift together. Mix well and store in an airtight container.

Sarah Raber

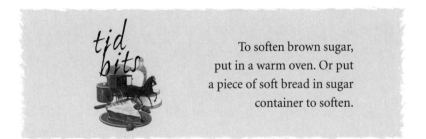

tid bits

To soften brown sugar, put in a warm oven. Or put a piece of soft bread in sugar container to soften.

Pies

Fruit Pie Filling

1/3 c. Mira-Clear
1 c. sugar
1 c. water
1 c. Sprite or 7-Up
2 Tbsp. Jell-O
2 c. fresh fruit

Cook Mira-Clear, sugar, water, and Sprite until thick. Add Jell-O and cool. Add fresh fruit and pour into crust. Garnish with Cool Whip.

Anna Miller

Thank-You Pie Filling

1/2 c. sugar
1 c. water
1/4 tsp. salt
1 tsp. lemon juice
1/4 c. clear jel
1/2 c. water
1/2 c. light Karo
2 c. fresh fruit

Heat sugar, water, salt, and lemon juice to dissolve sugar. Make a paste with clear jel and water. Stir into heated syrup and bring to a boil. When thick, remove from heat. Add Karo and fruit.

Savilla Mullet

Filling for Fruit Pie

4 oz. cream cheese, softened
1/2 c. sour cream
3 Tbsp. sugar
1/2 tsp. vanilla

Stir together. Put into a baked pie crust and top with your favorite fruit filling. Top with Cool Whip.

Mrs. Roman E. Raber

Shoestring Apple Pie

4 c. shredded apples
3/4 c. white sugar
3/4 c. brown sugar
1/4 c. milk
1 Tbsp. flour
2 eggs, beaten
1/2 tsp. maple flavoring

Mix all together and put into unbaked pie shells. Sprinkle with cinnamon. Bake at 350° until done.

Mrs. Mattie D. Miller

Apple Pie

4 c. water
2 c. white sugar
2 c. brown sugar
8 Tbsp. clear jel
8 c. chopped apples
4 tsp. butter
2 tsp. cinnamon or apple pie spice

Combine first 4 ingredients and cook until thickened. Add apples, then bring to a boil. Add butter and spice.

Anna Troyer

Apple Cream Pie

2 med. apples, sliced
$^1/_2$ c. brown sugar
$^1/_2$ c. white sugar
2 Tbsp. flour
1 c. sweet cream
1 egg
pinch salt
$^1/_2$ c. chopped nuts

Put apples in crust. Sprinkle with nuts. Mix remaining ingredients and pour over top. Bake slowly.

Mrs. Dan J.A. Yoder

Sour Cream Apple Pie

$^3/_4$ c. sugar
$^1/_2$ tsp. salt
1 egg
2 Tbsp. flour
2 c. chopped apples
1 c. sour cream
Crumbs:
$^1/_3$ c. brown sugar
1 tsp. cinnamon
$^1/_2$ c. flour
$^1/_4$ c. butter or margarine

Beat egg and add remaining ingredients. Bake at 350° for 30 minutes. Top with crumbs and bake for 15 minutes more. Yields 1 pie.

Anna Troyer

Mock Apple Pie

36 Ritz crackers, coarsely broken
2 c. water
2 c. sugar
2 tsp. cream of tartar
2 Tbsp. lemon juice
grated rind of 1 lemon
2 Tbsp. margarine
1/2 tsp. cinnamon

Place crackers in crust. Heat water, sugar, and cream of tartar. Simmer for 15 minutes. Add lemon juice and rind and cool. Pour over crackers. Dot with margarine. Sprinkle with cinnamon. Cover with top crust with slits. Bake at 425° for 30 minutes until crust is brown.

Mrs. Eli A. Mast

Streusel Topping for Apple Pie

1 c. quick rolled oats
1/3 c. brown sugar
1/3 c. chopped nuts
1/2 tsp. cinnamon
1/3 c. melted butter

Mix and sprinkle on top of apple pie before baking.

Susie Kuhns

Zucchini Pie

1 2/3 c. sugar
1/2 c. flour
1/2 tsp. cinnamon
1/8 tsp. salt
8 c. chopped zucchini
2 Tbsp. ReaLemon
4 Tbsp. margarine, divided

Mix sugar, flour, cinnamon, and salt. Set aside. Mix zucchini and lemon juice. Add dry ingredients and mix. Pour quickly into 2 unbaked pie crusts, dividing liquid evenly. Top each pie with 2 Tbsp. margarine, cut into 8 small pieces. Use a full top crust and seal edges tightly. Cut a few slits in center of pie with knife. Bake at 350° for 45–55 minutes. Note: I brush the top crust with milk and sprinkle with white sugar before baking. Many people have eaten this and thought it was apple pie since it tastes like apple pie.

Mrs. Eddie Raber

Green Tomato Pie

green tomatoes, thinly sliced
³/₄ c. brown sugar
³/₄ c. white sugar
2 Tbsp. flour
3 Tbsp. vinegar
1¹/₄ Tbsp. butter, melted
1 tsp. cinnamon

Fill unbaked pie shell with tomatoes. Mix remaining ingredients and pour on top. Cover with top crust and bake at 425° for 15 minutes. Reduce heat to 350° and bake for 30–40 minutes more. Delicious warm!

Mrs. Andrew A. Troyer

Rhubarb Crumb Pie

2 c. chopped rhubarb
1 egg, beaten
1 tsp. vanilla
2 Tbsp. flour
1 c. sugar
1 unbaked pie crust
Crumbs:
³/₄ c. flour
¹/₂ c. brown sugar
¹/₃ c. butter

Mix rhubarb, egg, vanilla, flour, and sugar. Put into pie crust. Top with crumbs. Bake at 425° for 15 minutes. Reduce heat to 350° and bake for 30 minutes more.

Mrs. Andrew A. Troyer

French Rhubarb Pie

1 egg
1 c. sugar
1 tsp. vanilla
2 c. diced rhubarb
2 tsp. flour
1 Tbsp. sour cream (heaping)
Topping:
³/₄ c. flour
¹/₂ c. brown sugar
¹/₃ c. margarine

Combine egg, sugar, vanilla, flour, rhubarb, and sour cream. Put into an unbaked pie shell. Cover with topping. Bake at 400° for 10 minutes. Reduce heat to 350° and bake for 30 minutes more or until done. Yields 1 (9") pie.

Mary Esther Miller

Rhubarb Custard Pie

2 c. rhubarb
1½ c. sugar
2 beaten eggs
5 tsp. flour
2 Tbsp. water
butter
cinnamon

Cut rhubarb thin. Put all ingredients except butter and cinnamon in a bowl and mix well. Pour into an unbaked pie shell. Sprinkle with cinnamon and dot with butter. Bake at 350° for 1 hour.

Anna Troyer

Delicious Peach Pie

2½ c. sliced peaches
1½ c. sugar
2 Tbsp. minute tapioca
1 Tbsp. butter
2 eggs, well beaten

Put 1 Tbsp. each of sugar and flour in crust. In a bowl, add sugar, butter, and tapioca to beaten eggs. Fold in peaches and bake at 450° for 15 minutes. Reduce heat to 350° and bake for 25 minutes longer.

Mrs. John D. Miller

Open-Face Peach Pie

1¼ c. sliced fresh peaches
½ c. brown sugar
½ c. white sugar
2 Tbsp. flour (rounded)
pinch salt
1 c. rich milk or cream

Put sliced peaches in unbaked pie shell. Mix remaining ingredients in order given and pour over peaches. Bake at 400° for 10 minutes. Reduce heat to 350° and bake until juice looks syrupy.

Mrs. Dan J.A. Yoder

Cherry Pie Filling

1½ c. water
1 c. sugar
clear jel
cherry Jell-O
food coloring
1 (21 oz.) can cherry pie filling

Mix water and sugar. Thicken with clear jel. Add food coloring and Jell-O. Add cherry pie filling.

Mrs. Arlene Hershberger

Blueberry Pie Filling

8 c. blueberries
3¹/₂ c. sugar
3 c. water
1 Tbsp. salt
1 tsp. lemon
¹/₄ c. butter
1 c. clear jel

Combine sugar, water, salt, lemon, butter, clear jel, and 4 c. blueberries. Cook until thick. Add remaining blueberries. Cold pack for 5–10 minutes. This is also good on ice cream or waffles or for pudding.

Mrs. Andy M.A. Troyer
Susie Keim

Blueberry Sour Cream Pie

1 c. sour cream
2 Tbsp. flour
³/₄ c. sugar
1 tsp. vanilla
¹/₄ tsp. salt
1 egg, beaten
2¹/₂ c. fresh blueberries
Crumbs:
3 Tbsp. flour
1¹/₂ Tbsp. butter
chopped nuts

Combine and beat until smooth. Fold in blueberries and pour into pie shell. Bake at 400° for 25 minutes. Remove from oven and sprinkle with crumbs. Bake for 10 minutes more.

Mrs. Jonas L. Miller

Sour Cream Cherry Pie

2¹/₂ c. cherry pie filling
1 c. sugar
1 c. sour cream
3 oz. cream cheese
3 Tbsp. flour
Crumbs:
1 c. flour
¹/₂ c. sugar
¹/₄ c. butter

Combine sugar and flour. Add sour cream and cream cheese. Blend well. Put fruit in unbaked pie shell. Pour mixture over fruit. Top with crumbs. Bake at 425° for 15 minutes. Reduce heat to 350° and bake for 25 minutes more. Also good with raspberry, blueberry, and pineapple. Delicious. Note: Always have cream cheese and sour cream at room temperature before using.

Mrs. Philip L. Yoder
Mrs. Ella Troyer

Raspberry Chiffon Pie

2 c. raspberries
3 Tbsp. ReaLemon
16 oz. Cool Whip
1 can Eagle Brand milk
8 oz. cream cheese, optional

Mix raspberries and ReaLemon. Thicken a little. When cool, add remaining ingredients. Pour into a baked pie shell.

Mrs. Abe Yoder
Mrs. Fred A. Raber
Mrs. Junior A. Troyer

Strawberry Pie Filling

8 c. water
5 c. sugar
2 pkgs. Danish dessert
1 pkg. strawberry Kool-Aid
1 c. clear jel
2 c. water
5 qts. partially chopped strawberries

Combine water and sugar. Bring to a boil. Mix Danish dessert, Kool-Aid, clear jel, and water. Add to first mixture and bring to a boil. Pour over strawberries. Put into jars and bring to boil. Let set for 10 minutes before removing. This is good in homemade yogurt.

Mrs. R.E. Weaver

Strawberry Pie

1 c. sugar
1 c. water
2 Tbsp. clear jel
2 Tbsp. strawberry Jell-O (heaping)
pinch salt
1 pkg. Danish dessert
strawberries
Cool Whip

Combine sugar, water and clear jel. Bring to a boil. Add Jell-O and salt. Mix Danish dessert according to package directions and add. Add strawberries. Put into crust. Top with Cool Whip.

Melvin Miller
Mandy Troyer

Orange Chiffon Pie

2 c. pineapple juice
3 oz. orange Jell-O
1 can Eagle Brand milk
12 oz. Cool Whip
3 Tbsp. lemon juice

Heat half of pineapple juice. Add Jell-O, then blend all together with a wire whip. Pour into baked pie shells.

Mrs. Felty J. Erb
Verna Yoder

Mary's Own Angel Pie

1 1/3 c. graham cracker crumbs
1/4 lb. melted butter or margarine
4 egg whites
1/4 tsp. salt
1 tsp. vinegar
1 c. sugar
1 1/2 c. heavy cream, whipped
1 c. shredded coconut
2 Tbsp. sugar
1 tsp. vanilla

Combine cracker crumbs and butter. Pat firmly into a 9" pie pan. Beat egg whites until frothy. Add salt and vinegar and beat until stiff. Add 1 c. sugar, 2 Tbsp. at a time, beating thoroughly after each addition. Spread in prepared crust and bake at 275° for 1 1/4 hours. Cool. Fold sugar, coconut, and vanilla into whipped cream. Spread over top of pie. Toast remaining coconut and sprinkle over whipped cream. Yields 6 servings.

Barbara Coblentz

Chiffon Pie

2 c. juice
3 oz. Jell-O
1 can Eagle Brand milk
12 oz. Cool Whip
3 Tbsp. lemon juice

Heat 1 c. juice and Jell-O until dissolved. Add milk, Cool Whip, remaining juice, and lemon juice. Blend all together with a wire whip. Flavor suggestions: Orange Jell-O with pineapple juice, grape Jell-O with grape juice, or raspberry Jell-O with raspberry juice. Yields 2 large or 3 small pies.

Mrs. Ben D. Miller

Lemon Chiffon Pie

1 pkg. gelatin
$1/4$ c. cold water
$1/2$ c. sugar
$1^1/4$ c. milk
pinch salt
$3/4$ tsp. lemon flavoring
1 c. Cool Whip
yellow food coloring

Soften gelatin in cold water. Set aside. Combine sugar, milk, and salt in a saucepan. Bring to a boil, stirring constantly. Remove from heat. Add gelatin mixture. Cool until slightly thick. Beat the cooked mixture in until smooth. Add lemon flavoring. Fold in Cool Whip and add food coloring for a light yellow color. Fill a baked pie crust.

Katie B. Yoder

Lemon Pie

1 tube lemon pie filling
1 tube cream cheese filling
$2^1/2$ c. topping

Whip topping, then beat all together and put into baked pie shells. Put topping on top. This is also good with other flavors of tube filling.

Mrs. Melvin Mast
Mrs. Henry A. Yoder

Old-Fashioned Lemon Pie

$1^1/2$ lemons
$1^1/2$ c. sugar
3 Tbsp. cornstarch or clear jel
3 eggs
$1^1/4$ c. boiling water

Juice lemons. Cook rind in water. Mix sugar, cornstarch, and lemon juice. Add beaten egg yolks. Remove lemon rind and pour mixture into boiling water. Stir constantly until boiling. Put into a baked crust. Beat egg whites until stiff. Add 6 Tbsp. sugar to egg whites. Spread over pie and brown. Note: I like to put Hi-N-Dri on top instead of egg whites.

Mrs. Ben R. Hershberger

Key Lime Pie

1 can Eagle Brand milk
1/2 c. ReaLime juice
8 oz. Cool Whip
green food coloring

Mix thoroughly and pour into baked pastry shell. Top with Cool Whip.

Mrs. Ben J. Troyer

Pennsylvania Shoo-Fly Pie

Crumbs:
1 c. flour
2/3 c. brown sugar
1 Tbsp. shortening
Syrup:
3/4 c. King syrup
1/4 c. baking molasses
1 egg, beaten
1 c. boiling water
1 tsp. soda

Mix crumb ingredients. Set aside 1/2 c. for topping. Mix molasses and egg. Combine soda and boiling water. Add to remaining crumbs and molasses. Pour into an unbaked pie shell. Top with remaining crumbs. Bake at 350° for 35–40 minutes.

Fannie Weaver

Shoo-Fly Pie

Syrup:
1 c. brown sugar
1 egg
1 c. molasses
1/2 tsp. soda
1/3 c. boiling water
2/3 c. cold water
Crumbs:
2 c. flour
2/3 c. brown sugar
1/3 tsp. baking powder
1/2 c. shortening or lard

Stir the egg into the sugar. Add the molasses. Dissolve the soda in the boiling water. Add the cold water. Combine with the sugar and egg mixture. Pour into an unbaked 9" pie shell. Mix crumb ingredients together until crumbly. Sprinkle on top. Bake at 350° for 10 minutes. Reduce heat to 325° and bake for 50 minutes longer or until done. Yields 1 (9") pie.

Barbara Raber

Creamy Vanilla Crumb Pie

2 (9") unbaked pie crusts
8 oz. cream cheese
1/2 c. sugar
1 egg, beaten
1/2 tsp. salt
1 tsp. vanilla
Filling:
2 c. water
1 c. sugar
1 Tbsp. flour
1 c. dark corn syrup
1 egg, beaten
1 tsp. vanilla
Crumb Topping:
2 c. flour
1/2 c. brown sugar
1/2 c. butter or margarine, softened
1 tsp. baking soda
1/2 tsp. cream of tartar
1/2 tsp. cinnamon

Beat together cream cheese, sugar, egg, salt, and vanilla. Spread in pie crusts. In a medium saucepan, bring 2 c. water to a boil. Combine sugar, flour, corn syrup, and egg. Stir into hot water. Bring to a boil, then set aside to cool. Add vanilla. When cooled, pour this over cream cheese layers. Mix topping ingredients until crumbly. Spread over top of pies. Bake at 375° for 30–40 minutes. Yields 2 pies.

Mrs. Abe E. Mast

Vanilla Crumb Pie

1 1/2 c. brown sugar
2 tsp. vanilla
3 c. water
3 Tbsp. clear jel (heaping)
1/2 c. butter
2 unbaked pie shells
Crumb Topping:
2 c. flour
1/2 c. margarine
1/4 tsp. cream of tartar
1/2 c. sugar
1/4 tsp. soda
1/2 tsp. salt

Cook sugar, clear jel, butter, and water together until thick. Cool. Add vanilla and pour into pie shells. Mix crumb ingredients until crumbly and pour over pie filling. Bake at 400° until crust is baked.

Mrs. Ivan Hershberger

Favorite Custard Pie

2 eggs
2 Tbsp. flour
$^1/_2$ c. white sugar
$^1/_2$ c. brown sugar
1 tsp. vanilla
1 c. evaporated milk
$^3/_4$ c. cream or half and half
1 c. milk

Separate eggs. Beat egg whites until fluffy. Add white sugar and beat again. Set aside. Beat egg yolks, brown sugar, and flour together. Add half of beaten egg whites. Mix well and add vanilla. Add evaporated milk, cream, milk, and the rest of the egg whites. Bake at 450° for 15 minutes. Reduce heat to 325° and bake for 20 minutes longer or until set.

Mrs. Aden Chupp

Custard Pie

10 eggs, separated
5 Tbsp. flour
5 tsp. vanilla
10 c. milk, heated
$1^3/_4$ c. white sugar
$1^3/_4$ c. brown sugar

Beat egg whites last and add to remaining ingredients. Bake at 450° for 10 minutes. Reduce heat to 325° and bake until done. Yields 4 pies.

Mrs. Mahlon R. Yoder

Custard Pie

4 c. milk, scalding
$^3/_4$ c. brown sugar
$^3/_4$ c. white sugar
2 Tbsp. flour
4 eggs, separated
$^1/_2$ can Eagle Brand milk
1 tsp. vanilla

Mix egg yolks, sugars, flour, and Eagle Brand milk. Add scalding milk and vanilla. Last, fold in beaten egg whites. Bake at 425° for 15 minutes. Reduce heat to 350° for 20 minutes or until done. Yields 2 pies.

Mrs. Ray Raber
Dora Schlabach
Dena Weaver

Custard Pie

3/4 c. white sugar
2 Tbsp. brown sugar
2 Tbsp. flour (slightly rounded)
pinch salt
3 eggs, separated
3 1/2 c. milk, including
  1/2 can evaporated milk
1 tsp. maple flavoring

Mix sugar, flour, and salt. Add egg yolks and a little of the milk. Do not heat the milk. Stir briskly. Gradually add the rest of the milk and maple flavoring with wire whip. Beat egg whites until stiff and fold in. Bake at 400° for 10 minutes. Reduce heat to 350° and bake for 30 minutes more. Yields 1 large pie.

Susie Ellen Yoder
Mrs. Mattie Miller

Cream Pie

2/3 c. sugar
2 eggs
2 Tbsp. flour
2 Tbsp. butter
3 c. milk
2 Tbsp. cornstarch
1/2 tsp. salt
1 tsp. vanilla

Heat milk to boiling. Mix other ingredients and add to milk, stirring constantly until it cooks. Cool. Yields 1 pie.

Mrs. John E. Troyer
Clara Hershberger

Coconut Cream Pie

First Layer:
1/3 c. brown sugar
1/3 c. butter or margarine
1/2 c. pecans
Second Layer:
2 c. milk
3 Tbsp. flour
1/2 tsp. salt
2 egg yolks
1 Tbsp. butter
3/4 c. brown sugar
1/2 c. fine coconut
3/4 tsp. coconut flavoring

For first layer: Combine ingredients in a saucepan and bring to a boil. Cook for 30 seconds, then put into a baked pie shell. *For second layer:* Heat milk. Mix other ingredients, except butter and flavorings. Add enough milk so you can stir. Bring to a boil. Add butter and flavoring. Cool. Stir in whipped topping when ready to use. This can also be used for raisin cream pie. We usually brown the butter a little bit.

Mrs. Adam Hershberger

Maple Cream Pie

1³/₄ c. milk, divided
¹/₄ c. cornstarch
³/₄ c. plus 1 Tbsp. maple
  syrup, divided
¹/₄ tsp. salt
2 egg yolks
2 Tbsp. butter or margarine
1 c. cream
almonds

Blend together cornstarch and ¹/₄ c. milk in a saucepan. Gradually stir in remaining milk, ³/₄ c. syrup, and salt. Cook over medium heat, stirring constantly, until it comes to a boil. Remove from heat. Stir ¹/₄ c. of the hot mixture into the egg yolks. Bring to boil. Cook, stirring constantly, until thick and bubbly. Remove from heat. Stir in butter. Cool, stirring frequently. Meanwhile, whip cream until stiff. Fold 1 cup whipped cream into cooled filling. Spoon into a prepared 9" pie crust. Fold remaining syrup into remaining cream. Spread over top of pie. Chill. Garnish with almonds.

Mrs. Dan E. Mast

Raisin Pie Filling

4 c. raisins
3 c. sugar
8 c. water
2 tsp. salt
1 Tbsp. ReaLemon
¹/₄ c. butter
1 c. clear jel

Cook raisins, sugar, water, salt, ReaLemon, and butter together. Add clear jel. It will thicken more when cool, so don't make it too thick.

Mrs. Jacob Yoder
Mrs. Andy M.A. Troyer

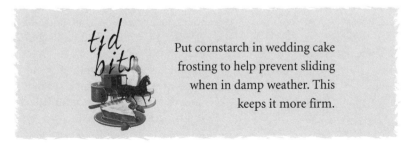

tid bits

Put cornstarch in wedding cake frosting to help prevent sliding when in damp weather. This keeps it more firm.

Raisin Cream Pie

2 c. milk
2 Tbsp. flour (heaping)
1 c. sugar
1 tsp. salt
4 egg yolks, well beaten
2 Tbsp. butter
1 c. raisins
2 tsp. vanilla
whipped topping

Heat milk in a saucepan. Mix flour, sugar, salt, and egg yolks together with a little milk. Add to hot milk. Boil a while, then add butter and raisins. When thickened, remove from heat and add vanilla. Fills 1 baked pie shell. Top with whipped topping.

Mrs. David A. Barkman
Mrs. Henry J.C. Yoder

Raisin Cream Pie

6 c. milk
9 Tbsp. flour (heaping)
1¹/₂ tsp. salt
6 egg yolks
3 Tbsp. butter, slightly browned
3 c. cooked raisins
2¹/₄ c. brown sugar

Heat milk and butter. Mix other ingredients except raisins. Add enough milk so you can stir. Bring to a boil. Add raisins. Cool. Add 1 can Rich's topping when ready to use. Variation: Omit raisins and browned butter and use melted butter and coconut. Yields 4 pies.

Mrs. Abe Yoder

Caramel Raisin Pie

3 c. raisins
2 c. brown sugar
3 c. water
1 can evaporated milk
2 Tbsp. butter
2 c. water
¹/₂ c. water
7 Tbsp. clear jel (heaping)
1¹/₂ c. milk
salt
1 tsp. maple flavoring

Cook raisins and 3 c. water in a saucepan. In another pan, cook ¹/₂ c. water and brown sugar. Cook each for 7–10 minutes. Add sugar and water mixture to raisins. Add 2 c. water. Bring to a boil again and add clear jel. Immediately add milk and evaporated milk. Cook for several minutes. Add butter and salt. More sugar may be used to suit taste. May be used for 2-crust pies or for baked crusts. Yields 3 pies.

Mrs. Ivan Hershberger

Fluffy Caramel Pie

1½ c. crushed gingersnaps
¼ c. melted butter
Filling:
¼ c. cold water
1 env. unflavored gelatin
28 caramels
1 c. milk
salt
½ c. chopped pecans
1 tsp. vanilla
1 c. whipping cream, whipped
caramel ice cream topping
pecans

Combine cookie crumbs and butter. Press into a 9" pie plate and chill. Place cold water in a saucepan and sprinkle with gelatin. Let set for 1 minute. Add caramels, milk, and salt. Cook and stir over low heat until gelatin is dissolved and caramels are melted. Refrigerate until mixture mounds when stirred with a spoon. Stir in pecans and vanilla. Fold in whipped cream. Pour into crust and refrigerate overnight. Garnish with caramel ice cream topping and pecans.

Mrs. Atlee (Lizzie) Raber

Old-Fashioned Butterscotch Pie

½ c. butter
1 c. water
⅛ tsp. soda
2 egg yolks
1 c. brown sugar
3 Tbsp. cornstarch
1½ c. milk
1 tsp. vanilla

Brown butter in saucepan. Add sugar and cook, stirring constantly, until sugar is melted. Add boiling water. Stir slowly and cook until sugar is again dissolved. Add soda. Combine cornstarch, egg yolks, and milk. Add to first part. Cook until thickened. Yields 1 (9") pie.

Our Favorite Peanut Butter Pie

8 oz. cream cheese, softened
¾ c. peanut butter
2½ c. powdered sugar
3 c. whipped topping
1 tsp. vanilla

Combine cream cheese and peanut butter. Add vanilla and powdered sugar. Beat well and add topping. Pour into a baked pie shell. Top with peanut butter and powdered sugar crumbs. Yields 2 pies.

Mrs. Philip L. Yoder

Peanut Butter Cup Pie

First Layer:
$^1/_2$ c. sugar
1 Tbsp. flour
1 Tbsp. cocoa
$^1/_4$ c. milk
1 egg, beaten
$1^1/_2$ tsp. vanilla
Second Layer:
4 oz. cream cheese
$^1/_4$ c. peanut butter
$^1/_2$ c. powdered sugar
4 oz. whipped topping
$^1/_2$ tsp. vanilla

Mix first layer ingredients together and pour into an unbaked pie shell. Bake at 350° for 20 minutes or until set. Cool and chill. Mix together second layer ingredients. Pour over chocolate mixture. Spread whipped topping on top and sprinkle with grated chocolate.

Mrs. Ben J. Troyer
Mrs. John E. Troyer
Mrs. Henry A. Yoder

Peanut Butter Pie Filling

1 qt. milk
1 c. white sugar
3 egg yolks
3 Tbsp. flour (heaping)
milk
$1^1/_2$ c. Rich's topping, whipped
8 oz. cream cheese
vanilla

Combine milk and sugar. Bring to a boil. Add egg yolks. Mix flour with milk to make a paste. Add. Bring to a boil, then remove from heat. Cool. Combine whipped topping, cream cheese, and vanilla. Add to pudding mixture. Put into baked pie shells. This can also be used for cracker or Oreo cookie pudding.

Mrs. Aden L. Yoder

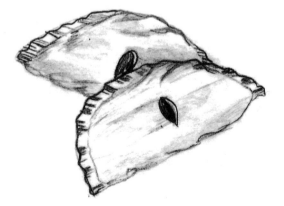

Esther's Peanut Butter Pie

1 baked pie shell
8 oz. cream cheese, room temp.
1 c. creamy peanut butter
1 c. powdered sugar
2 Tbsp. butter, room temp.
$^1/_2$ c. whipping cream
2 Tbsp. powdered sugar
1 Tbsp. vanilla
Fudge Topping:
$^1/_2$ c. whipping cream
6 oz. semi-sweet chocolate, chopped

Beat cream cheese and peanut butter in a large bowl until well blended. Add 1 c. powdered sugar and butter. Beat until fluffy. In a medium bowl, beat $^1/_2$ c. cream until soft peaks form. Gradually add 2 Tbsp. powdered sugar and vanilla and beat to stiff peaks. Fold $^1/_3$ of cream mixture into peanut butter mixture to lighten. Gently fold in remaining cream. Spoon into pie shell and refrigerate until firm, about 3 hours. *For fudge topping:* Bring $^1/_2$ c. cream to simmer in a heavy saucepan over low heat. Add chocolate and stir until smooth. Cool until lukewarm. Spread topping over pie. Refrigerate until firm. Cut into small pieces and enjoy. This is very rich and good.

Mrs. Edwin N. (Ruth) Weaver

White Christmas Pie

1 can Meadow Gold milk
$^1/_3$ c. lemon juice
$^1/_3$ c. coconut
$^1/_2$ c. chopped nuts
1 (16 oz.) can crushed
    pineapple, drained
$^1/_4$ c. pineapple juice
12 oz. Cool Whip

Mix all together. Put into 2 baked crusts. Put whipped topping on top, if desired.

Katie Hershberger
Mrs. Mose A. Miller

Rice Krispie Ice Cream Pie

1/2 c. marshmallow topping
2 c. Rice Krispies
1 Tbsp. melted butter

Mix together. Press into pie pan and freeze. Fill with softened vanilla ice cream and freeze again. Top with your favorite pie filling or strawberries cooked with Danish dessert.

Mary Hostetler

Frozen Chocolate Pie

4 oz. cream cheese, softened
1/2 c. powdered sugar
1 tsp. vanilla
2 1/2 Tbsp. cocoa
1/4 c. milk
8 oz. Cool Whip
9" baked pie crust

Beat cream cheese, sugar, and vanilla until smooth. Add cocoa alternately with milk. Fold in Cool Whip. Pour into pie crust. Freeze. Serve directly from freezer. Pie does not need to be thawed to cut.

Mrs. Roman E. Raber

Chocolate Cream Pie

3 oz. cream cheese, softened
1/2 c. sugar
1 tsp. vanilla
1/3 c. cocoa
1/3 c. milk
8 oz. whipped topping

Combine first 3 ingredients. Add cocoa and milk alternately. Add whipped topping. Put into a baked pie crust.

Mrs. Andy E. Yoder

Chocolate Pie

3 pkgs. chocolate instant pudding
4 1/2 c. milk
16 oz. cream cheese, softened
2 c. powdered sugar
16 oz. Cool Whip

Heat milk. When milk is cool, add pudding. Let set until thick. Mix cream cheese, powdered sugar, and Cool Whip. Mix all together. Pour into 4 pie crusts. Good!

Mrs. Marion Miller
Mrs. Mosie Yoder
Mrs. Susan Miller

Chocolate Mocha Pie

½ c. sugar
8 oz. Baker's chocolate
8 oz. cream cheese, softened
½ c. milk
3½ c. Cool Whip
9" baked pie crust

Melt chocolate and ¼ c. milk over very low heat, stirring constantly. Beat in cream cheese, sugar, and remaining milk. Cool. Carefully fold in Cool Whip. Put in pie crust.

Mrs. Neva J. Hershberger

Oreo Pie

For 3 pies:
3 pkgs. instant vanilla pudding
4½ c. milk
16 oz. cream cheese, softened
16 oz. whipped topping
2 c. powdered sugar
For 1 pie:
1 pkg. instant vanilla pudding
1½ c. milk
5¼ oz. whipped topping
5 oz. cream cheese
⅔ c. powdered sugar

Beat together milk and pudding. Add whipped topping. Mix cream cheese and powdered sugar. Add to pudding mixture. Add crushed Oreo cookies. Pour into baked pie crust.

Mrs. Leroy Miller

tid bits

There is no need to grease cake pans. Just swish water over pan and pour out. Put batter in and it will come out nicely.

Chocolate Cream Cheese Pie

For 1 pie:
8 oz. whipped topping
3 oz. cream cheese, softened
$^1/_2$ c. sugar
1 Tbsp. cocoa
2 Tbsp. milk
1 tsp. vanilla
For 10 pies:
4 boxes cream cheese
4 c. white sugar
10 Tbsp. cocoa
$^1/_2$ c. milk
3 tsp. vanilla
3 boxes Hi-N-Dri Topping

Combine cream cheese, sugar, and vanilla. Add cocoa and milk. Beat until smooth. Add whipped topping. Spoon into baked pie shell. Top with whipped topping and grated chocolate candy bar, if desired.

Mrs. Melvin Mast
Mrs. Jacob Yoder

Turtle Pie

3 baked pie crusts
First Layer:
45 caramels
$^1/_2$ c. butter
1 can Eagle Brand milk
Second Layer:
3 pkgs. cook & serve
    chocolate pie filling
$1^1/_2$ c. Rich's topping, whipped
8 oz. cream cheese

Cook first layer ingredients until caramels are melted. Put in bottom of crusts. Cook pudding. Cool, then add whipped topping and cream cheese.

Susie Keim

Pecan Cream Pie

$^1/_3$ c. brown sugar
$^1/_3$ c. butter or margarine
$^1/_2$ c. pecans

Put all together and cook for 30 seconds. Pour into a baked pie shell. Top with vanilla, coconut, or peanut butter pie filling.

Mrs. Abe Yoder

Chocolate Fudge Pecan Pie

1/2 c. butter
3/4 c. hot water
1/2 c. flour
1 tsp. vanilla
3 Tbsp. cocoa
3/4 c. white sugar
3/4 c. brown sugar
1/8 tsp. salt
1/2 can evaporated milk
1 1/2 c. pecans

Melt butter and cocoa together. Add other ingredients. Bake at 350° for 1 hour or until set.

Mary Schlabach

Cream Cheese Pecan Pie

8 oz. cream cheese, softened
1/2 c. sugar
1 egg, beaten
1/2 tsp. vanilla
1 c. chopped pecans
Topping:
3 eggs
1/4 c. sugar
1 c. light corn syrup
1 tsp. vanilla

Mix first 4 ingredients. Spread into bottom of an unbaked pie shell. Top with pecans. Mix topping ingredients and beat until smooth. Pour over pecan layer. Bake at 375° for 35–40 minutes or until golden brown. Serve slightly warm.

Mrs. David Yoder

Pecan Praline Pie

1/3 c. butter
1/3 c. brown sugar
1/2 c. pecans
Filling:
1 pkg. instant vanilla pudding
1 1/4 c. milk
2 c. whipped topping

Combine butter, sugar, and pecans. Heat until bubbly. Pour into baked pie shell and bake at 350° for 3–5 minutes. Mix filling and put on top. Yields 1 pie.

Mrs. Alvin H. Hershberger
Mrs. Eddie E. Miller

Butterscotch Praline Pie

1 c. butter or margarine
1 c. brown sugar
1 c. chopped pecans or walnuts
Filling:
2 c. brown sugar
$1/2$ c. butter or margarine
$3^1/2$ c. hot water
3 eggs
1 c. white sugar
1 c. cornstarch
4 c. milk
pinch salt
$1^1/2$ c. whipped topping

Combine butter and brown sugar in saucepan. Cook, stirring constantly, until mixture bubbles. Remove from heat. Add nuts and gently spread in 3 lightly baked pie crusts. Return crusts to oven until mixture starts to bubble. Remove immediately. Cool. Combine brown sugar, butter, and hot water in saucepan. Cook until you have combined eggs, sugar, milk, cornstarch, and salt. Beat these and add to boiling mixture, stirring constantly until it thickens. Cool. Add whipped topping.

Mrs. John E. Troyer

Holiday Walnut Pie

4 tsp. butter, melted
$1/2$ c. sugar
$1/2$ c. brown sugar
2 eggs
$1/2$ c. canned milk
$1/4$ c. light corn syrup
1 c. chopped walnuts or pecans
$1/4$ tsp. salt

Combine butter, sugar, and salt. Add eggs and mix well. Stir in milk, corn syrup, vanilla, and nuts. Pour into 1 unbaked pie shell. Bake at 400° for 30 minutes.

Mrs. Levi Yoder

Favorite Pecan Pie

3 eggs, beaten
1 c. dark Karo
$1/2$ c. light Karo
1 tsp. vanilla
$1/4$ tsp. salt
1 Tbsp. flour
1 c. chopped pecans

Mix first 5 ingredients together. Mix nuts and flour. Add butter and mix all together. Bake at 350° for 40 minutes.

Mrs. Edward M. Hershberger

Coconut Oatmeal Pie

3 eggs, beaten
²/₃ c. sugar
1 c. brown sugar
2 Tbsp. margarine, softened
²/₃ c. quick oats
²/₃ c. coconut
1 c. milk
1 tsp. vanilla

Mix together. Bake at 400° for 8 minutes. Reduce heat to 350° and bake until done.

Mrs. David J. Troyer

Oatmeal Pie

4 eggs
2 c. sugar
2 Tbsp. clear jel
1 c. light corn syrup
1 c. maple syrup
1 c. water
1¹/₂ c. quick oats
1 c. butter
1 tsp. salt
1 tsp. vanilla
1 c. coconut or pecans

Beat eggs. Combine sugar and clear jel. Add to eggs. Add remaining ingredients. Bake at 450° until slightly browned. Reduce heat to 350° and bake until done. If you don't have maple syrup, pancake or waffle syrup may be used. Yields 2 pies.

Mrs. John D. Miller

Pumpkin Pecan Pie

4 eggs, slightly beaten
2 c. canned or mashed, cooked pumpkin
1 c. sugar
¹/₂ dark corn syrup
¹/₂ tsp. cinnamon
¹/₄ tsp. salt
1 tsp. vanilla
1 c. chopped pecans
1 unbaked 9" crust

Combine all ingredients except pecans. Pour into pie shell. Top with pecans. Bake at 350° for 40 minutes or until set.

Barbara Coblentz

Pumpkin Pie

³/₄ c. sugar
2 Tbsp. brown sugar
2 tsp. cornstarch
pinch salt
¹/₄ tsp. nutmeg
¹/₂ tsp. cinnamon
¹/₂ tsp. pumpkin pie spice
2 eggs, separated
³/₄ c. cooked pumpkin
1 c. milk
1 c. evaporated milk
1 tsp. vanilla

Mix dry ingredients. Add egg yolks and a little milk. Stir well and add pumpkin. Add remaining milk and vanilla. Add beaten egg whites last. Bake at 425° for 10 minutes. Reduce heat to 325° and bake 30 minutes longer.

Mrs. Dan Mast

Pumpkin Pie

3 c. milk
1¹/₄ c. brown sugar
3 Tbsp. flour
³/₄ c. pumpkin
3 egg yolks, separated
¹/₄ tsp. cloves
¹/₄ tsp. nutmeg
¹/₄ tsp. cinnamon

Heat milk to boiling point. Cool. Mix brown sugar, flour, egg yolks, pumpkin, and spices. Add cooled milk. Beat egg whites until stiff. Add to mixture and beat all together. Pour into unbaked shells and bake at 425° for 10 minutes. Reduce heat to 325° and bake until done.

Mrs. Ben R. Hershberger

Pumpkin Pie

2 c. white sugar
6 Tbsp. brown sugar
4 Tbsp. flour
pinch salt
1 tsp. cinnamon
1 tsp. pumpkin pie spice
2 c. milk, heated
2 c. evaporated milk
6 eggs, separated
1¹/₂ c. pumpkin
1 tsp. vanilla

Add beaten egg whites last. Bake at 400° for 15 minutes. Reduce heat to 350° and bake for 25 minutes more. Yields 2 large pies.

Mrs. Monroe N. Miller
Mrs. Marion Miller

Sensational Double-Layer Pumpkin Pie

Part One:
4 oz. cream cheese, softened
1 Tbsp. milk or half and half
1 Tbsp. sugar
1 1/2 c. Cool Whip
Part Two:
1 c. milk or half and half
2 pkgs. instant vanilla pudding
16 oz. pumpkin
1 3/4 tsp. pumpkin pie spice

Combine ingredients for part one. Mix well and spread in bottom of crust. Mix part two ingredients well and spread over cream cheese layer. Garnish with whipped topping.

Mrs. Aden Chupp

Cream Cheese Pastries

1 c. butter, softened
8 oz. cream cheese, softened
2 c. flour
1/2 tsp. salt
pie filling
Glaze:
1 1/2 c. powdered sugar
2–4 Tbsp. water

Mix together and chill dough for 1 hour. Roll out to 1/4" thickness and cut into 4" squares. Put pie filling in from one corner to the other across the center and fold in the other two corners. Fasten with a toothpick. Bake at 375° for 15 minutes. Cool and drizzle with glaze.

Jerilyn Miller

Pecan Tarts

Crust:
2 1/2 c. flour
6 oz. cream cheese
1 c. butter or margarine
1 1/4 tsp. salt
Syrup:
1 c. brown sugar
1/2 c. light Karo
2 Tbsp. melted butter
1 tsp. vanilla
2 eggs
1/2 c. chopped pecans

Mix crust ingredients. Shape into balls the size of a walnut. Place each into a greased tart pan, shaping it like the pan. *For the syrup:* Beat eggs into melted butter. Add sugar, Karo, vanilla, and a pinch of salt. Add nuts. Pour syrup into each tart. Bake at 350° for 20 minutes.

Luella Wengerd

Cheese Tarts

Crust:
2^{1}/$_{2}$ c. pastry flour
1 c. shortening
8 oz. cream cheese
pinch salt
Filling:
16 oz. cream cheese
1 c. sugar
1 c. powdered sugar
2 eggs
2 Tbsp. melted butter

Mix crust like pie crust.

Erma Mast

Dolly's Pie Crust

4 c. sifted flour
1 Tbsp. sugar
1^{1}/$_{2}$ tsp. salt
1^{1}/$_{2}$ c. lard or Crisco
1 egg
1 tsp. vinegar
^{1}/$_{2}$ c. water

Blend flour, sugar, and salt. Cut lard until particles are the size of peas. Beat egg. Blend in vinegar and water. Sprinkle over flour mixture, 1 Tbsp. at a time, tossing with a fork. Gather dough together with fingers so it cleans the bowl. Yields enough for 2 (9") double-crust pies and 1 (9") shell.

Dora Schlabach
Katie Mae Troyer

Pie Crust

6 c. flour
2 Tbsp. sugar
2 c. shortening
pinch salt
1 egg
1 tsp. vinegar
water

Put egg in a 1 c. measure and add vinegar. Fill cup with water. Crumble flour, shortening, salt, and sugar together. Add water mixture. Yields 9 pie crusts.

Mrs. Mattie Miller

Pie Crust

6 c. flour
$^1/_2$ c. lard
$^3/_4$ c. Crisco
1 tsp. soda
pinch salt
2 eggs
1 Tbsp. vinegar
$^1/_2$ c. cold water

Mrs. Dan Mast

Push Pastry

1$^1/_2$ c. flour
1 Tbsp. sugar
1 tsp. salt
2 Tbsp. milk
$^1/_2$ c. oil

Mix all together and press into pan.
Yields 1 crust.

Pie Crust

5 lbs. Flaky Pie Crust flour
$^1/_2$ c. sugar
2 Tbsp. salt
1 can regular or butter Crisco

Blend ingredients. Store in a plastic container. Mix will keep indefinitely and needs no refrigeration. When ready to make pie crust, mix 1$^1/_2$ c. crumbs with 2 Tbsp. ice water. Roll out as usual to make a 9" crust. Bake at 400° for 13–14 minutes. Use flour generously while rolling.

Mrs. Aden B. Miller
Mrs. Emanuel J. Miller
Mrs. Edward M. Hershberger
Mrs. Arlene Hershberger

Pie Dough

7 c. flour
1 tsp. salt
1 c. shortening
1 Tbsp. sugar
¹/₄ tsp. baking powder
1 c. shortening
1 c. lard

Mix to form crumbs. Put an egg in a cup and fill with water. Add 1 Tbsp. corn oil and 1 Tbsp. vinegar. Beat with egg beater and add crumbs. If using shortening instead of lard, use more than 1 cup.

Mrs. David A. Barkman

tid bits

Set foil pie pans into Pyrex pans to bake pies. This will make the crust brown better.

To beat eggs quickly, add a pinch of salt.

When measuring shortening, take a larger pitcher than you need and put in a few cups of water. The shortening will float and the pitcher is a lot easier to wash.

To keep icing soft, add a pinch of soda to the whites before beating them. Beat and pour the hot syrup over beaten egg whites. It will be soft and creamy.

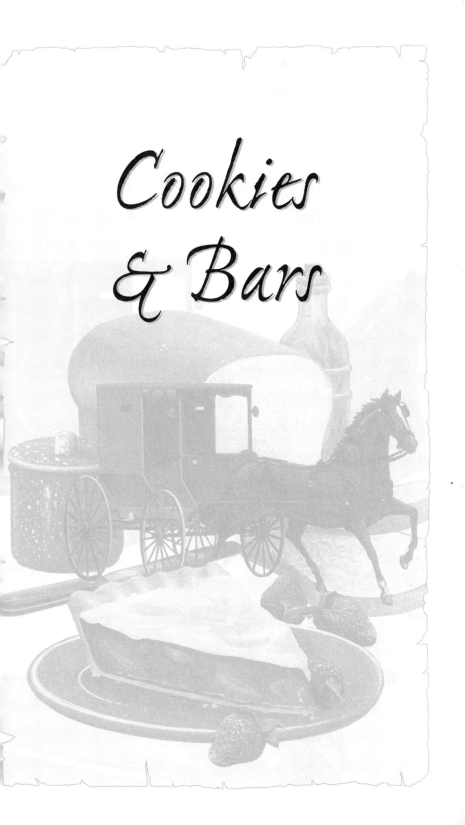

Cookies & Bars

Simple Cookies

2 c. margarine
1 c. brown sugar
1 tsp. soda
2 pkgs. instant vanilla pudding
1 c. sugar
4 eggs
5 c. flour
chocolate chips

Mix in order listed.

Mrs. Aden A. Raber

Cliff's Chocolate Chip Cookies

1 c. Crisco
$^1/_2$ c. sugar
1 c. brown sugar
2 eggs, well beaten
$2^1/_2$ c. flour
1 tsp. soda
1 tsp. salt
1 tsp. vanilla
12 oz. chocolate chips

Cream together shortening, sugar, and brown sugar. Add eggs, flour, soda, salt, vanilla, and chocolate chips. Bake at 350°. Shape into balls. Do not flatten for chewy cookies. Yields 35 cookies.

Mrs. Wayne Yoder

Soda Box Chocolate Chip Cookies

2 eggs
$^3/_4$ c. brown sugar
$^3/_4$ c. white sugar
1 c. soft margarine
1 tsp. soda
1 tsp. salt
1 tsp. vanilla
$2^1/_4$ c. flour
1 c. chocolate chips
$^1/_2$ c. nuts

Mix all together. Drop and flatten. Bake at 375° until lightly browned. Fill with whoopie pie filling.

Mrs. David A. Barkman

Soft Chocolate Chip Cookies

4 c. brown sugar
4 eggs
4 Tbsp. hot water
2 c. Crisco
1¹/₂ tsp. vanilla
6 c. flour
3 tsp. soda
¹/₂ tsp. salt
2 (12 oz.) pkgs. chocolate chips

Beat with mixer for 10 minutes. Stir in chocolate chips by hand. Bake at 375°. Do not overbake.

Mrs. John L. Erb
Mrs. Alvin I. Yoder
Mrs. David J. Troyer

Pudding Chip Cookies

³/₄ c. brown sugar
1 c. margarine
1 pkg. instant vanilla pudding
2 eggs
1 tsp. soda
1 tsp. vanilla
1 c. chocolate chips
2¹/₄ c. flour
1 c. nuts

Bake at 350°.

Mrs. Ivan A. Miller

Soft Batch Chocolate Chip Cookies

2 c. margarine
¹/₂ c. sugar
1¹/₂ c. brown sugar
2 pkgs. instant vanilla pudding
4¹/₂ c. flour
1 c. oatmeal
2 tsp. baking soda
4 eggs
12 oz. chocolate chips
2 tsp. vanilla

Cream margarine and sugar. Add pudding and vanilla. Beat until smooth and creamy. Beat in eggs. Combine flour with oatmeal and soda. Beat in gradually. Add chips. Drop by teaspoonfuls on a cookie sheet. Bake at 350° for 8–10 minutes.

Melvin Miller

Esther's Emergency Chocolate Chip Cookies

2 c. butter
2 c. margarine
2 c. brown sugar
4 eggs
2 tsp. vanilla
4 c. flour
5 c. rolled oats (grind)
1 tsp. salt
2 tsp. baking powder
2 tsp. soda
24 oz. semisweet chocolate chips
6 oz. milk chocolate chips

Using a cookie scoop, form balls and freeze. Bake, frozen, at 350° for about 8 minutes. Do not overbake. These are really good and are always ready for any emergency when you want to serve warm chocolate chip cookies.

Mrs. Edwin N. (Ruth) Weaver

$250 Cookie Recipe

2 c. butter
2 c. white sugar
2 c. brown sugar
4 eggs
2 tsp. vanilla
4 c. flour
5 c. blended oatmeal
1 tsp. salt
2 tsp. baking powder
2 tsp. soda
24 oz. chocolate chips
1 (8 oz.) Hershey's
    chocolate bar, grated
3 c. chopped nuts

Measure oatmeal and blend in a blender to a fine powder. Mix all together. Bake at 375°.

Mrs. Albert M.L. Yoder

Heavenly Chocolate Chip Cookies

1/2 c. butter, softened
2/3 c. Crisco
1 c. white sugar
1 c. brown sugar
2 eggs
1 tsp. vanilla
3 1/2 c. flour
1 tsp. salt
1 tsp. soda
1 pkg. chocolate chips
3/4 c. mini M&M's, optional

Mix in order given. Bake at 350° for 10 minutes.

Mrs. Philip L. Yoder
Mrs. Samuel Bowman, Jr.

Favorite Chocolate Chip Cookies

1 c. white sugar
2/3 c. brown sugar
1 c. butter or margarine
1 c. peanut butter
1 tsp. vanilla
2 eggs
2 c. flour
1 c. quick oats
2 tsp. soda
1/2 tsp. salt
6 oz. chocolate chips

Beat sugar, butter, peanut butter, vanilla, and eggs until well blended. Mix in flour, oats, soda, and salt. Stir in chocolate chips. Drop on cookie sheets and bake at 350° for 10 minutes. Do not overbake.

Mrs. Abe Miller
Mrs. Roman Hershberger

Chocolate Krinkle Cookies

1 c. cocoa
1 c. vegetable oil
4 c. sugar
8 lg. eggs
4 tsp. vanilla
4 c. bread flour
1 tsp. salt
4 tsp. baking powder

Mix all together. Chill. Drop by teaspoonful in powdered sugar and roll into balls. Do not flatten. Bake at 350° for 8–10 minutes. Do not overbake.

Mrs. Sylvanus Raber
Mrs. Andy M.A. Troyer

Double Chocolate Jumbo Crisps

2 c. margarine
3 c. sugar
2 tsp. vanilla
2 eggs
2 c. flour
1 tsp. soda
1 tsp. salt
6 Tbsp. cocoa
$^1/_2$ c. water
6 c. rolled oats
12 oz. chocolate chips
Filling:
2 egg whites
1 Tbsp. vanilla
2 c. powdered sugar
$1^1/_2$ c. Crisco

Cream margarine, sugar, and vanilla. Add eggs and beat until fluffy. Blend in dry ingredients. Add water. Add oats gradually, then chocolate chips. Drop by spoonfuls onto ungreased cookie sheets. Bake at 350° for 15 minutes. *For filling:* Beat egg whites until stiff. Add powdered sugar. Cream together, then add Crisco and vanilla.

Mrs. Eli Burkholder

Chocolate Sandwich Cookies

2 devil's food cake mixes
4 eggs, lightly beaten
$^2/_3$ c. vegetable oil
Filling:
8 oz. cream cheese, softened
$^1/_2$ c. butter or margarine, softened
3–4 c. powdered sugar
$^1/_2$ tsp. vanilla extract
food coloring, optional

In a mixing bowl, beat cake mixes, eggs, and oil. Batter will be very stiff. Roll into 1" balls. Place on ungreased cookie sheets and flatten slightly. Bake at 350° for 8–10 minutes or until a slight indentation remains when lightly touched. Cool. In another mixing bowl, beat cream cheese and butter. Add sugar and vanilla. Mix until smooth. If desired, tint with food coloring. Spread on bottom of half of the cookies. Top with remaining cookies. Yields 4 doz.

Barbara Coblentz
Mrs. Junior A. Troyer

Whoopie Pies

4 c. flour
2 c. sugar
1 c. shortening
1 c. cocoa
1 c. sour milk
2 eggs plus 1 egg yolk
2 tsp. soda
1 c. water

Bake at 350°. Fill with your favorite filling.

Mrs. David J. Troyer

Chocolatey Double Crunchers

$^{1}/_{2}$ c. white sugar
$^{1}/_{2}$ c. brown sugar
$^{1}/_{2}$ c. butter, softened
1 egg
$^{1}/_{2}$ tsp. vanilla
$^{1}/_{2}$ tsp. soda
$^{1}/_{4}$ tsp. salt
1 c. oats
1 c. all-purpose flour
$^{1}/_{2}$ c. coconut
Filling:
6 oz. cream cheese
2 c. chocolate chips, melted
$1^{1}/_{2}$ c. powdered sugar

Combine sugar, butter, egg, and remaining ingredients. Bake at 350°. *For filling:* Melt chocolate chips and cream cheese. Add powdered sugar.

Mrs. Aden Burkholder

Chocolate Pixie Cookies

$^{1}/_{2}$ c. margarine
2 c. sugar
2 eggs
3 c. flour
$^{1}/_{2}$ c. chopped nuts, optional
$^{1}/_{2}$ tsp. salt
1 tsp. vanilla
2 tsp. soda
1 c. cocoa

Melt margarine with cocoa over low heat. Cool slightly. Blend in sugar and eggs, one at a time, beating after each addition. Add dry ingredients, vanilla, and nuts. Chill for 30 minutes. Shape into balls and roll in powdered sugar. Bake at 350°. Do not overbake or they will be hard.

Mrs. R.E. Weaver

Double Chocolate Jumbo Cookies

1 c. margarine
1 1/2 c. sugar
1 egg
1 tsp. vanilla
1/2 tsp. salt
1/2 tsp. soda
3 Tbsp. cocoa
1/2 c. water
3 c. rolled oats
1 c. Thesco flour
3/4 c. chocolate chips

Put together like a sandwich, using frosting for filling.

Mrs. Susan Miller

Cocoa Cheese Sandwich Cookies

6 c. flour
1 tsp. salt
2 1/4 c. sugar
1 c. cocoa
2 1/4 c. butter or margarine
3 eggs
3 tsp. vanilla
3 tsp. soda
Filling:
1/2 c. butter
3 Tbsp. cream or milk
8 oz. cream cheese
6 c. powdered sugar
3/4 tsp. salt

Combine all ingredients. Mix well and shape into balls. Flatten with a glass dipped in sugar. Bake at 350°. Do not overbake!

Mrs. Owen Yoder

Buckeye Crunches

1 c. peanut butter
1 1/2–2 lbs. powdered sugar
1 tsp. vanilla
1 c. butter
1 pkg. Heath toffee bits
1 pkg. chocolate chips
1 pkg. butterscotch chips

Mix first 5 ingredients together until smooth. Roll into balls. Chill in refrigerator. Melt chocolate chips and butterscotch chips in double boiler. Dip chilled balls into chocolate mixture. Place on wax paper to cool.

Mrs. Wayne Schrock

Peanut Butter Cookies

1 c. margarine
1 c. white sugar
1 c. brown sugar
2 eggs
1 c. peanut butter
1 tsp. vanilla
4 c. flour
2 tsp. baking soda
Icing: (optional)
$^1/_4$ c. peanut butter
$^1/_4$ c. Crisco
1 tsp. vanilla
3 c. powdered sugar
milk

Shape into balls and flatten with a potato masher. Can be made into a sandwich cookie with icing in between.

Mrs. Eli N. Hershberger
Mrs. John E. Troyer
Lovina Raber

Triple Treat Cookies

2 c. brown sugar
2 c. white sugar
2 c. margarine
4 eggs
2 tsp. vanilla
6 c. flour (half Robin Hood)
2 c. peanut butter
4 tsp. soda
3 tsp. salt
3 c. chocolate chips
Filling:
1 c. peanut butter
$^2/_3$ c. milk
2 tsp. vanilla
6 c. powdered sugar

Mix and bake at 350°. Put filling between 2 cookies.

Mrs. Jerry Miller
Clara Hershberger
Mrs. David M. Miller
Mrs. Alvin I. Yoder

Peanut Butter Chocolate Chip Cookies

1 1/2 c. margarine
2 c. peanut butter
2 c. white sugar
2 c. brown sugar
4 eggs
4 tsp. vanilla
4 c. flour
1 tsp. salt
3 tsp. soda
2 tsp. baking powder
2 c. chocolate chips

Cream together margarine, sugar, and peanut butter. Add eggs and mix well. Add dry ingredients and vanilla. Shape into balls. Do not flatten.

Mrs. Vernon Mast
Mrs. Alvin I. Yoder

Chocolate Peanut Butter Cookies

1 1/2 c. brown sugar
1 c. peanut butter
3/4 c. margarine
1/3 c. water
1 tsp. vanilla
3 c. quick oats
1 1/2 c. flour
1/2 tsp. soda
1 egg
Topping:
1 1/2 c. chocolate chips
4 tsp. vegetable oil

Chill for 1 hour. Shape into 1" balls. Flatten to 1/4" thick with a glass dipped in white sugar. Melt oil and chocolate chips. Stir until smooth. Top each cookie with 1/2 tsp. mixture.

Mrs. Ben D. Miller

Peanut Butter Temptations

1/2 c. peanut butter
1/2 c. margarine
1/2 c. sugar
1/2 c. brown sugar
1 egg
1/2 tsp. vanilla
1 1/4 c. flour
3/4 tsp. soda
1/2 tsp. salt
48 Reese's peanut butter cups

Cream margarine, peanut butter, and sugar. Add egg and vanilla. Beat until creamy. Stir in dry ingredients until well blended. Chill. Roll into balls 1" thick. Press into small muffin tins. Bake at 350° for 12 minutes. Remove from oven and immediately press 1 peanut butter cup into each hot cookie. Cool.

Mrs. Roy N. Miller

Peanut Butter Pinwheels

1/2 c. shortening
1 c. sugar
1/2 c. peanut butter
1 egg
2 Tbsp. milk
1 1/4 c. flour
1/2 tsp. baking soda
1/2 tsp. salt
6 oz. semisweet chocolate chips

Cream shortening, sugar, and peanut butter. Add egg and milk. Sift together flour, soda, and salt. Add to peanut butter mixture. Mix well. Place dough on lightly floured piece of wax paper about 20" long. Roll to 15 X 8 rectangle. Melt chocolate chips and spread over dough. Roll in jellyroll fashion. Refrigerate until firm enough to cut into 1/4" slices. Bake at 375° for 8–10 minutes.

Mrs. Myron Miller

Peanut Blossoms

2 c. white sugar
2 c. brown sugar
2 c. butter
4 eggs
1 1/4 lb. peanut butter
1/2 c. milk
1 tsp. vanilla
2 lb. flour
1 1/2 Tbsp. soda
1 tsp. salt
chocolate stars

Cream together sugars and butter. Add eggs, peanut butter, milk, and vanilla. Add flour, soda, and salt. Shape into balls and flatten with a glass dipped in sugar. Top with a chocolate star as soon as removed from oven.

Mrs. Jacob Yoder

Caramel Drops

8 c. brown sugar
2 c. margarine
8 eggs
2 tsp. salt
4 tsp. soda
4 tsp. cream of tartar
4 tsp. vanilla
14 c. Softex flour (scant)
12 Tbsp. water
2 c. butterscotch chips

Drop on cookie sheet and bake.

Mrs. Eli N. Hershberger

Spellbinder Cookies

1 c. soft margarine
1 c. brown sugar
1 egg
1 1/2 c. flour
1 tsp. soda
1 1/2 tsp. baking powder
1 c. coconut
1 c. oats
1 c. chocolate chips or nuts
1/2 c. finely crushed corn flakes
Glaze:
2 Tbsp. butter, melted
1 Tbsp. hot water
1/2 tsp. vanilla
1 c. powdered sugar

Cream margarine and sugar. Add egg. Add dry ingredients. Flatten with a glass with a greased bottom dipped in corn flake crumbs. Bake at 350°. *For glaze:* Melt butter. Add hot water and vanilla. Add powdered sugar. Drizzle over cooled cookies.

Butterscotch Sandwich Cookies

2 c. margarine
4 c. brown sugar
4 eggs
2 tsp. vanilla
1/2 tsp. salt
7 1/2 c. flour
2 tsp. baking soda
1 c. coconut
Creme Frosting:
3/4 c. shortening
2 c. marshmallow creme
3–4 Tbsp. milk
1 tsp. vanilla
4 c. powdered sugar

Cream margarine, sugar, eggs, salt, and vanilla. Blend in flour and soda. Stir in coconut. Shape dough into a roll. Wrap and refrigerate overnight. Slice into 1/8" thick slices and bake on greased baking sheet at 350° for 8–10 minutes. Beat together frosting ingredients. Spread between cooled cookies.

Katie B. Yoder

Butterscotch Chip Pudding Cookies

4¹/₂ c. flour
2 tsp. soda
2 c. butter
¹/₂ c. white sugar
1¹/₂ c. brown sugar
2 tsp. vanilla
4 eggs
2 pkgs. instant butterscotch pudding
2 c. butterscotch chips
nuts, optional

Melt butter and mix with sugar, vanilla, and instant pudding. Mix well. Add eggs, then remaining ingredients. Bake on ungreased cookie sheet at 350°. For a softer cookie, do not overbake.

Mrs. Ivan Hershberger

Monster Cookies

6 eggs
2 c. brown sugar
2 c. white sugar
4 tsp. soda
1 c. margarine
1 c. peanut butter
4 c. quick oats
1 tsp. vanilla
5 c. flour
chocolate chips
M&M's

Mix in order given. Drop by spoon on cookie sheet. Bake at 350°.

Mrs. Wayne Yoder
Marlene Troyer
Mrs. Monroe N. Miller

Maple Sandwich Cremes

¹/₂ c. butter
1 c. brown sugar
2 eggs
1 Tbsp. maple flavoring
1 tsp. baking soda
¹/₂ tsp. salt
2 Tbsp. cream
2¹/₂ c. flour
Filling:
2 egg whites, beaten
1¹/₂ c. butter, softened
2 c. powdered sugar
1 tsp. maple flavor

Mix together in order given. Chill for a few hours. Roll out in size of sandwich cookies or put dough through cookie press. Bake at 400° for 10–12 minutes. Variation: Add 2 tsp. cinnamon to batter instead of maple flavoring. Also omit maple flavoring in filling.

Mrs. Abe Yoder

Children's Delights

2 c. margarine
2 c. brown sugar
2 c. white sugar
2 tsp. maple flavoring
2 tsp. baking powder
4 c. quick oats
1 c. chopped nuts
4 eggs
4 c. flour
2 tsp. soda
1 tsp. salt
2 c. chocolate chips

Do not overbake. Flatten slightly.
Bake at 350° for 12 minutes.

Mrs. Mahlon R. Yoder

Best Ever Cookies

2 c. brown sugar
1 c. butter or margarine
2 eggs
1 Tbsp. hot water
1 tsp. vanilla
$^1/_2$ tsp. salt
2 c. flour
1 tsp. soda
1 tsp. baking powder
2 c. oatmeal
1 c. coconut
1 c. chocolate chips

Cream sugar, margarine, and eggs.
Add hot water, vanilla, and salt. Sift
flour, soda, and baking powder; add.
Add oatmeal, coconut, and chocolate
chips. Mix well. Refrigerate 1 hour.
Shape into 1–2" balls, then roll in
powdered sugar. Bake at 375° for 9
minutes. Do not overbake. Leave
cookies on sheet about 2 minutes.

Barbara Raber

Bushel Cookies

5 lbs. brown sugar
2 lbs. seedless raisins
6 lbs. flour
2$^1/_2$ lbs. lard or butter
1 qt. sweet milk
2 lbs. quick oats
4 Tbsp. soda
4 Tbsp. baking powder
12 eggs
1 c. maple syrup

Mix all together. Use chocolate chips
instead of raisins, if desired. Or use
half of each. Drop by tablespoons.
These are very good with milk.

Mrs. Raymond D. (Edna) Miller

Vanishing Oatmeal Raisin Cookies

Mrs. Eli A. Mast

1 c. margarine
1 c. brown sugar
1/2 c. white sugar
2 eggs
1 tsp. vanilla
1 1/2 c. flour
1 tsp. soda
1 tsp. cinnamon
1/2 tsp. salt
3 c. quick oats
1 c. chopped raisins

Chocolate Chewy Oatmeal Cookies

3 c. brown sugar
2 c. margarine
2 eggs
1/2 c. water
2 tsp. vanilla
6 c. oatmeal
2 tsp. soda
1 tsp. salt
2/3 c. cocoa
2 1/2 c. flour
Filling:
2 c. powdered sugar
2 egg whites, beaten
1 1/2 c. Crisco
1 tsp. vanilla

Mix in order listed. Drop by teaspoonful on cookie sheet. Bake at 350°. Fill with filling, making a sandwich cookie.

Mrs. Ben J. Troyer

Chewy Oatmeal Cookies

2¼ c. margarine
4½ c. brown sugar
6 eggs
3 c. flour
2¼ tsp. soda
1½ tsp. salt
3 tsp. cinnamon
¾ tsp. nutmeg
3 tsp. vanilla
6 c. oatmeal
Filling:
2 c. powdered sugar
2 egg whites, beaten
1½ c. Crisco
1 tsp. vanilla

Mix together. Drop by teaspoons on cookie sheet. Bake at 350° for 10–12 minutes. Fill with filling, making a sandwich cookie.

Mrs. Ben J. Troyer
Mrs. Eli E. Yoder
Mrs. Andrew A. Troyer

Chocolate Chip Oatmeal Cookies

2 c. brown sugar
2 eggs
1 c. margarine
5 Tbsp. sour cream
1 tsp. soda
1 tsp. vanilla
½ tsp. salt
2 c. flour
1 c. chocolate chips
3 c. oatmeal

Mix all together. Let set for 1 hour. Shape into balls, then roll in powdered sugar. Do not flatten. Bake at 350°.

Katie Hershberger

tid bits

Marshmallows can be cut nicely by using a scissors dipped in water.

Oatmeal Chippers

2 c. shortening
4 c. brown sugar
4 eggs
4 c. pastry flour
4 c. quick oats
2 tsp. vanilla
2 tsp. soda
2 tsp. salt
2 tsp. cinnamon
2 tsp. nutmeg
1 pkg. chocolate chips
1 c. nuts
Filling:
2 eggs, beaten
2 c. powdered sugar
1 tsp. vanilla
1¹/₂ c. Crisco

Mix together. Chill. Bake at 350°. Do not overbake. *For filling:* Mix eggs, powdered sugar, and vanilla. Beat well. Add shortening and beat until smooth.

Mrs. David J. Troyer

Raisin Top Cookies

2 c. brown sugar
2 eggs
1 Tbsp. vanilla
1 tsp. soda
¹/₄ tsp. salt
1 c. margarine
¹/₄ c. milk
4 c. flour
Raisin Filling:
1¹/₂ c. raisins
1¹/₂ c. water
¹/₂ tsp. salt
clear jel
1¹/₂ tsp. maple flavoring

Roll dough into balls and place on cookie sheets. Indent with fingers. *For filling:* Cook raisins, water, and salt together. Thicken with clear jel and add maple flavoring. Fill cookie indentation with 1 tsp. filling. Bake at 350°.

Mrs. Mahlon R. Yoder

Trilby Cookies

3 c. brown sugar
2 c. butter
1 c. buttermilk or sour milk
2 tsp. soda
1 tsp. vanilla
$^1/_2$ tsp. salt
4 c. quick oatmeal
6 c. flour
Filling:
2 c. sugar
2 c. water
4 Tbsp. flour
4 c. chopped dates

Mix butter and sugar. Add soda to milk. Dissolve and add remaining ingredients. Roll thin. Use round cookie cutter or press very flat if you use a cookie dipper. Bake at 375°.
For filling: Cook ingredients together until thick. Put between 2 cookies to make a sandwich cookie.

Mrs. Leroy C. Miller

Date Oatmeal Cookies

$1^1/_2$ c. shortening
2 c. brown sugar
1 c. white sugar
2 eggs
$^1/_2$ c. water
2 tsp. vanilla
3 c. flour
2 tsp. salt
1 tsp. soda
4 c. quick oats
2 tsp. cinnamon
$^1/_2$ tsp. nutmeg
1 c. chopped nuts
$^1/_2$ lb. dates

Cook dates and 1 c. water over medium heat until the dates are soft. Combine shortening, sugar, eggs, water, and vanilla. Mix thoroughly and add cooled dates. Add dry ingredients. Drop by teaspoon on a greased cookie sheet. Bake at 350°–400° for 10–15 minutes. Yields 8 doz.

Mrs. Wayne A. Weaver

Rolled Date-Filled Cookies

4 c. margarine
6 c. brown sugar
8 eggs
8 c. Gold Medal flour
4 tsp. baking powder
2 tsp. soda
2 tsp. salt
10 c. rolled oats
4 tsp. vanilla
Filling:
2 c. chopped dates
1 c. sugar
2 c. water

Mix together and roll out or drop and flatten. Bake. *For filling:* Cook for 15 minutes. Thicken with 2 Tbsp. flour and a little water to make a paste.

Mrs. Wayne Yoder

Date-Filled Cookies

Filling:
1 pkg. dates, cut fine
1 c. brown sugar
1 c. water
1 tsp. grated orange rind, optional
$^3/_4$ c. finely chopped nuts
Dough:
1 c. butter or margarine
1$^1/_2$ c. brown sugar
2 eggs
1$^1/_2$ c. quick oats
3$^1/_4$ c. sifted flour
1 tsp. cream of tartar
$^1/_2$ tsp. salt
1 tsp. vanilla

For filling: Combine dates, sugar, and water. Cook for 10 minutes, stirring constantly. Beat until smooth while cooling, then add orange rind and nuts. *For dough:* Cream butter and sugar well. Add eggs and beat until light and fluffy. Add oatmeal, then remaining sifted dry ingredients and vanilla. Chill several hours. Roll to $^1/_8$" thickness on a well floured surface. Cut with a 2$^1/_2$" cutter. Spread 1 Tbsp. filling on half of each cookie and fold over like a moon pie. There is no need to seal the edge. Place on ungreased cookie sheet and bake at 375° for 8–10 minutes or until a delicate brown.

Biena Schlabach

Honey Delights

2 c. honey
1 c. margarine
4 tsp. soda
2 eggs, beaten
$^{1}/_{2}$ tsp. cinnamon
$^{1}/_{2}$ tsp. cloves
$^{1}/_{2}$ tsp. allspice
2 tsp. vanilla
$7^{1}/_{2}$–8 c. flour

Cook honey and margarine for 1 minute. Add soda. Add remaining ingredients. Cut out cookies. Bake at 350°.

Mrs. Mahlon R. Yoder

Ginger Cookies

3 c. brown sugar
$2^{1}/_{4}$ c. shortening or half margarine
$^{3}/_{4}$ c. baking molasses
3 eggs
$4^{1}/_{2}$ tsp. ginger
6 tsp. soda
3 tsp. cinnamon
$1^{1}/_{2}$ tsp. salt
6 c. flour

Cream together sugar, shortening, molasses, and eggs. Combine dry ingredients and add to creamed mixture. Stir well. Chill. Shape into balls and roll in white sugar. Bake at 375°. Frost and put together as sandwich cookies.

Gingerbread Boys

$^{1}/_{2}$ c. shortening
$^{1}/_{2}$ c. sugar
$^{1}/_{2}$ c. dark molasses
$^{1}/_{4}$ c. water
$2^{1}/_{2}$ c. flour
$^{3}/_{4}$ tsp. salt
$^{1}/_{2}$ tsp. soda
$^{3}/_{4}$ tsp. ginger
$^{1}/_{4}$ tsp. nutmeg
$^{1}/_{8}$ tsp. allspice

Cream shortening and sugar. Blend in molasses, water, flour, soda, salt, and spices. Cover. Chill for 2–3 hours. Heat oven to 375°. Roll dough to $^{1}/_{4}$" thick on a lightly floured board. Cut with gingerbread boy cutter. Place on ungreased baking sheet. Bake for 10–12 minutes. Immediately remove from cookie sheet. Decorate with raisins, cherries, citron, licorice, and icing.

Mrs. David J. Troyer

Cane Cookies

2 c. brown sugar
1 c. lard
3 eggs
1 c. sour cream
1 c. cane molasses
3 tsp. soda
$1/2$ tsp. cloves
1 tsp. nutmeg
1 tsp. cinnamon
8 c. sifted flour
pinch salt
Frosting:
1 c. sugar
1 egg white
4 Tbsp. cold water
$1/2$ tsp. vanilla

Mix together and let set overnight. Roll out and cut or drop onto cookie sheets. Bake at 400°. *For frosting:* Mix sugar, egg white, and cold water in top of double boiler. Bring water in bottom to a boil. Beat with egg beater for 7–10 minutes until soft peaks form. Remove from heat and add vanilla. Beat with a spoon for several minutes longer.

Katie B. Yoder

Soft Molasses Cookies

$1/2$ c. butter, softened
$1/2$ c. shortening
$1 1/2$ c. sugar
$1/2$ c. molasses
2 eggs, lightly beaten
4 c. all-purpose flour
$1/2$ tsp. salt
$2 1/4$ tsp. baking soda
$2 1/4$ tsp. ground ginger
$1 1/2$ tsp. ground cloves
$1 1/2$ tsp. ground cinnamon
additional sugar

Cream together butter, shortening, and sugar until light colored and fluffy. Beat in molasses and eggs. Combine dry ingredients, then add to creamed mixture. Roll into $1 1/2$" balls. Dip tops in sugar. Bake at 350° for 11 minutes. Do not overbake. Store in a tightly covered container to maintain softness. These are super delicious!

Mrs. David A. Yoder
Mrs. Marion Miller

Molasses Crinkle Cookies

4 c. margarine
8 c. brown sugar
1 c. Brer Rabbit molasses (light)
8 eggs
1 c. sour cream
16 c. flour
1 tsp. ginger
8 tsp. cinnamon
2 tsp. salt
12 tsp. soda
4 tsp. baking powder
Filling:
1 c. milk
2 Tbsp. cornstarch
1 tsp. vanilla
1 c. sugar
$1/2$ c. Crisco
$1/2$ c. margarine

Mix and refrigerate overnight. Shape into balls, then roll in white sugar. Fill with filling.

Mrs. Mary Miller

Grandma's Molasses Cookies

2 c. molasses
1 c. lard
3 tsp. soda
2 tsp. ginger
1 tsp. cinnamon
3 eggs
6 c. flour
Icing:
6 Tbsp. butter, lightly browned
3 Tbsp. hot water
1 tsp. vanilla
powdered sugar

Mix and bake at 350° until done.
For icing: Mix butter, hot water, and vanilla. Thicken with powdered sugar. If too thick, add a little milk.

Mrs. Jerry Miller

Sandwich Molasses Cookies

2 c. margarine, softened
4 c. brown sugar
$^1/_2$ c. sour cream or yogurt
$^1/_2$ c. molasses
4 eggs
1 tsp. salt
$^1/_2$ tsp. ginger
4 tsp. cinnamon
6 tsp. soda
2 tsp. baking powder
8 c. flour
Filling:
5 Tbsp. flour
$1^1/_4$ c. milk
1 c. powdered sugar
$^3/_4$ c. Crisco

Mix in order given. Refrigerate overnight. Bake at 350°. *For filling:* Cook flour and milk until thick. Cool. Combine sugar and Crisco. Cream well. Add to flour mixture and mix until creamy.

Esther Mast
Mrs. Mahlon R. Yoder
Mrs. Felty L. Raber

Sorghum Cookies

3 c. margarine or shortening
$2^1/_2$ c. white sugar
$2^1/_2$ c. brown sugar
4 eggs
2 tsp. baking powder
4 tsp. cinnamon
10 c. flour
8 tsp. soda
1 c. buttermilk or sour milk
1 c. sorghum or Brer Rabbit molasses
Filling:
3 egg whites, beaten, or 2 whole eggs
$4^1/_2$ c. powdered sugar
$1^1/_2$ c. Crisco
1 tsp. vanilla
$^1/_2$ tsp. salt

Chill. Shape into balls and roll in white sugar. Bake at 350° for 15 min.

Mrs. Arlene Hershberger
Mrs. Leroy Miller
Mrs. Ray Raber

Favorite Cookies

2 c. brown sugar
2 c. white sugar
9 c. flour
6 eggs, beaten
1 c. lard or margarine
1 tsp. cinnamon
2 tsp. soda
2 tsp. baking powder
2 tsp. vanilla

Mix together and shape into rolls. Let set overnight. Slice and bake.

Mrs. Mattie Miller

Soft Cut-Out Cookies

1 c. butter, softened
2 c. sugar
3 eggs
1 c. whipping cream or
  evaporated milk
1 tsp. salt
1 tsp. baking soda
5 tsp. baking powder
3 tsp. maple flavoring
5 c. flour
Frosting:
1 1/2 c. Crisco
2 tsp. vanilla
1/2 c. hot water
3/4 c. marshmallow creme
4 c. powdered sugar

Chill dough. Bake at 350°. Do not overbake. Beat frosting ingredients well.

Mrs. Philip L. Yoder

Christmas Cookies

1 c. butter or margarine
1 1/2 c. powdered sugar
1 egg
1 tsp. vanilla
2 1/2 c. flour
1 tsp. baking soda
1 tsp. cream of tartar

Mix in order listed. Chill. Roll out and cut with cookie cutters. Bake at 350°. Do not overbake.

Chocolate Cut-Out Cookies

1 c. butter
2 c. sugar
4 eggs
1/4 c. cocoa
4 Tbsp. cream or milk
2 Tbsp. vanilla
1 Tbsp. soda
2/3 tsp. cinnamon
1 tsp. salt
5 1/2 c. flour

Cut out and bake. Delicious with caramel filling.

Mrs. David J. Troyer

Holiday Cut-Outs

2 c. margarine
3 c. sugar
5 eggs
1 c. sour cream
1 tsp. soda
1 tsp. vanilla
1 tsp. baking powder
1/4 c. boiling water
6 1/2 c. bread flour

Mix together. Chill. Roll and cut out.

Mrs. David J. Troyer

Rolled Christmas Cookies

3 c. sugar
2 c. margarine, softened
3/4 c. cream
1 tsp. salt
7 eggs
2 tsp. soda
3 tsp. cream of tartar
10 c. flour

Best if dough is chilled.

Mrs. Paul J. Hochstetler

Sour Cream Cut-Out Cookies

1 c. brown sugar
1 c. white sugar
1 c. margarine
2 eggs
5½ c. flour
1 tsp. baking powder
2 tsp. baking soda
1 c. sour cream
1 tsp. vanilla

Cream sugars and margarine. Add eggs and mix well. Sift together dry ingredients. Combine sour cream and vanilla. Add alternately with dry ingredients to creamed mixture. Chill. Roll out on floured surface and cut with desired cookie cutter. Do not roll dough too thin if you want a thick, soft cookie. Bake at 350°–375° until set, not brown.

Mrs. Alvin I. Yoder

Sour Cream Cookies

3 eggs
2 c. brown sugar
³/₄ c. lard
1 c. sour cream
2 tsp. baking powder
1 tsp. soda
3 c. Gold Medal flour

Bake at 350°.

Mrs. Adam Hershberger

Lemon Cookies

4 c. brown sugar
2 c. butter and lard
5 eggs, beaten
1 c. sweet milk
3 tsp. baking powder
1 tsp. soda
vinegar
4–6 Tbsp. lemon flavoring
8 c. flour

Mix soda with a little vinegar.

Verna Yoder

Orange Cookies

2 c. sugar
1 c. butter
3 eggs
1 c. sour milk
2 tsp. baking powder
4 c. flour
1 orange, ground
Frosting:
1 orange, ground
powdered sugar

Mix all together. Use whole orange, including peel. *For frosting:* Add powdered sugar to ground orange to thicken.

Mrs. Eli A. Mast

Cherry Wink Cookies

2¹/₄ c. flour
1 tsp. baking powder
¹/₂ tsp. soda
¹/₂ tsp. salt
³/₄ c. shortening
2 eggs
2 Tbsp. milk
1 tsp. vanilla
1 c. sugar
1 tsp. almond extract
1 c. chopped pecans
1 c. chopped dates
¹/₃ c. maraschino cherries, chopped
2¹/₂ c. corn flakes, crushed

Sift together flour, baking powder, soda, and salt. Combine shortening, eggs, milk, vanilla, sugar, and almond extract. Blend in dry ingredients and mix well. Add pecans, dates, and cherries. Shape into balls, using 1 Tbsp. dough for each cookie. Roll into cornflake crumbs. Place on greased cookie sheet and bake at 375°. Top with ¹/₄ cherry. Do not stack until cold.

Mrs. Mary Miller

Butter Pecan Cookies

1 butter pecan cake mix
2 eggs
3 Tbsp. water
2 Tbsp. cooking oil
¹/₂ c. flour

Mix in order listed. Let set for 20 minutes. Shape into balls. Flatten with a glass dipped in white sugar. Bake at 350° for 8 minutes. Fill with your favorite filling.

Mrs. Ben D. Miller

Butter Pecan Thumbprints

1 c. butter, softened
$^1/_3$ c. powdered sugar
1 egg
1 tsp. vanilla
1 tsp. almond extract
2 c. flour
$^2/_3$ c. butter pecan instant pudding
$^1/_2$ c. mini chocolate chips
2 c. finely chopped pecans
Filling:
2 Tbsp. butter, softened
2 c. powdered sugar
1 tsp. vanilla
2–3 Tbsp. milk
Glaze:
$^1/_2$ c. chocolate chips

Cream butter and sugar until smooth. Add egg and extracts. Mix well. Combine flour and pudding mix. Stir in chocolate chips and pecans. Use hands to mix well. Make indentation in each cooke with thumb. Bake at 350° for 10 minutes. Mix filling ingredients and fill indentation. Melt glaze ingredients together and drizzle over cookies.

Mrs. Philip L. Yoder

Sugarless Cookies

$^1/_2$ c. chopped dates
$^1/_2$ c. chopped apples
1 c. raisins
1 c. water
3 eggs
$^1/_2$ c. shortening or $^1/_3$ c. oil
$^1/_2$ c. chopped nuts
1 tsp. soda
1 tsp. cinnamon
1 tsp. vanilla
$^1/_2$ tsp. salt
$1^1/_2$ c. white flour or
    $1^1/_3$ c. whole wheat flour
2 tsp. Crisco

Cook dates, apples, raisins, and water together for 3 minutes. Cool. Add remaining ingredients and mix well. Chill for 15 minutes. Drop on greased cookie sheet. Bake at 350°. Do not overbake. Store in a cool place, since they get moldy easily.

Mrs. Katie Hershberger

Melting Moments

1 c. butter
$^1/_3$ c. powdered sugar
$^3/_4$ c. cornstarch
1 c. flour
Icing:
3 oz. cream cheese
1 c. powdered sugar
1 tsp. vanilla
food coloring

Mix. Do not overbake. Ice.

Anna Troyer

Sandwich Filled Cookies

$^1/_2$ c. butter
1 c. brown sugar
2$^3/_4$ c. flour
1 tsp. vanilla
$^1/_3$ tsp. cinnamon
1 tsp. soda
2 eggs, beaten
2 tsp. cream
pinch salt

Can be put in a cookie press or cut out with cookie cutters. Put together like a sandwich or decorate.

Mrs. Nelson L. Miller

Grandmother's Cookies

1$^1/_2$ c. brown sugar
$^1/_2$ c. white sugar
1$^1/_2$ c. margarine
4 eggs
$^3/_4$ c. milk
4 tsp. baking powder
2 tsp. soda
2 tsp. vanilla
1 tsp. salt
6 c. flour

Drop on cookie sheet and bake at 350°.

Mrs. Mahlon R. Yoder

Cream Wafers

2 c. lard or butter
8 eggs, beaten
4 tsp. cream
6 tsp. soda
4 c. brown sugar
10^1/$_2$ c. flour
4 tsp. cinnamon
vanilla
salt

Mix and roll out. Cut out with cookie cutters or put through a cookie press. Bake at 350°. When done, spread with your favorite frosting. Top with another cookie.

Mrs. Harry M. Miller

Mim's Filled Cookies

4 c. flour
2 c. brown sugar
1 tsp. soda
1 tsp. cream of tartar
^{1}/$_2$ tsp. salt
1 c. shortening
3 eggs, beaten
Filling:
2^1/$_2$ Tbsp. cornstarch
^{1}/$_2$ c. dates, chopped
1 c. cold water
1 c. brown sugar
lemon juice, optional

Mix flour, sugar, soda, salt, and cream of tartar. Blend in shortening. Add eggs and mix like pie dough. If still too crumbly, add another egg. Chill. Roll thin and cut out. Bake in hot oven for 5–7 minutes. Cool. *For filling:* Cook until thickened. Cool, then spread between 2 cookies.

Mary Hostetler

Parker Cookies

2 c. brown sugar
1 c. butter
3 eggs
9 Tbsp. milk
2 tsp. soda
2 tsp. baking powder
1 tsp. vanilla
3^1/$_2$ c. Gold Medal flour

Cream butter and sugar. Add eggs and mix well. Add soda to milk and add remaining ingredients. Drop on cookie sheets and flatten with a glass dipped in cookie decorations. Bake at 350°. Ice, if desired. This is a good brown sugar cookie.

Newcomer Sugar Cookies

1 c. cooking oil
2 c. white sugar
1 c. brown sugar
4 eggs
2 c. milk or buttermilk
2 tsp. soda
6 c. flour
6 tsp. baking powder
1 tsp. vanilla
$^1/_4$ tsp. salt

Beat oil, sugar, and eggs. Mix milk and soda. Add to creamed mixture. Add flour, baking powder, vanilla, and salt. Drop on ungreased cookie sheet. Bake at 450°. Yields 5 dozen.

Katie Yoder

Sugar Cookies

2 c. margarine
3 c. sugar
4 eggs
10 c. flour
$^1/_2$ tsp. salt
2 tsp. soda
6 tsp. baking powder
2 c. cream or rich milk

Roll out or drop.

Mrs. John E. Troyer
Lovina Raber

Soft Sugar Cookies

2 c. margarine
2 c. white sugar
1 c. brown sugar
4 eggs
2 c. cream
$^1/_2$ tsp. salt
2 tsp. soda
6 tsp. baking powder
8–10 c. Thesco flour

Frost with frosting of your choice. This recipe is also very good to use for cut-outs.

Mrs. Susan Miller

Brown Sugar Cookies

4 c. brown sugar
1 c. butter
1 c. lard
4 eggs
2 tsp. soda
4 tsp. baking powder
1 Tbsp. vanilla
1 tsp. salt
2 c. evaporated milk
8 c. flour
Icing:
$^1/_2$ c. butter
3 c. powdered sugar
5 Tbsp. evaporated milk
$^1/_2$ tsp. salt
$^1/_2$ c. brown sugar

Bake at 350° until done. *For icing:*
Cook butter and sugar until sugar
dissolves. Add remaining ingredients.
Mrs. Mahlon R. Yoder

Buttermilk Cookies

2 eggs
1 c. margarine
2 c. brown sugar
2 tsp. soda
2 tsp. baking powder
1 c. buttermilk or evaporated milk
$4^1/_2$ c. flour

For chocolate cookies, use $^1/_4$–$^1/_2$ c.
cocoa and not as much flour.
Mrs. David A. Yoder

Cookies

2 c. brown sugar
$^1/_2$ c. margarine
2 eggs
2 tsp. soda
1 Tbsp. water
1 tsp. cream of tartar
3 c. flour
1 c. chocolate chips
vanilla

Put soda in water. Bake at 350°.
Mrs. Jonathan N. Raber

Butter Cream Drops

2 1/2 c. brown sugar
1/2 c. butter
1/2 c. soft shortening or lard
4 eggs
4 2/3 c. flour
2 tsp. soda
1 tsp. baking powder
1 tsp. salt
2 c. sour cream
2 tsp. vanilla
1 c. chocolate chips
Frosting:
3/4 c. butter
3 c. powdered sugar
2 tsp. vanilla
1/2 c. hot water

Cream sugar, butter, and shortening thoroughly. Add eggs and mix well. Combine dry ingredients and add alternately with sour cream. Add vanilla and chocolate chips. Bake at 350° for 10–12 minutes. *For frosting:* Melt butter in saucepan over medium heat. Brown lightly. Remove from heat and stir in sugar and vanilla. Add water. Beat until of spreading consistency. Frost cookies while warm.

Mrs. Levi (Susan) Troyer

Good Soft Drop Cookies

1 c. shortening
3 eggs
2 c. brown sugar
1 c. sour milk
4 1/2 c. flour
1 tsp. soda
1 tsp. baking powder
1 tsp. salt
1 tsp. vanilla

Cream sugar and shortening. Add eggs and milk. Add dry ingredients and mix well. Frost with caramel frosting. Bake at 400°.

Mrs. Ivan Hershberger

tid bits

Mix equal parts soda and salt.
Use occasionally to brush teeth.
This will make them feel
very clean.

Pumpkin Chocolate Chip Cookies

1 c. soft butter
³/₄ c. brown sugar
³/₄ c. white sugar
1 egg, beaten
1 tsp. vanilla
2 c. flour
1 c. quick oats
1 tsp. soda
1 tsp. cinnamon
1 c. canned pumpkin
1¹/₂ c. chocolate chips

Drop and bake at 350°. These are soft cookies.

Mrs. Fannie Mae Barkman

Ice Cream Cookies

2 c. shortening
1¹/₂ c. brown sugar
1¹/₂ c. white sugar
4 eggs
5 c. oatmeal
2 c. macaroon coconut
4 c. flour
¹/₂ c. cocoa
2 tsp. soda
2 tsp. vanilla
2 tsp. baking powder

Mix well. Chill. Roll out and cut with cookie cutter. Mix in more flour, if needed. Bake in ungreased pans at 350°. Cool. Spoon vanilla ice cream between 2 cookies. Freeze. May wrap in plastic wrap.

Mrs. Wayne M. Yoder

Filling for Cookies

2 eggs, beaten
2 tsp. vanilla
2 c. powdered sugar
1¹/₂ c. Crisco

Beat egg whites until stiff. Add yolks. Beat again. Cream Crisco; add eggs and powdered sugar alternately. Add vanilla. Mix well.

Mrs. David A. Yoder

Bar Cookies

Cookie Sheet Whoopie Pies

1 1/2 c. margarine
4 eggs
4 c. flour
1 1/2 c. cocoa
2 2/3 c. water
3 1/2 c. sugar
2 tsp. vanilla
2 1/2 tsp. soda
1 tsp. salt
Filling:
1 egg white, unbeaten
2 Tbsp. milk
2 c. powdered sugar
1 tsp. vanilla
1/2 c. shortening

Cream margarine and sugar. Add eggs and vanilla. Add flour, cocoa, soda and salt. Gradually add water. Mix and divide into 2 cookie sheets. Bake at 375° until done. Cool. *For filling:* Mix egg white, milk, and vanilla. Beat in powdered sugar and then shortening. Spread over half of cake. Top with remaining cake.

Mrs. John L. Erb

Yum Yum Cookies

Crust:
2 c. flour
1/2 c. butter or margarine
1/2 c. brown sugar
Filling:
3 eggs
2 c. brown sugar
1/2 tsp. salt
1 c. coconut
1/2 c. chopped nuts
2 Tbsp. flour
1/4 tsp. baking powder
1 tsp. vanilla

Mix crust ingredients and press firmly in bottom of large cookie sheet. Mix remaining ingredients. Spread over crust. Bake at 350° for 20 minutes or until nicely browned. Cut into bars when cool.

Mrs. Henry J.C. Yoder
Mrs. Emanuel J. Miller

Banana Bars

3 c. flour
2 tsp. baking powder
1 c. butter
2 c. sugar
2 eggs
2 tsp. soda
2 Tbsp. water
2²/₃ c. mashed bananas
7 oz. marshmallow creme

Dissolve soda in water. Mix like a cake. Add bananas with flour. Bake on a cookie sheet. Spread marshmallow creme on top while bars are still warm. Frost with caramel frosting.

Mrs. Mary Miller

Lemon Bars

Crust:
2 c. flour
¹/₄ c. powdered sugar
1 c. butter
Filling:
2 c. sugar
4 Tbsp. flour
4 Tbsp. fresh lemon juice
4 eggs, beaten fluffy

For crust: Mix like pie crust and press into pan. Bake at 325° for 20 minutes. *For filling:* Mix sugar, flour, and lemon juice. Add beaten eggs. Mix well. Pour over hot crust. Bake at 325° for 25 minutes. Remove from oven and dust with powdered sugar while still hot.

Miriam Yoder

Cream Cheese Lemon Bars

1 yellow cake mix
2 eggs, divided
¹/₃ c. vegetable oil
8 oz. cream cheese
¹/₃ c. sugar
1 Tbsp. lemon juice

Mix cake mix, 1 egg, and oil until crumbly. Reserve 1 c. crumbs. Press remaining crumbs in greased jellyroll pan. Bake at 350° for 10 minutes. Meanwhile, beat cream cheese, egg, sugar, and lemon juice until light and creamy. Spread on top of crust and sprinkle reserved crumbs on top. Bake 12–14 minutes more. Cut into small squares when cool.

Mrs. Arlene Hershberger

Rhubarb Custard Bars

Crust:
2 c. all-purpose flour
1/4 c. brown sugar
1 c. cold butter
Filling:
1 1/2 c. sugar
7 Tbsp. all-purpose flour
3 eggs, beaten
1/2 c. milk
1/2 c. cream
5 c. finely chopped fresh
    or frozen rhubarb
Topping:
6 oz. cream cheese
1/2 tsp. salt
1/2 c. sugar
1 c. whipped topping

For crust: Make crumbs like pie dough and press into a greased 9 X 13 pan. Bake at 350° for 10 minutes. For filling: Mix and pour over hot crust. Bake at 350° for 40–45 minutes or until custard is set. For topping: Mix and spread over top of cooled custard.

Mrs. Junior (Dora) Miller
Mandy Troyer

Marble Squares

2 c. plus 2 Tbsp. Gold Medal flour
1 tsp. soda
1/2 tsp. baking powder
1/2 tsp. salt
1 c. soft margarine or butter
2/3 c. sugar
3/4 c. brown sugar
1 Tbsp. water
1 tsp. vanilla
3 eggs, beaten
1 c. chocolate chips
1 c. chopped nuts
1 c. coconut

Sift together dry ingredients. Blend together butter, sugar, vanilla, and water. Add eggs, nuts, and coconut. Mix in flour mixture. Spread in a greased 12 X 16 cookie sheet. Sprinkle with chocolate chips. Place in oven for 1 minute, then run knife through dough to marbleize. Bake at 350° until done. Cut into squares when cool. If you use pastry flour, use 1/4 c. more.

Anna Troyer

Fruit Bars

1 c. margarine
1³/₄ c. sugar
4 eggs
1 tsp. vanilla
1 tsp. almond extract
3 c. flour
1 tsp. salt
¹/₄ tsp. baking powder
4 c. pie filling, any flavor

Cream together butter and sugar. Add beaten eggs. Stir in flavorings. Add flour, salt, and baking powder. Spread ²/₃ of batter on greased baking sheet. Cover with pie filling. Drop spoonfuls of remaining batter over pie filling. Bake at 350° for 35–40 minutes. Drizzle with icing.

Mrs. Dennis (Rosie) Miller
Mrs. Vernon Mast

Pumpkin Pie Squares

Crust:
1¹/₄ c. flour
¹/₂ c. quick oats
¹/₂ c. brown sugar
¹/₂ c. butter
Filling:
1¹/₂ c. pumpkin
1 can evaporated milk
2 eggs, beaten
³/₄ c. sugar
¹/₂ tsp. salt
2 tsp. pumpkin pie spice
Topping:
¹/₂ c. flour
¹/₂ c. pecans
¹/₂ c. brown sugar
2 Tbsp. butter

For crust: Mix ingredients to form crumbs. Press into a 9 X 13 pan and bake at 350° for 10 minutes. *For filling:* Mix and pour over hot crust. Bake 20 minutes more. *For topping:* Sprinkle over pumpkin filling and bake for 10–15 minutes or until set.

Mrs. Aden Chupp

Pumpkin Crunch

First Layer:
3 eggs
1 1/2 c. sugar
12 oz. evaporated milk
3 tsp. pumpkin pie spice
pinch salt
Second Layer:
1 yellow cake mix
Third Layer:
1 c. melted butter
1 c. chopped nuts

Mix first layer ingredients and put in a 9 X 13 pan. Sprinkle dry cake mix over top. Sprinkle with chopped nuts and drizzle with melted butter. Bake at 350° for 1 hour or until done.

Mrs. David A. Yoder

Raisin Bars

3 1/2 lbs. bread flour
2 lbs. brown sugar
1 lb. shortening
1 tsp. salt
1 1/2 lb. raisins
5 eggs, beaten
2 c. cane molasses
3 Tbsp. soda
1/2 c. boiling water
1 egg
milk

Cook raisins in as little water as possible. Cool. Mix flour, sugar, salt, and shortening like pie dough. Add raisins. Make a well in mixture. Mix soda and boiling water. Add soda, eggs, and molasses to raisin mixture. Mix well. Use your hands since dough is stiff and sticky. Using 1/2 lb. dough, roll out on a floured cookie sheet along the long side. Press flat with fingers. You can get 2 rolls in one sheet. Beat egg and add a little milk. Brush over top. Bake at 350°. When done, let set for a little while before taking out and cutting. Store between layers of wax paper when cooled. These freeze well.

Biena Schlabach

Sour Cream Raisin Bars

1¾ c. oatmeal
½ c. sugar
½ c. brown sugar
1¾ c. flour
1 c. margarine
1 tsp. soda
1 tsp. baking powder
pinch salt
1 tsp. vanilla
Filling:
4 egg yolks
1 c. sugar
2 Tbsp. clear jel
2 c. sour cream
1½ c. raisins

Mix ingredients. Put ⅔ of batter in bottom of 9 X 13 pan. Bake at 350° for 15 minutes. Cool slightly. *For filling:* Combine eggs, sugar, and clear jel. Beat well. Add sour cream and raisins. Cook for 3 minutes, stirring constantly. Pour over baked crumbs, then top with remaining crumbs. Bake 15 minutes more.

Mrs. Roy M. Kuhns

Love Bars

1 c. raisins or dates
1 c. sugar
1 c. water
2 tsp. cinnamon
7 Tbsp. margarine
1 tsp. soda
3 Tbsp. boiling water
2 c. flour
nuts
1 tsp. salt
1 tsp. baking powder
Vanilla Glaze:
2 c. powdered sugar
dash salt
¼ tsp. vanilla
3–4 Tbsp. boiling water

Cook raisins, sugar, water, cinnamon, and margarine slowly for 5 minutes. Remove from heat. Mix soda with boiling water and add to raisin mixture. Cool. Add flour, nuts, salt, and baking powder. Mix. Spread thinly on greased cookie sheet. Bake at 375° for 20 minutes or until done. Mix glaze ingredients and drizzle over bars. Very good.

Biena Schlabach

Twinkies

1 yellow or chocolate cake mix
4 eggs
3 Tbsp. vegetable oil
$^3/_4$ c. water
1 pkg. instant vanilla pudding
Frosting:
3 egg whites, beaten
$4^1/_2$ c. powdered sugar
$1^1/_2$ c. Crisco
1 tsp. vanilla
salt

Pour in cookie sheet lined with wax paper. Bake at 350°. Slice lengthwise and fill with frosting.

Mrs. Arlene Hershberger

Zucchini Brownies

4 eggs
$1^1/_2$ c. oil
2 c. sugar
2 c. flour
2 tsp. soda
2 tsp. cinnamon
1 tsp. salt
4 Tbsp. cocoa
1 tsp. vanilla
3 c. shredded zucchini
1 c. nuts

Beat eggs, oil, and sugar. Sift flour, soda, cinnamon, salt, and cocoa. Mix well. Add vanilla, zucchini, and nuts. Mix all together and spread on a 10 X 15 jellyroll pan. Bake at 350° for 30 minutes. These are good plain, but you may frost them.

Mrs. Andy M.A. Troyer

Peanut Butter Brownies

$^3/_4$ c. shortening
$^3/_4$ c. peanut butter
$2^1/_4$ c. sugar
5 eggs
$1^1/_2$ tsp. vanilla
$1^1/_2$ c. all-purpose flour
$1^1/_2$ tsp. baking powder
$^3/_4$ tsp. salt
$1^1/_2$ c. chocolate chips
$^3/_4$ c. chopped peanuts

Put in a 10 X 15 pan. Bake at 350° for 30 minutes.

Tri-Level Brownies

Crust:
1 1/4 c. flour
1 1/4 c. brown sugar
1 1/4 c. melted margarine
2 1/2 c. oatmeal
3/4 tsp. baking powder
Filling:
1/4 c. cocoa
1 3/4 c. sugar
3/4 c. melted margarine
3 eggs
1 2/3 c. flour
1/2 tsp. baking powder
1/2 tsp. salt
1/2 c. milk
Icing:
3/8 c. cocoa
3 1/2 c. powdered sugar
1/2 c. melted margarine
2 1/2 tsp. vanilla
3/8 c. hot water

Mix crust and press lightly in large cookie sheet. Mix filling and pour over crust. Bake at 350° for 25 minutes. Ice.

Mrs. Ivan A. Miller

Chocolate Chip Cream Cheese Bars

1 chocolate cake mix
1 egg
1/3 c. vegetable oil
Filling:
8 oz. cream cheese, softened
1/3 c. sugar
1 egg
1 c. chocolate chips

Mix cake mix, egg, and oil until crumbly. Reserve 1 c. crumbs. Pat remaining crumb mixture into greased 9 X 13 pan. Bake at 350° for 8–10 minutes. Beat cream cheese, sugar, and egg until smooth. Spread over baked layer. Sprinkle chocolate chips and reserved crumbs on top. Bake 10–15 minutes longer. Cool before cutting.

Mrs. Jonas L. Miller

Double Decker Brownies

Chocolate Layer:
2 eggs, lightly beaten
1 c. sugar
3/4 c. all-purpose flour
1/2 c. chopped walnuts
pinch salt
1/2 c. butter or margarine, melted
1/4 c. baking cocoa
Butterscotch Layer:
1 1/2 c. brown sugar
1/2 c. butter or margarine, melted
2 eggs
2 tsp. vanilla
1 1/2 c. all-purpose flour
1/4 tsp. salt
1/2 c. chopped walnuts
Frosting:
1/2 c. brown sugar
1/4 c. butter or margarine
3 Tbsp. milk
1 1/2 c. powdered sugar
1/3 c. chocolate chips
1/3 c. butterscotch chips
1 Tbsp. shortening

In a bowl, combine eggs, sugar, flour, walnuts, and salt. In another bowl, stir butter and cocoa until smooth. Add to egg mixture and blend well with a wooden spoon. Pour into a greased 9 X 13 pan. Set aside. *For butterscotch layer:* Cream sugar and butter in a mixing bowl. Beat in eggs and vanilla. Stir in flour, salt, and walnuts. Spoon over chocolate layer. Bake at 350° for 30–35 minutes or until brownies begin to pull away from sides of pan. Cool. *For frosting:* Combine sugar, butter, and milk in a small saucepan. Bring to a boil for 2 minutes. Remove from heat. Stir in powdered sugar until smooth and quickly spread over brownies. In a small saucepan over low heat, melt chocolate chips, butterscotch chips, and shortening, stirring frequently. Drizzle on top. Yields 3 dozen.

Mrs. Henry J.C. Yoder

Cream Cheese Brownies

1 German chocolate cake mix
1/2 c. oil
1 1/3 c. water
2 eggs
Filling:
8 oz. cream cheese
1 egg
1/2 c. sugar
1/2 c. milk chocolate chips
nuts

Heat oven to 325°. Grease and flour a jellyroll pan. Mix cake mix, oil, water, and eggs. Pour into pan. Mix cream cheese, egg, and sugar. Drop by teaspoon onto batter. Cut through batter with a knife or spatula several times for a marble effect. Sprinkle with chocolate chips and nuts. Bake for 25–30 minutes.

Mrs. Roman Hershberger

Swirl of Chocolate Cheesecake Triangles

Crust:
2 c. graham cracker crumbs
$^1/_2$ c. melted margarine
$^1/_3$ c. sugar
Filling:
16 oz. cream cheese, softened
1 c. sugar
$^1/_4$ c. flour
$1^1/_2$ c. evaporated milk
2 eggs
1 Tbsp. vanilla
1 c. chocolate chips

Mix crust ingredients and press into a 9 X 13 pan. Beat cream cheese, sugar, and flour gradually. Beat in evaporated milk, eggs, and vanilla. Melt chocolate chips in double boiler and add 1 c. cream cheese mixture. Pour remaining cream cheese mixture over the crust. Pour chocolate mixture over top and swirl mixture with spoon, pulling plain cream cheese mixture up to surface. Bake 40–45 minutes or until set. Cool until firm. Cut in 15 rectangles. Cut each rectangle in half diagonally to form triangles.

Mrs. David E. Beachy

Chocolate Streusel Bars

$1^3/_4$ c. flour
$1^1/_2$ c. powdered sugar
$^1/_2$ c. unsweetened cocoa
1 c. cold margarine or butter
8 oz. cream cheese, softened
1 can Eagle Brand milk
1 egg
1 tsp. vanilla
$^1/_2$ c. chopped nuts

Preheat oven to 350°. In a large bowl, combine flour, sugar, and cocoa. Cut in margarine until crumbly. Mixture will be dry. Reserve 2 c. crumbs. Press remaining crumbs firmly on bottom of 9 X 13 pan. Bake for 15 minutes. In large mixing bowl, beat cream cheese until fluffy. Gradually beat in Eagle Brand milk until smooth. Add egg and vanilla. Mix well. Pour over prepared crust. Add nuts to reserved crumb mixture. Bake 25 minutes or until bubbly. Cool, then chill. Cut into bars. Store covered in refrigerator.
Yields 24–36 bars.

Katie Mae Troyer

Maple Pecan Bars

Crust:
3 c. flour
1/2 c. brown sugar
1 c. butter
Filling:
1 c. white sugar
1/3 c. brown sugar
1 c. dark Karo
1 c. light Karo
4 eggs, beaten
4 Tbsp. flour
1/2 tsp. salt
1 tsp. vanilla

Mix crust ingredients well and press on a cookie sheet. Bake at 350° for 15 minutes. Mix filling ingredients and pour over baked crust. Sprinkle 2 c. chopped pecans over top. Bake for 20–25 minutes more.

Mrs. Aden Chupp

Chocolate Caramel Bars

2 1/4 c. all-purpose flour, divided
2 c. quick-cooking oats
1 1/2 c. brown sugar
1 tsp. baking soda
1/2 tsp. salt
1 1/2 c. butter, room temp.
2 c. chocolate chips
1 c. chopped pecans
1 (12 oz.) jar caramel
   ice cream topping

In a bowl, combine 2 c. flour, oats, brown sugar, baking soda, and salt. Cut in butter until crumbly. Set half aside for topping. Press remaining crumb mixture into a greased cookie sheet. Bake at 350° for 15 minutes. Sprinkle with chocolate chips and pecans. Whisk caramel topping and remaining flour until smooth. Drizzle over top. Sprinkle with the reserved crumb mixture. Bake for 18–20 minutes or until golden brown. Cool on wire rack for 2 hours before cutting. Yields 4 1/2 dozen.

Mrs. Atlee (Lizzie) Raber

Goodie Bars

1 yellow cake mix
1/2 c. butter, melted
3 eggs
3 1/2 c. powdered sugar
8 oz. cream cheese

Combine cake mix, butter, and 1 egg. Mix well and put into a 9 X 13 pan. Combine remaining ingredients. Beat well and pour over first layer. Bake at 350° for 40–45 minutes.

Mrs. Wayne Yoder

Caramel Bars

Crust:
1½ c. oatmeal
1½ c. flour
½ tsp. salt
1 c. brown sugar
¾ tsp. soda
½ c. butter, melted
½ c. margarine, melted

Topping:
1 c. chocolate chips
¾ c. chopped nuts
14 oz. caramels
⅔ c. evaporated milk

Mix crust until crumbly. Press ⅔ of mixture into 9 X 13 pan. Bake at 350° for 8 minutes. Top with nuts and chocolate chips. Melt caramels and evaporated milk. Spread over chips and nuts. Sprinkle remaining crumbs on top. Bake for 12–15 minutes more.

Mrs. Susan Miller

Butterscotch Cake Bars

1 yellow cake mix
2 eggs
½ c. oil
½ c. water
1 c. chocolate chips
2 c. butterscotch chips
1 c. fine nuts, optional
powdered sugar
water
vanilla
butter flavoring

Mix cake mix, eggs, oil, and water. Spread in a cookie sheet. Sprinkle chocolate chips, butterscotch chips, and nuts on top. Bake at 350° for 15–20 minutes. Mix remaining ingredients. Drizzle on top of cooled cake.

Mrs. Aden W. Chupp

Surprise Bars

1 c. brown sugar
4 c. quick rolled oats
1 c. margarine, melted
1½ c. chocolate chips
1½ c. crunchy peanut butter
3 c. Rice Krispies

Mix sugar, oats, and margarine. Press in 10 X 15 cookie sheet. Bake at 350° for 12–15 minutes. Melt chocolate chips. Add peanut butter and Rice Krispies. Put on top of baked crust.

Mrs. Roman E. Raber

Can't-Leave-Alone Bars

1 white cake mix
2 eggs
1/3 c. oil
1/4 c. butter
1 c. chocolate chips
1 can sweetened condensed milk

Mix cake mix, eggs, and oil together with a fork. Reserve 3/4 c. for crumbs. Press remaining mixture in bottom of cake pan. Melt butter, chocolate chips, and sweetened condensed milk together, then pour over crust. Top with reserved crumbs. Bake at 350° for 20–30 minutes until brown on top. These are rich, but good.

Mrs. R.E. Weaver

Open House Bars

3/4 c. butter
2 c. brown sugar
2 eggs
2 tsp. vanilla
2 1/2 c. Bisquick
3 c. oatmeal
Topping:
2 Tbsp. margarine
12 oz. chocolate chips
1 can Eagle Brand milk
1/2 tsp. salt
1 c. nuts

Cream together butter, sugar, eggs, and vanilla. Stir in Bisquick and oatmeal. Spread 3/4 of the mixture in a jellyroll pan. Melt topping ingredients, then spread on top. Dot with remaining oatmeal mixture. Bake at 350° for 30–35 minutes.

Mrs. Allen R. Troyer

Esther's Butterscotch Bars

1 c. sugar
1 c. light corn syrup
2 c. peanut butter
6 c. Rice Krispies
6 oz. chocolate chips
6 oz. butterscotch chips

Over low heat, melt sugar, peanut butter, and corn syrup. Crush Rice Krispies and add to peanut butter mixture. Mix well. Spread into an 11 X 16 pan. Melt chips and spread onto bars. Chill and cut.

Mrs. Edwin N. (Ruth) Weaver

Holiday Chocolate Bars

1¹/₂ c. flour
²/₃ c. sugar
³/₄ c. butter
1¹/₂ c. chocolate chips, divided
1 can Eagle Brand milk
1 egg
2 c. nuts
¹/₂ tsp. vanilla extract
1 tsp. solid shortening

Preheat oven to 350°. Combine flour and sugar. Cut in butter until crumbly. Press on bottom of 9 X 13 pan. Bake for 20 minutes. Melt 1 c. chocolate chips with Eagle Brand milk. Remove from heat and cool slightly. Beat in egg. Stir in nuts and vanilla. Spread over baked crust. Bake for 25 minutes or until set. Cool. Melt remaining chocolate chips with shortening. Drizzle over bars. Chill 10 minutes. Cut into bars.

Mrs. Allen R. Troyer

Mud Hen Bars

¹/₂ c. melted butter
1 c. sugar
3 eggs
1¹/₂ c. flour
1 tsp. baking powder
¹/₄ tsp. salt
1 tsp. vanilla
1 c. brown sugar
1 c. semisweet chocolate chips
1 c. miniature marshmallows

Cream shortening and sugar. Add 1 whole egg and 2 egg yolks. Beat. Add flour, baking powder, salt, and vanilla. Mix thoroughly. Spread in greased 9 X 13 pan. Place chips and marshmallows over batter. Beat 2 egg whites and add brown sugar while beating. Spread over top of batter. Bake at 350° for 30–40 minutes until golden brown. Cool and cut into squares.

Savilla Mullet

Scotcharoos

1 c. sugar
1 c. light Karo
1 c. peanut butter
6 c. Rice Krispies
6 oz. chocolate chips
6 oz. butterscotch chips

Combine sugar and Karo. Cook over medium heat, stirring until it boils. Remove from heat. Stir in peanut butter. Pour over Rice Krispies. Press into buttered pan. Let cool. Melt chips in double boiler and spread over mixture.

Peanut Butter Dream Bars

2 c. quick oats
1 1/2 c. flour
1 c. chopped nuts
1 c. brown sugar
1 tsp. baking soda
3/4 tsp. salt
1 c. butter, melted
1 can sweetened condensed milk
1/3 c. peanut butter
1 c. chocolate-coated candies
  or chocolate chips

Combine oats, flour, nuts, sugar, soda, and salt. Mix. Add butter and mix until dry ingredients are moist and mixtures resembles coarse crumbs. Reserve 1 1/2 c. and press in greased jellyroll pan. Bake at 375° for 10 minutes. Combine milk and peanut butter and pour over crust. Add candies to remaining crumbs and sprinkle on top. Bake 20 minutes more on top rack. Cool and cut into bars. Very good!

Mrs. Fannie Mae Barkman
Mrs. Vernon Mast

Yellow Chocolate Crumble Bars

1 c. flour
4 eggs, separated
4 Tbsp. butter, melted
1 tsp. baking powder
1/4 tsp. salt
1 c. brown sugar
2 tsp. vanilla
2 c. marshmallows
1 1/2 c. chocolate chips
1/2 c. peanut butter
1 1/2 c. Rice Krispies

Beat egg whites until stiff. Add yolks and beat again. Add sifted flour, salt, baking powder, and brown sugar. Add butter and vanilla. Bake, then spread marshmallows on top. Cool. Melt chocolate chips and peanut butter in a double boiler. Stir in Rice Krispies. Spread on top.

Mrs. Eli N. Hershberger
Mrs. Leroy Miller

Scrunch Bars

1 3/4 c. peanut butter
2 c. powdered sugar
3/4 c. margarine
4 c. Rice Krispies

Chill. Cut into 1" squares and dip in chocolate.

Mrs. Felty L. Raber

Deluxe Krispy Bars

24 oz. marshmallows
1/2 c. honey
1/4 c. vegetable oil
5 c. quick oats
1/4 c. margarine
1/4 c. peanut butter
9 1/2 c. Rice Krispies
1 c. raisins, chocolate chips,
    or nuts, optional

In large saucepan, melt margarine and marshmallows. Add remaining ingredients. Press into buttered pan. Cut into squares when cool.

Mrs. Albert Barkman

No-Bake Bars

4 c. Cheerios
2 c. crispy rice cereal
2 c. dry roasted peanuts
2 c. M&M's
1 c. light corn syrup
1 c. sugar
1 1/2 c. creamy peanut butter
1 tsp. vanilla

In a saucepan, bring sugar and syrup to a boil. Stir in peanut butter and vanilla. Pour over cereal mixture and toss to coat evenly.

Mrs. Aden A. Yoder
Katie B. Yoder
Mrs. Atlee (Lizzie) Raber

Granola Bars

1/4 c. butter
1/4 c. vegetable oil
1 1/2 lb. marshmallows
1/4 c. honey
1/4 c. peanut butter
4 1/2 c. Rice Krispies
1 c. graham cracker crumbs
5 c. oatmeal
1 c. crushed peanuts or
    roasted sunflower seeds
1 1/2 c. raisins
1 c. coconut
1 c. chocolate chips

Heat butter and oil over low heat until butter is melted. Add marshmallows and stir until melted. Remove from heat and add honey and peanut butter. In a large bowl, mix remaining ingredients. Add marshmallow mixture. Stir immediately. Press into a greased cookie sheet. Cool and cut into bars. These are great for a snack.

Mrs. Allen Jay Beechy
Mrs. Leroy (Barbara) Erb

Granola Bars

1/4 c. margarine or butter
1 pkg. marshmallows
1/2 c. peanut butter
1 c. oatmeal
5 c. Rice Krispies or Cheerios
1 c. chocolate chips

Melt margarine, marshmallows, and peanut butter together. Add remaining ingredients. Press into a 9 X 13 pan. Cool and cut into bars.

Mrs. Eli Burkholder
Mrs. Roy A. Troyer
Mrs. Edwin N. (Ruth) Weaver
Mrs. Wayne Yoder

Pumpkin Roll

3 eggs
1 c. sugar
2/3 c. pumpkin
3/4 c. flour
1/2 tsp. salt
1 tsp. baking powder
1 tsp. cinnamon
1 tsp. ginger
1/2 tsp. nutmeg
1/2 c. nuts, optional
Filling:
1 1/4 c. powdered sugar
8 oz. cream cheese
4 Tbsp. butter
1/2 tsp. vanilla

Mix all ingredients. Grease jellyroll pan and line with wax paper. Pour batter in pan and bake at 375° for 15 minutes. Put on towel sprinkled with powdered sugar. Trim off hard edges and roll up. Cool. Beat together filling ingredients. Unroll cake and spread with filling. Roll up again.

Mrs. Levi (Susan) Troyer
Mrs. Eli E. Yoder

Use fabric softener sheets for removing dust, etc. from window screens. This way they do not always need to be washed.

Cream Roll

4 egg whites
$^1/_2$ c. sugar
4 egg yolks
$^1/_4$ c. sugar
$^1/_2$ tsp. vanilla
$^3/_4$ c. flour
$^1/_4$ tsp. salt
1 tsp. baking powder
Filling:
$^1/_2$ c. milk
1 Tbsp. flour
$^1/_4$ c. margarine
$^1/_4$ c. Crisco
$^1/_2$ c. sugar
$^1/_2$ tsp. vanilla

Mrs. Levi Yoder

Glaze for Donuts & Fry Pies

2 lbs. powdered sugar
3 Tbsp. butter or honey glaze
3–4 Tbsp. cornstarch
pinch salt
1 Tbsp. vanilla
hot water

Adjust the water to your liking.
Glaze donuts while still hot.

Martha A. Hershberger

Use hair spray to remove ink marks
on clothes. Spray several times
before putting in wash machine.

Desserts

Cherry Cheese Squares

Crust:
1 c. walnuts, divided
1 1/4 c. flour
1/2 c. brown sugar
1/2 c. butter
Filling:
8 oz. cream cheese, softened
1/3 c. sugar
1 egg
1 tsp. vanilla
1 (21 oz.) can cherry pie filling

Mix crust ingredients together, adding only 1/2 c. nuts. Reserve 1/2 c. crumbs and set aside. Press remaining crumbs in bottom of greased pan. Bake at 350° for 8–12 minutes. Mix cream cheese, sugar, egg, and vanilla until smooth. Spread over hot, baked crust and bake 10 minutes more. Spread cherry filling over cheese layer. Combine reserved crumbs and reserved nuts. Sprinkle evenly over cherries and bake 15 minutes longer.

Mrs. Jonas L. Miller

Crumb Crunch

3/4 c. margarine
1 1/2 c. brown sugar
2 1/4 c. flour
1 tsp. salt
3/4 tsp. soda
1 1/2 c. oatmeal
4 c. thickened fruit filling, any flavor

Mix all except fruit filling. Put 2/3 of crumbs in bottom of 9 X 13 pan. Top with thickened fruit. Top with remaining crumbs. Bake at 350° for 30–35 minutes. Very good with ice cream.

Mrs. Susan Miller

Fruit Cobbler

1/2 c. margarine
3/4 c. sugar
2 c. flour
4 tsp. baking powder
1/2 tsp. salt
1 c. milk
fresh fruit
3/4 c. sugar
2 c. water

Cream together margarine and sugar. Add flour, baking powder, salt, and milk. Stir until blended. Put in cake pan. Top with fruit, sugar, and water. Or use 1 qt. canned fruit with juice. Bake at 350° for 40–45 minutes.

Mrs. Ben N. Weaver

Peach Cobbler

1/2 c. melted butter
2 c. flour
2 c. sugar
pinch salt
2 tsp. baking powder
1 1/3 c. milk
1 qt. peaches, fresh or canned
1/2 tsp. nutmeg
1/2 tsp. cinnamon

Combine all ingredients except peaches and pour into a cake pan. Place peaches and pour juice on top. Do not stir. Bake at 350° for 40 minutes or until brown.

Mrs. David Miller

Raspberry Cobbler

2 c. raspberries
1/4 c. shortening
1 c. sugar
1 egg
1 1/2 c. flour
1/2 tsp. salt
2 tsp. baking powder
1/3 c. milk

Put raspberries in bottom of square cake pan. Make a dough with the remaining ingredients. Put on piles on top of raspberries. Bake at 350° for 45–60 minutes. Serve warm with milk.

Mrs. Felty L. Raber

Apple Crunch

1 c. sugar
4 Tbsp. margarine
2 eggs
1 tsp. soda
1 c. sour milk
2 c. flour
1 tsp. salt
1 tsp. baking powder
1 tsp. vanilla
3 c. diced apples
Crumbs:
3/4 c. brown sugar
3 Tbsp. flour
1 tsp. cinnamon
2 Tbsp. melted butter

Cream sugar and shortening. Add eggs and beat. Add soda to sour milk and stir into mixture. Add dry ingredients and stir thoroughly. Add diced apples. Mix together crumbs. Put apple mixture into a 9 X 13 cake pan and sprinkle crumbs on top. Bake at 350° for 35–40 minutes. Serve hot with milk.

Apple Crisp

24 apples
²/₃ c. brown sugar
²/₃ c. flour
salt
Crumbs:
2¹/₂ c. flour
1 c. brown sugar
2 c. oatmeal
1 tsp. soda
¹/₈ tsp. salt
³/₄ c. plus 2 Tbsp.
   margarine, softened

Peel and chop apples. They should almost fill a 9 X 13 pan. Sprinkle brown sugar, flour, and salt over apples. Mix dry crumb ingredients, then add margarine. Mix until crumbly and put on top. Bake at 350° for 30–50 minutes or until apples are soft and crumbs are browned. Note: Baking time depends on the type of apples used. We like Grimes or Yellow Delicious.

Mrs. Eddie Raber

Caramel Dumplings

2 Tbsp. butter or margarine
1¹/₂ c. water
1¹/₂ c. brown sugar
Dumplings:
1¹/₄ c. all-purpose flour
¹/₂ c. sugar
2 tsp. baking powder
¹/₂ tsp. salt
¹/₂ c. milk
2 Tbsp. butter or magarine, softened
2 tsp. vanilla
¹/₂ c. apples, chopped

In skillet, heat butter, brown sugar, and water to boiling. Reduce heat to simmer. Drop dumplings by tablespoon into simmering sauce. Cover tightly and simmer for 20 minutes. Do not lift lid. Serve hot with milk or ice cream.

Mrs. Abe Yoder

Rhubarb Pudding

4 c. rhubarb, cut up
1 c. sugar
1 (3 oz.) pkg. cherry Jell-O
1 white or yellow cake mix
2 c. cold water

Layer in cake pan in order given. Pour water over top and bake at 350° for 30–35 minutes. When ready to serve, top with Rich's topping. Serve with ice cream or warm with milk.

Mary Schlabach

Rhubarb Torte

Crust:
1 c. flour
2 Tbsp. sugar
$^1/_2$ c. butter
pinch salt
Filling:
$2^1/_4$ c. rhubarb
$1^1/_4$ c. sugar
$^1/_2$ c. half & half
2 Tbsp. flour
3 egg yolks
Topping:
3 egg whites
$^1/_4$ tsp. cream of tartar
6 Tbsp. sugar

Combine crust and press into 8 X 10 pan and bake at 325° for 20–25 minutes. In a saucepan, combine filling ingredients. Cook until thick, then pour over baked crust. Beat topping ingredients until stiff. Spread over rhubarb mixture. Brown at 325° for 10–15 minutes.

Mrs. Atlee Mast

Rhubarb Delicious

Crust:
$^1/_2$ c. margarine
1 c. flour
5 Tbsp. brown sugar
$^1/_2$ c. nuts
Filling:
3 eggs, beaten
$1^1/_2$ c. sugar
$^3/_4$ tsp. salt
$^1/_4$ c. flour
2 c. chopped rhubarb

Mix crust and press into pan. Bake at 350° for 15 minutes. Mix filling ingredients and pour on top of crust. Bake at 350° for 40–45 minutes. Beaten egg whites can be baked on top, or serve with whipped topping.

Marlene Troyer
Esta Raber

Apple Torte

Crust:
¹/₂ c. butter, softened
¹/₃ c. sugar
¹/₄ tsp. vanilla
1¹/₂ c. flour
Filling:
8 oz. cream cheese
¹/₄ c. sugar
1 egg, beaten
1 tsp. vanilla
Topping:
¹/₃ c. sugar
¹/₂ tsp. cinnamon
4 c. chopped apples
¹/₄ c. chopped pecans

For crust: Cream butter, vanilla, and sugar. Blend in flour. Spread dough on bottom and sides of pan. *For filling:* Combine sugar and cream cheese. Mix well. Add beaten egg and vanilla. Pour over dough. *For topping:* Combine sugar and cinnamon. Toss apples in sugar. Mix. Spoon mixture over cheese layer. Sprinkle with nuts. Bake at 350° until done. Loosen torte from rim of pan. Cool before removing.

Mrs. Philip L. Yoder

Zucchini Pudding

4 eggs
2 c. sugar
1¹/₂ c. oil
1 tsp. vanilla
2 c. flour
4 Tbsp. cocoa
2 tsp. soda
2 tsp. cinnamon
1 tsp. salt
3 c. grated zucchini
1 c. nuts

Beat together eggs, oil, sugar, and vanilla. Add flour, cocoa, soda, salt, and cinnamon. Fold in zucchini and nuts. Bake in jellyroll pan at 350° for 30 minutes. Cut in squares and serve with whipped cream.

Mrs. Mary Miller

Pluckets

1 (16 oz.) loaf frozen bread
   dough, partially thawed
$1/2$ c. chopped walnuts
1 pkg. cook & serve
   butterscotch pudding
1 c. brown sugar
$1/2$ c. margarine
1 tsp. cinnamon
1 tsp. vanilla
$1/2$ c. milk

Grease an 8 X 8 pan. Sprinkle nuts on bottom. In a medium saucepan, combine pudding, sugar, margarine, cinnamon, vanilla, and milk. Bring to a boil and cook for 3–5 minutes. Cool, then pour 1 c. pudding mixture over nuts. Cut bread dough into cubes and place on top. Pour rest of pudding mixture over dough. Cover with wax paper and refrigerate overnight. Bake, uncovered, at 350° for 30 minutes. Remove from oven and invert onto serving plate almost immediately.

Mrs. Eli E. Yoder

Hot Fudge Pudding

$1^2/3$ c. water
$3/4$ c. sugar
$1/2$ tsp. salt
2 Tbsp. cocoa
2 Tbsp. butter
1 c. sifted flour
2 Tbsp. butter
$1/2$ c. milk
1 tsp. baking powder
$3/4$ c. sugar
2 Tbsp. cocoa
1 tsp. vanilla
$1/2$ tsp. salt
nuts, optional

Combine water, sugar, salt, cocoa, and butter in saucepan and cook for 5 minutes. Pour into a 9 X 13 pan. Mix remaining ingredients like cake and drop by Tbsp. in hot sauce. Bake at 350° for 45 minutes. Very good with whipped cream or warm with ice cream. I always double this for a 9 X 13 pan. It make a much nicer dish.

Mrs. Abe A. Yoder
Mrs. Mosie Yoder
Mrs. Emma Hershberger

Cheesecake Pie

8 oz. cream cheese
8 oz. sour cream
³/₄ c. milk
1 pkg. instant pudding

Cream the cream cheese and sour cream. Add milk and pudding. Pour into a 9" pie pan, lined with graham cracker crust. Top with your favorite topping.

Mrs. David M. Miller

Peanut Butter Cheesecake

Crust:
chocolate graham crackers, crushed
sugar
butter, melted
Filling:
8 oz. cream cheese
1 c. peanut butter
1¹/₂ c. powdered sugar
1¹/₂ c. milk
16 oz. Cool Whip
Topping:
Reese's peanut butter cups, chopped

Mix crust and line a 9 X 13 pan with crumbs. Cream together cream cheese and peanut butter. Add powdered sugar and milk. Stir in whipped cream. Pour over graham cracker crust. Put topping over filling. Freeze or refrigerate.

Mrs. Myron Miller

Lemon Cheesecake

Crust:
1 c. flour
¹/₂ c. butter
¹/₂ c. nuts
Filling:
8 oz. cream cheese, softened
³/₄ c. powdered sugar
12 oz. Cool Whip
Topping:
3 c. cold milk
2 pkgs. instant lemon pudding

Blend flour and butter well. Add nuts. Put in 9 X 13 pan and bake at 375° for 12 minutes. Mix cream cheese and powdered sugar well. Add Cool Whip, ¹/₂ c. at a time. Spread over cooled crust. Mix milk and pudding. Pour over top.

Mrs. Susan Miller
Mrs. Eli S. Miller

Angel Food Cake Dessert

1³/₄ c. egg whites
2 tsp. cream of tartar
¹/₄ tsp. salt
1 c. sugar
1 tsp. vanilla
1¹/₄ c. cake flour
1¹/₄ c. powdered sugar

Beat egg whites, cream of tartar, and salt together. Slowly add sugar and vanilla. Sift flour and powdered sugar. Fold into egg white mixture. Bake at 325°. For dessert, cut into cubes and serve with your favorite fruit with glaze and Cool Whip.

Anna Troyer

Cherry Chip Delight

1 cherry chip cake mix
8 oz. cream cheese
2 c. powdered sugar
2 c. Rich's topping, whipped
vanilla

Mix cake mix according to directions and bake in 2 cake pans. Cool. Mix cream cheese and powdered sugar. Beat topping and add to cream cheese mixture. Add vanilla and spread over cooled cakes. Top with cherry pie filling.

Mrs. Raymond Wengerd

Angel Food Cake Dessert

1 qt. vanilla ice cream, softened
1 pkg. instant vanilla pudding
1 c. milk

Mix pudding and milk. Add to ice cream and mix well. Layer with pie filling and angel food cake. Fresh strawberry filling is delicious. Best if eaten soon after made.

Mary Esther Miller

Lemon Trifle

1 can Eagle Brand milk
8 oz. lemon yogurt
¹/₃ c. ReaLemon juice
2 c. Cool Whip

Mix together. Layer with angel food cake and put thickened strawberries on top.

Mrs. Roman E. Raber

Date Pudding

1 c. chopped dates
1 tsp. soda
1 Tbsp. butter
1 egg
pinch salt
1 tsp. vanilla
1 c. boiling water
1 c. sugar
1¹/₂ c. flour
¹/₂ c. chopped nuts

Pour boiling water over dates and soda. Let set until cold. Add to other mixture. Bake at 350° for 40 minutes. Serve with whipped cream and date pudding sauce.

Amanda Mast

Sauce for Date Pudding

2 tsp. butter
1 c. brown sugar
3 tsp. clear jel
1¹/₂ c. water
³/₄ tsp. vanilla
¹/₂ tsp. maple flavor

Brown butter. Add brown sugar and 1 c. water. Mix ¹/₂ c. water and clear jel. Cook for 10 minutes. Add flavor and a little salt.

Amanda Mast

Caramel Sauce for Date Pudding

1 c. butter
4 c. brown sugar
4 c. water
³/₄ c. clear jel
2 c. cold water
4 tsp. vanilla

Combine butter and sugar. Brown a little, then add water and bring to a boil. Combine clear jel and water. Add to first mixture and cook until thickened. Add vanilla. Yields 6 cups.

Mrs. Sylvanus Raber

Strawberry Cracker Pudding

1 pkg. strawberry Jell-O
1 c. hot water
8 oz. cream cheese
1/2 c. sugar
2 c. whipped topping or 1
   can evaporated milk, whipped

Combine Jell-O and hot water. Let set until it thickens, then whip. Combine cream cheese and sugar. Add to Jell-O mixture. Add whipped topping. Mix crushed crackers with melted butter. Put in pan and spread pudding on top with some crumbs on top.

Mrs. Mattie D. Miller

Graham Cracker Pudding

1/2 c. butter
1 c. brown sugar
1 1/2 c. water
2 Tbsp. flour (rounded)
2 Tbsp. cornstarch
1/2 c. white sugar
2 egg yolks
1 c. milk
12 graham crackers, crushed
1/4 c. sugar
2 Tbsp. melted butter

Mix butter and brown sugar. Brown a little. Add water and cook together. Combine flour, cornstarch, sugar, egg yolks, and milk. Add and cook until thick.

Mrs. Sylvanus Raber

Old-Fashioned Cracker Pudding

1/2 c. flour
1 c. brown sugar
4 egg yolks
1 c. milk
4 c. milk
vanilla
1/2 c. whipped topping
1 pkg. graham crackers, crushed
2 Tbsp. melted butter
1 Tbsp. brown sugar

Combine flour, brown sugar, egg yolks, and 1 c. milk. Beat until smooth. Heat 4 c. milk and add. Cook until thick. Add vanilla. Add whipped topping when cool. Mix graham crackers, butter, and sugar. Layer crumbs with pudding in a dish. Reserve whipped topping to put on top of pudding.

Mrs. David A. Barkman

Sweetheart Pudding

Crust:
12 graham crackers
²/₃ c. sugar
¹/₂ c. melted butter
Filling:
4 c. milk
³/₄ c. sugar
³/₄ c. flour
4 egg yolks
1 c. milk
2 tsp. vanilla
Meringue:
3 egg whites
¹/₂ c. sugar

Crush crackers. Add sugar and butter. Line 8 X 11 pan, pressing firmly, and set aside. Heat 4 c. milk to boiling. Combine flour, sugar, egg yolks, and 1 c. milk. Beat until smooth. Add egg yolk mixture to boiling milk. Heat to boiling, stirring constantly. Remove from heat and add vanilla. Pour into pan. Beat egg whites until soft peaks form. Add sugar. Spread on top of pudding. Sprinkle a handful crackers on top. Bake at 325° for 25 minutes.

Mrs. Vernon Schmucker
Mrs. Dan Mast

Quick 'N' Easy Pudding

2 c. milk
2 Tbsp. butter
2 egg yolks
2 Tbsp. sugar
2 Tbsp. clear jel
pinch salt
1 tsp. vanilla
3 oz. cream cheese
¹/₂ c. Hi 'N' Dri
graham crackers
4 Tbsp. butter
2 Tbsp. brown sugar

Melt butter in kettle. Add milk and heat to boiling. While heating, mix sugar, clear jel, salt, and egg yolks. Add to milk and bring to a boil. Remove from heat. Add vanilla, cream cheese, and more sugar to suit your taste. Stir until cream cheese melts. Cool, then fold in whipped topping. Add butter and sugar to crushed graham crackers to keep them from getting soggy. Save some crackers to put on top. Variations: Use Ritz crackers instead of graham crackers. Or make peanut butter crumbs by mixing 1 c. powdered sugar and ¹/₃ c. peanut butter. Put on crackers before adding filling. This recipe doubled fills a large Tupperware pan.

Mrs. Ben R. Hershberger

Orange Dessert

Crust:
3 c. crushed Ritz crackers
4 Tbsp. sugar
3 tsp. gelatin
1¼ c. melted butter
Filling:
12 oz. cream cheese
³/₈ c. orange Jell-O
³/₈ c. peach Jell-O
2 c. boiling water
1 c. cold water
¾ c. sugar
1 can crushed pineapple, drained
1½ c. topping
mandarin oranges

Mix crust and press in pan. Mix filling and spread over top. Top with mandarin oranges.

Mrs. John E. Troyer

Lemon Cheese Pudding with Pretzel Crust

Crust:
2 c. crushed pretzels (not too fine)
1 c. sugar
½ c. melted butter
Filling:
8 oz. cream cheese
1 c. sugar
2 tsp. vanilla
1 pkg. lemon Jell-O
¼ c. boiling water
1 can evaporated milk, chilled
  or Rich's topping

Mix crust and line bottom of 9 X 13 Tupperware pan. Save a little for top. Cream together cream cheese, sugar, and vanilla. Mix Jell-O with water. Add to cream cheese mixture. Whip milk until it forms peaks. Combine with cream cheese mixture and pour over crust. Sprinkle with remaining crumbs. Chill.

Mrs. Emma Hershberger

Cherry Berry on a Cloud

Layer One:
$1/2$ c. egg whites
$1/8$ tsp. vinegar
$1/2$ tsp. vanilla
1 c. sugar
Layer Two:
1 c. whipping cream
3 oz. cream cheese
$1/2$ c. powdered sugar
Layer Three:
Fruit filling of your choice

Beat egg whites until foamy. Add vinegar and vanilla and beat until stiff peaks form. Slowly add sugar while beating. Beat until very stiff. Cover baking sheet with a brown paper bag cut to size of pan. Spread egg white mixture on paper in a round or heart shape. Bake at 300° for 15 minutes. Reduce heat to 250° and bake for 1 hour more. Mix layer two ingredients. Spread on top. Mix layer three ingredients and put on top.

Mrs. Aden E. Schlabach

Chocolate Peanut Torte

2 c. vanilla wafer crumbs
$1/4$ c. butter, melted
1 c. peanuts, finely chopped, divided, optional
8 oz. cream cheese, softened
1 c. powdered sugar
$1/2$ c. peanut butter
4 c. Cool Whip, divided
3 c. cold milk
2 pkgs. instant chocolate pudding
1 milk chocolate candy bar, grated

Combine wafer crumbs, butter, and peanuts. Press into 9 X 13 pan and bake for 8–10 minutes. Cool. In mixing bowl, beat cream cheese, sugar, and peanut butter until smooth. Fold in Cool Whip. Spread over crust. Beat milk and pudding. Spread over cream cheese layer. Cover and refrigerate 4–6 hours. Spread remaining topping over pudding layer and sprinkle with grated chocolate and remaining peanuts.

Mrs. Jonas L. Miller

Sunny South Pudding

1/2 c. flour
1/4 c. margarine
1/2 c. nuts
8 oz. cream cheese
2 c. Cool Whip (heaping)
2 c. powdered sugar
3 c. milk
1 pkg. instant butterscotch pudding
1 pkg. instant vanilla pudding
Cool Whip
nuts

Mix flour, nuts, and margarine. Press into a 9 X 13 cake pan. Bake at 375° until brown, about 15 minutes. Cool. Cream the powdered sugar and cream cheese together. Add Cool Whip. Spread on top of crumbs. Mix milk with puddings. Pour on top of creamed mixture. Finish off with Cool Whip. Sprinkle with nuts. Very yummy!

Mrs. Ray Raber

Pumpkin Torte

Crust:
12 whole graham crackers
1/3 c. sugar
1/2 c. butter
Filling:
2 eggs, beaten
8 oz. cream cheese
3/4 c. sugar
Topping:
2 c. pumpkin
3 egg yolks
1/2 c. sugar
1/2 c. milk
1/2 tsp. salt
1 tsp. cinnamon
1 Tbsp. gelatin
1/4 c. cold water
3 egg whites, beaten
1/4 c. sugar

Mix crust and press into pan. Mix eggs, cream cheese, and sugar. Pour over crackers and bake at 350° for 20 minutes. Cook pumpkin, egg yolks, sugar, milk, salt, and cinnamon. Soak gelatin in water. Add to pumpkin mixture. Cool. Add egg whites and sugar. Pour over cooled filling. When ready to serve, top with whipped topping.

Mrs. Ben N. Weaver

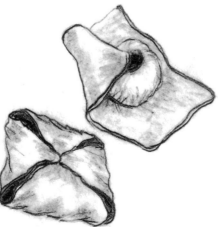

Pumpkin Dessert

1 yellow cake mix
$^1/_2$ c. melted butter or margarine
1 egg
Filling:
3 c. pumpkin
$2^1/_2$ tsp. pumpkin pie spice
2 eggs
$^2/_3$ c. milk
$^1/_2$ c. brown sugar
Topping:
1 c. reserved cake mix
$^1/_4$ c. sugar
1 tsp. cinnamon
$^1/_4$ c. butter

Grease a 9 X 13 pan. Reserve 1 c. cake mix for topping. Combine remaining cake mix, butter, and egg. Press into pan. Mix filling ingredients until smooth. Pour over crust. Mix topping ingredients and sprinkle over filling. Bake at 350° for 45–50 minutes or until knife comes out clean. Cool. Serve with whipped cream.

Mrs. Atlee Hershberger
Mrs. Felty L. Raber

Fluffy Pistachio Dessert

Crust:
$^1/_2$ c. margarine, softened
1 c. all-purpose flour
$^1/_2$ c. powdered sugar
$^1/_2$ c. chopped walnuts
First Layer:
8 oz. cream cheese, softened
1 c. sour cream
8 oz. whipped topping
Second Layer:
3 c. cold milk
2 pkgs. instant pistachio pudding
Topping:
8 oz. whipped topping
2 Tbsp. ground walnuts

Cream margarine. Add flour and sugar. Blend until crumbly. Stir in walnuts. Press onto bottom of a 9 X 13 baking dish coated with non-stick cooking spray. Bake at 375° for 10–12 minutes or until set. Cool. In a mixing bowl, beat cream cheese and sour cream. Fold in whipped topping. Spread over crust. In another mixing bowl, combine milk and pudding mixes. Beat on low speed for 2 minutes. Spread over first layer. Carefully spread whipped topping over second layer. Sprinkle with walnuts. Chill at least 1 hour. Yields 24 servings.

Barbara Coblentz

Chocolate Pudding Pizza

1 (17¹/₂ oz.) pkg. peanut butter
   cookie mix or your own recipe
12 oz. cream cheese, softened
1³/₄ c. cold milk
1 pkg. instant chocolate pudding
8 oz. frozen whipped topping
¹/₄ c. mini semisweet chocolate chips

Prepare cookie mix dough according to package directions. Press into a greased 12" pizza pan. Bake at 375° for 15 minutes. Cool. In a mixing bowl, beat cream cheese until smooth. Spread over crust. Beat milk and pudding on medium speed for 2 minutes. Spread over cream cheese layer. Refrigerate 20 minutes or until set. Spread with whipped topping and sprinkle with chocolate chips. Chill 1–2 hours.

Mrs. Atlee (Lizzie) Raber

Layered Dessert

Crust:
1 c. flour
¹/₂ c. margarine, softened
1 c. chopped nuts
First Layer:
1 c. powdered sugar
8 oz. cream cheese
1 c. Cool Whip
Second Layer:
1 pkg. vanilla instant pudding
2 c. milk

Mix crust and press into 9 X 13 pan. Bake at 350° for 20 minutes. Cool. Mix powdered sugar, cream cheese, and Cool Whip. Spread on cooled crust. Mix pudding and milk. Spread over first layer and top with Cool Whip.

Mrs. Henry J.C. Yoder

Pudding

2 pkgs. instant vanilla pudding
1 (20 oz.) can pineapple
9 oz. Cool Whip
2 c. miniature marshmallows

Mix all together. Chill and serve cold.

Mandy Troyer

Basic Vanilla Cream Pudding

8 c. milk
2 c. sugar
1 c. cornstarch
$^1/_2$ tsp. salt
5 egg yolks
2 tsp. vanilla
$^1/_2$ c. margarine

Heat 7 c. milk. Combine sugar, salt, cornstarch, egg yolks, and 1 c. milk. Add to milk when almost boiling. Cook over low heat for 2–3 minutes. Add margarine and vanilla. This is also very good for peanut butter pie.

Mrs. Emanuel J. Miller

Orange Danish Dessert

4 c. water
$^1/_2$ c. clear jel
$1^1/_4$ c. sugar
1 pkg. orange or cherry Kool-Aid
fresh or canned fruit

Combine water, clear jel, sugar, and Kool-Aid. Bring to boil. Cool, then add fruit.

Mrs. Edward M. Hershberger

Frozen Cheesecake

Crust:
1 pkg. graham crackers, crushed
$^1/_2$ c. melted butter or margarine
3 Tbsp. brown sugar
Filling:
8 oz. cream cheese
1 c. sugar
4 eggs, beaten
1 c. whipped topping
1 tsp. vanilla
Topping:
fruit glaze of your choice

Mix crust and press into a 9 X 13 pan. Mix filling and pour over crust. Freeze. Remove from freezer 15 minutes before serving. Top with fruit glaze.

Mrs. Atlee Hershberger
Mrs. Felty J. Erb
Mrs. John L. Erb
Mrs. Ivan Hershberger

Fruit Salad Pie

32 large marshmallows,
cut into pieces
$^1/_2$ c. milk
1 can fruit cocktail, drained
$^1/_2$ c. chopped nuts
1 c. whipping cream, whipped

Heat milk and stir in marshmallows until light and fluffy. Let cool. Add fruit cocktail, nuts, and whipped cream. Blend all together. Pour into a graham cracker crust. Freeze until hardened.

Frozen Strawberry Salad

12 oz. whipped topping
8 oz. cream cheese, softened
1 qt. sweetened, mashed
strawberries
1 (20 oz.) can crushed pineapple,
drained
4–6 bananas, thinly sliced
2–3 c. thinly sliced peaches,
canned or fresh

Blend gently until mixed, then freeze. To serve, unmold and cut into slices. Note: Almost any variety of fruit may be substituted and amount can be adjusted to your taste.

Mrs. Eddie Raber

Frosty Strawberry Dessert

First Layer:
$1^1/_2$ c. flour
$^1/_2$ c. nuts
$^1/_2$ c. butter
$^1/_4$ c. brown sugar
Second Layer:
2 egg whites
2 c. crushed strawberries,
fresh or frozen
$^3/_4$ c. sugar
2 Tbsp. lemon juice
1 c. whipped topping

Mix flour, nuts, butter and brown sugar. Spread in pan and bake at 350° for 20 minutes, stirring occasionally. Place $^2/_3$ of crumbs into a 9 X 13 Tupperware pan. In a large bowl, beat egg whites, strawberries, sugar, and lemon juice for 10 minutes. Beat whipped topping and fold into mixture. Pour over crumbs in pan. Sprinkle remaining crumbs evenly on top. Freeze at least 6 hours. Refreshing!

Mrs. Dennis (Rosie) Yoder

Frozen Strawberry Dessert

Crumbs:
1 c. margarine
1/2 c. brown sugar
2 c. flour
1 c. nuts or oatmeal
Filling:
1 Tbsp. lemon juice
1 c. sugar
1 pt. fresh or frozen strawberries
1/2 tsp. salt
1 tsp. vanilla
2 egg whites, beaten

Mix crumbs. Bake on cookie sheet at 325°, stirring often. Cool and crumble. Put 3/4 of mixture in pan and save rest for top. Mix filling and add 1 c. whipped topping. Put on top of crumbs. Top with remaining crumbs. Freeze.

Mrs. Reuben Mast

Frozen Ice Cream Delight

2 1/2 c. Oreo cookie crumbs, divided
1/2 c. butter, melted
1/2 gal. vanilla ice cream
1 1/2 c. salted peanuts
8 oz. Cool Whip
Chocolate Sauce:
2 c. powdered sugar
2/3 c. semisweet chocolate chips
1 can evaporated milk
1/2 c. butter
1 tsp. vanilla

Combine 2 c. cookie crumbs with butter. Press into bottom of 9 X 13 pan. Freeze for 15 minutes. Spread ice cream over crumbs. Freeze until firm. Mix chocolate sauce and bring to a boil. Cook for 8 minutes. Add vanilla; cool. Pour sauce over ice cream and sprinkle with peanuts. Freeze until firm. Spread Cool Whip over nuts and top with crumbs. Freeze at least 3 hours before serving.

Mrs. Roman E. Raber

Caramel Ice Cream Dessert

3/4 c. oatmeal
1/2 c. brown sugar
2 c. flour
1 c. butter
3/4 c. pecans
caramel ice cream topping
1/2 gal. vanilla ice cream

Mix oatmeal, sugar, flour, butter, and pecans. Bake at 350° for 20–25 minutes. Put half of crumbs in a 9 X 13 pan. Drizzle with caramel topping. Slice ice cream and put on top. Layer remaining topping and crumbs. Freeze.

Mrs. Allen R. Troyer

Cookie Crumbs & Ice Cream

Crumbs:
6 c. all-purpose flour
1¹/₂ c. chopped nuts
1¹/₂ c. firmly packed brown sugar
1 lb. butter or margarine, softened
Ice Cream Dessert:
3¹/₂ c. crumbs
2¹/₂ qts. ice cream
additional crumbs

Preheat oven to 375°. Combine flour, sugar, and nuts. Blend well. Cut in margarine until crumbs are fine. Press firmly into 2 shallow ungreased baking pans. Bake for 15 minutes. Cool, crumble, and store in an airtight container. Use in 4–6 weeks. Yields 10¹/₂ cups. For dessert, press crumbs onto bottom of 9 X 13 pan. Whip ice cream and spread over crust. Top with more crumbs. Freeze until firm. We love to mix fresh strawberries in our ice cream.

Susie Ellen Yoder

Esther's Brownie Baked Alaska

¹/₂ gal. ice cream
1 pkg. brownie mix
Meringue:
6 egg whites
12 Tbsp. sugar

Mix brownies according to package directions and put into a 9"–10" round pan. Line a bowl (about 7" across top) with plastic wrap. Make sure that the bowl is just a little smaller than the brownie pan. Spoon softened ice cream into lined bowl. Press down well. Freeze. When brownie is cold and ice cream is hard, make meringue by beating egg whites until frothy. Gradually beat in sugar until stiff peaks form. Put brownie in oven-proof dish. Invert ice cream onto brownie. Peel off plastic wrap and frost with meringue, sealing edges well. Freeze. When frozen solid, bake at 500° for 2–3 minutes until peaks brown. Freeze again until serving time. Let set for 15 minutes before cutting with a heavy knife.

Mrs. Edwin N. (Ruth) Weaver

Frozen Pumpkin Dessert

1 1/2 c. graham cracker crumbs
1/8 tsp. salt
1/4 c. brown sugar
1/3 c. melted butter
Filling:
1 c. canned pumpkin
1 c. brown sugar
1 tsp. cinnamon
1/4 tsp. salt
1/8 tsp. nutmeg
8 oz. Cool Whip
1 qt. softened vanilla ice cream

Mix crumbs, salt, sugar, and butter. Line a 9 X 13 pan with crumbs. Mix pumpkin, sugar, cinnamon, salt, nutmeg, and Cool Whip. Add ice cream. Pour over crumbs. Freeze.

Mrs. John A. Miller

Chocolate Malt Dessert

1 1/2 c. chocolate cookie crumbs
1/4 c. butter, melted
2 c. vanilla ice cream, softened
1/2 c. crushed malted milk balls
2 Tbsp. milk, divided
3 Tbsp. instant chocolate
  malted milk powder
3 Tbsp. marshmallow creme
1 c. whipped cream

Combine crumbs and butter. Press into a 9" pie pan. Freeze while preparing filling. In bowl, blend ice cream, crushed malted milk balls, and 1 Tbsp. milk. Spoon over crust. Freeze for 1 hour. Blend malted milk powder, marshmallow creme, and 1 Tbsp. milk. Stir in whipped cream and whip until soft peaks form. Spread over ice cream. Freeze several hours or overnight. Garnish with whipped cream and malted milk balls, if desired.

Mrs. Levi (Susan) Troyer

Caramel Ice Cream Cake

1 caramel cake mix
3 qts. vanilla ice cream, softened
1 pkg. instant vanilla pudding
2 c. milk
16 oz. Cool Whip
4 Snickers candy bars, chopped
caramel ice cream topping

Mix cake according to directions on box. Bake in a jellyroll pan. Cool. Invert into a large Tupperware pan. Mix pudding and milk. Blend in ice cream. Pour over cake. Spread Cool Whip on top. Sprinkle with Snickers and drizzle caramel topping over all. Freeze. Thaw slightly before serving. Variation: Use chocolate cake and cookies and cream ice cream, with Oreo crumbs and chocolate syrup on top.

Mrs. Dennis (Rosie) Yoder

Peanut Butter Ice Cream Pudding

50 Ritz crackers, crushed
6 Tbsp. butter, melted
1 qt. softened ice cream
8 oz. cream cheese, softened
$1/2$ c. peanut butter
$1^1/2$ c. whipped topping
$1/2$ c. powdered sugar
3 c. softened ice cream
chocolate syrup

Mix cracker crumbs with butter. Spread $2/3$ of mixture in pan. Spread 1 qt. ice cream on top. Mix cream cheese, peanut butter, whipped topping, and powdered sugar. Spread over ice cream. Top with 3 c. ice cream and swirl with chocolate syrup. Sprinkle remaining crumbs. Freeze. Thaw slightly before serving.

Mrs. Atlee Mast

Ice Cream Sandwiches

3 eggs, separated
$1^1/3$ c. powdered sugar
2 c. whipping cream or
    Rich's Topping, whipped
graham crackers

Beat egg yolks until light and fluffy. Whip egg whites. Fold together egg yolks, whites, powdered sugar, and whipped cream. Line a cookie sheet with whole graham crackers. Pour filling over crackers and top with more crackers. Freeze. Cut into sandwiches while frozen.

Dora Schlabach

Ice Box Sandwiches

1 pkg. instant vanilla pudding
2 c. cold milk
2 c. whipped topping
1 c. mini chocolate chips
48 graham cracker squares

Mix pudding and milk according to package directions and refrigerate until set. Fold in whipped topping and chocolate chips. Place 24 graham crackers on baking sheet. Top each with about 3 Tbsp. filling. Place another cracker on top. Freeze for 1 hour or until firm. Wrap individually in plastic wrap. Freeze. Enjoy!

Mrs. David A. Yoder
Mrs. Marion Miller

Cherry Vanilla Ice Cream

1 gal. milk
3 pkgs. gelatin
4 Tbsp. cornstarch (rounded)
5 c. sugar
1 can evaporated milk
$1/2$ tsp. salt
6 egg yolks
3 egg whites
1 Tbsp. vanilla
$1^1/2$ c. whipped topping

Heat half of milk. Pour some over sugar. Mix cornstarch with milk and stir in remaining warm milk. Bring to a boil. Soak gelatin in $1/2$ c. cold water. Add to warm mixture. Beat eggs with a little milk and add to sugar. Put all together. Add 1 jar maraschino cherries. Yields 2 gal.

Mrs. Aden A. Raber

Ice Cream

5 pkgs. instant vanilla pudding
$1^1/2$ c. sugar
3 tsp. vanilla
1 gal. milk
2 c. whipping cream

Mix and put in ice cream freezer. Yields 2 gallons.

Mrs. Ivan A. Miller

Ice Cream

1 1/2 c. sugar
1 1/2 c. brown sugar
2 pkgs. instant pudding
6 eggs
2 Tbsp. gelatin
3 qts. milk
vanilla
pinch salt

Soak gelatin in a little milk. Mix 4 c. milk and pudding. Heat remaining milk. Dissolve gelatin mixture in hot milk. Mix all together. Cool. Add 12 oz. evaporated milk. Yield 6 qts.

Mrs. David J. Troyer

Ice Cream

2 pkgs. vanilla instant pudding
4 c. milk
4 eggs
1 1/2 c. sugar
1/2 c. brown sugar
1 can Eagle Brand milk
  or Meadow Gold
1 tsp. vanilla
6 c. milk

Mix pudding and 4 c. milk. Set aside. Beat eggs. Add sugar, Eagle Brand milk, and vanilla. Add pudding and mix all together. Add more milk until ice cream freezer can is about 3/4 full. May add several drops maple flavoring, if you wish. Yields 6 qts.

Katie Hershberger

Vanilla Ice Cream

3 pts. milk
1 1/2 c. sugar
3 Tbsp. cornstarch (rounded)
1/2 tsp. salt
6 eggs, beaten
3/4 c. sugar
vanilla
1 pkg. instant vanilla pudding
cream
milk

Cook a custard with milk, sugar, salt, and cornstarch. Remove from heat and add eggs, sugar, and vanilla. Cool, then add pudding and cream. Fill ice cream freezer can with milk. Yields 6 qts.

Mrs. Atlee M. Shetler

Fudgesicles

1 pkg. instant chocolate pudding
$^1/_2$ c. sugar
3 eggs
4 c. milk

Beat all together and freeze.

Mrs. Fannie Mae Barkman

Popsicles

1 pkg. Jell-O
1 pkg. Kool-Aid
$^1/_2$ c. sugar
2 c. boiling water
2 c. cold water

Add boiling water to sugar, Jell-O, and Kool-Aid. Stir until dissolved. Add cold water. Pour into popsicle trays and freeze.

Mrs. Roy E. Mast

Crunchy Chocolate Sauce

1 c. chopped walnuts or pecans
$^1/_2$ c. butter
1 c. chocolate chips

In a skillet, sauté nuts in butter until golden. Remove from heat. Stir in chocolate chips until melted. Serve warm over ice cream. Sauce will harden. Delicious!

Mrs. Roy A. Troyer

Crispy Ice Cream Topping

2 c. Rice Krispies, slightly crushed
$^1/_2$ c. peanuts
$^1/_2$ c. brown sugar
$^1/_3$ c. melted butter

Mix cereal and peanuts on cookie sheets. Brown at 350°. Mix sugar and butter. Mix in cereal and nuts. Put half in bottom of pan. Add vanilla ice cream and put remaining crumbs on top. Freeze. Thaw slightly before serving.

Katie Hershberger

Hot Fudge

1 pkg. cook and serve
    chocolate pudding
$1/2$ c. brown sugar
1 c. water
2 Tbsp. butter

Mix pudding, sugar, and water. Cook until thick. Add butter.

Mrs. Allen R. Troyer

24-Hour Salad Dessert

2 eggs, beaten
$1/2$ c. sugar
2 Tbsp. flour
1 c. orange juice
8 oz. cream cheese
10 oz. miniature marshmallows
1 can crushed pineapple, drained
1 can mandarin oranges, drained
12 oz. Cool Whip

Mix eggs, sugar, flour, and orange juice. Cook until thick. While still hot, add cream cheese and marshmallows. Beat well. Add pineapple and oranges. Mix well and chill for 2 hours. Add Cool Whip. Mix well. Top with mandarin oranges and nuts, if desired.

Mrs. Ben D. Miller

Apple Fruit Salad

1 c. pineapple chunks
1 c. apple chunks
1 c. grapes
1 c. miniature marshmallows
Dressing:
1 c. pineapple juice
1 egg, beaten
$1/2$ c. sugar
2 Tbsp. cornstarch

Mix dressing ingredients and cook until thick, stirring constantly. Cool and mix with fruit.

Marlene Troyer

Fruit Slush

12 oz. orange juice concentrate
8 bananas, mashed
1 c. crushed pineapple
2 c. sugar
1 c. hot water

Mix juice according to directions. Mix water and sugar until sugar is dissolved. Mix all together. Stir once or twice while freezing. Remove from freezer 1 hour before serving.

Mrs. Mattie Miller

Crust Salad

2 c. flour
1 c. butter
$1/2$ c. brown sugar
$1/2$ c. nuts
$1/2$ c. boiling water
$1/2$ c. orange Jell-O
$1/2$ c. cold water
1 can crushed pineapple
8 oz. cream cheese
1 c. sugar
$1^1/2$ c. Rich's topping, whipped

Mix flour, butter, sugar, and nuts. Press into pan. Bake until brown. Mix boiling water and Jell-O. Add cold water. Add pineapple and let set. Mix cream cheese and sugar. Add to Jell-O. Add whipped topping and put on crust.

Mrs. Albert Barkman

Grapefruit Salad

3 c. sugar
2 c. water
$3^1/2$ pkgs. gelatin
1 c. cold water
4 c. whole grapefruit, cut up
1 c. orange juice
$1/2$ c. lemon or ReaLemon
$1/2$ tsp. salt

Cook sugar and water together for 3 minutes. Mix gelatin and cold water. Let set for 5 minutes before adding to hot sugar water. Add remaining ingredients.

Mrs. Roy M. Kuhns

Tropical Fruit Dessert

1 1/4 c. sugar
1/2 c. clear jel
1 pkg. tropical punch Kool-Aid
4 c. water
1 can pineapple tidbits, drained
1 1/2 c. grapes
2–3 bananas

In saucepan, combine sugar, clear jel, and Kool-Aid. Stir in water. Bring to a boil over medium heat, stirring constantly until clear and thick. Cool and add fruit. May use any kind of fruit you wish. Very good!

Katie Hershberger
Mary Esther Miller

Company Fruit Salad

4 med. Golden Delicious
 apples, diced
4 med. Red Delicious apples, diced
2 c. seedless green grapes, halved
2 c. seedless red grapes, halved
1 (20 oz.) can mandarin
 oranges, drained
Dressing:
3 oz. cream cheese, softened
1/2 c. sour cream
1/2 c. mayonnaise
1/2 c. sugar

Combine all fruit in a mixing bowl. Beat dressing ingredients until smooth. Pour over fruit and toss gently to coat. Serve immediately. Yields 16–20 servings.

Mrs. Lovina Schlabach

Grape Salad

1 1/2 c. whipped topping
3/4 c. cream cheese in a tube
1/4 c. powdered sugar
3 lbs. seedless grapes,
 washed, drained
bananas, if desired

Mix whipped topping and cream cheese together. Add powdered sugar, then add grapes. Also good without sugar for diabetics.

Mrs. Mattie Miller

Carrot Pudding

6 Tbsp. cold water
2 pkgs. unflavored gelatin
1 c. sugar
1 can pineapple
2 lg. carrots, grated fine
1 c. celery
1½ c. cottage cheese
1 lg. container Cool Whip

In a saucepan, heat water and add gelatin. Heat to boiling. Remove from heat and add remaining ingredients. Chill.

Mrs. Mary Miller

Festive Fruit Salad

1 (15 oz.) can mandarin
   oranges, drained
1½ c. red seedless grapes, halved
1½ c. green seedless grapes, halved
1 (10 oz.) jar maraschino cherries,
   rinsed, drained, optional
1 can pineapple chunks, drained
2 c. miniature marshmallows
1 c. flaked coconut, optional
1 c. sour cream

Combine all ingredients except sour cream. Just before serving, add sour cream. Toss to coat. This makes a great holiday dish.

Mrs. Ivan Hershberger

Fruit Dessert

2 (20 oz.) cans pineapple tidbits
2 (11 oz.) cans mandarin oranges
4 c. grapes
4 c. whipped topping or
   12 oz. Cool Whip
1½ c. instant vanilla pudding

Combine fruit. Mix with remaining ingredients.

Mrs. Arlene Hershberger

Festive Cranberry Salad

1 can Eagle Brand milk
1/4 c. ReaLemon
1 can crushed pineapple, drained
1 (16 oz.) can whole
   cranberry sauce
2 c. miniature marshmallows
1/2 c. chopped nuts
red food coloring, optional
8 oz. Cool Whip

In a bowl, combine milk and lemon juice. Mix well. Stir in the pineapple, cranberry sauce, marshmallows, nuts, and food coloring. Fold in Cool Whip. Spoon into a 9 X 13 pan. Freeze until firm. Cut in squares.

Mrs. Arlene Hershberger

Date Balls

2 eggs
1/2 c. butter or margarine
1 c. sugar
1 pkg. dates, chopped
2 c. Rice Krispies
1 c. chopped nuts
coconut

Beat eggs. Add butter and sugar. Melt over low heat, stirring all the time. Add dates. Cook over low heat. Take off when mixture leaves pan clear. Add Rice Krispies and nuts. Shape into balls. Roll in coconut and cool. Delicious!

Mrs. Andy A. Troyer

Warm Minute Tapioca

2 1/4 c. milk
1 egg yolk
1/2 tsp. salt
6 Tbsp. minute tapioca
3 Tbsp. sugar
1 egg white, beaten
chocolate chips

Combine milk and egg yolk. Put in a saucepan and add salt, tapioca, and sugar. Cook together for 1 minute or until thickened. Take off heat and add beaten egg white. Cool a bit, then toss with chocolate chips. This is a favorite for our little ones.

Mrs. Andrew A. Troyer

Fruity Tapioca

4 c. water
1 c. sugar
1/3 c. quick-cooking tapioca
1 (6 oz.) can frozen orange
   juice concentrate, thawed
1 can peaches
1 can mandarin oranges

Combine water, sugar, and tapioca. Let set for 5 minutes. Bring to a full rolling boil. Remove from heat. Stir in orange juice concentrate. Cool for 20 minutes. Stir in peaches and oranges.

Mrs. Roy E. Mast

Jell-O Tapioca Dessert

2 pkgs. orange Jell-O
2 pkgs. instant vanilla pudding
2 pkgs. tapioca pudding
4 c. boiling water
Cool Whip
oranges or peaches, cut up

Pour boiling water over Jell-O and puddings. Stir well. Let set until it starts to thicken. Beat in Cool Whip and add fruit. Note: May use sugar-free Jell-O and pudding.

Mary Schlabach

Grape Tapioca Pudding

2¹/₂ c. grape juice
4 Tbsp. granulated tapioca
1/2 c. sugar
pinch salt
whipped topping

Mix together first 4 ingredients. Bring to a full boil, stirring constantly. Remove from heat and chill thoroughly without stirring. Fold in desired amount of whipped topping.

Mrs. Roy E. Mast

Tapioca

4 c. water
1/2 c. plus 1 Tbsp. baby pearl tapioca
1 pkg. Jell-O, any flavor
2/3 c. sugar
pinch salt
1 c. whipped topping
fresh fruit

Heat water to boiling. Add tapioca and cook for 15 minutes. Turn off heat and let set until tapioca is clear. Add Jell-O, sugar, and salt. Let set overnight, then add topping and fruit that matches with your flavor Jell-O. Good!

Mrs. Norman H. Mast

Broken Glass Salad

1 pkg. lime Jell-O
1 pkg. orange Jell-O
1 pkg. strawberry Jell-O
4¹/₂ c. boiling water, divided
1 pkg. pineapple Jell-O
1 pkg. lemon Jell-O
3 c. boiling water
2 c. whipped cream

Dissolve strawberry, orange, and lime Jell-O in 1¹/₂ c. boiling water each. Gel in a flat dish or pan. Mix pineapple and lemon Jell-O in 3 c. boiling water. When this starts to gel, add whipped cream and mix well. Cut other Jell-O in squares and fold into pineapple mixture. Put in Jell-O mold or other dish and let set.

Mrs. Paul J. Hostetler

Crown Jewel Jell-O

1 pkg. raspberry Jell-O
1 pkg. lime Jell-O
1 pkg. orange Jell-O
3 c. hot water, divided
1¹/₂ c. cold water, divided
¹/₄ c. sugar
pineapple juice
1 pkg. strawberry Jell-O
¹/₂ c. cold water
2 c. cream, whipped

Prepare raspberry, lime, and orange Jell-O separately, using 1 c. hot water and ¹/₂ c. cold water for each. Pour into 3 shallow pans and chill until firm. Cut into ¹/₂" cubes. Heat sugar with pineapple juice and bring to a boil. Dissolve strawberry Jell-O in this liquid. Add ¹/₂ c. cold water and chill until syrupy. Fold in whipped cream. Fold in Jell-O cubes. Chill and serve.

Katie Mae Troyer

12-Layer Jell-O Salad

6 pkgs. Jell-O, each a different flavor
6 c. boiling water
3 c. sour cream
6 Tbsp. cold water

Dissolve 1 pkg. Jell-O in 1 c. boiling water. Reserve ¹/₂ c. Jell-O. Add ¹/₂ c. sour cream to remaining Jell-O. Stir until dissolved. Pour into 9 X 13 pan and let set for 30 minutes or until firm. Add 1 Tbsp. cold water to reserved Jell-O. Pour over first layer. Repeat with next color.

Mrs. Wayne Yoder

Refreshing Jell-O Dessert

1 pkg. cook & serve vanilla pudding
1 pkg. apricot Jell-O
2 c. water
2 c. Cool Whip
1 can mandarin oranges

Cook pudding and Jell-O with water for 5 minutes. Cool and add Cool Whip and oranges. You may change Jell-O and fruit to any combination.

Mae Mast

Ribbon Salad

1 pkg. green Jell-O
1³/₄ c. hot water
1 pkg. orange Jell-O
1¹/₂ c. hot water
8 oz. cream cheese
1¹/₂ c. sugar
²/₃ c. Rich's topping, whipped
1 pkg. red Jell-O
2 c. hot water

Mix green Jell-O and water. Put into a pan and let harden. Mix orange Jell-O and water. Cream sugar and cream cheese. Add to partially thickened orange Jell-O. Add whipped topping. Pour over green Jell-O and let harden. Mix red Jell-O and water and let set until no longer very hot. Pour slowly over top.

Mrs. John Yoder

Triple Orange Salad

1 pkg. orange Jell-O
1 pkg. vanilla instant pudding
1 pkg. tapioca pudding
2¹/₂ c. water
1 can mandarin oranges
2 c. Cool Whip

Bring water to boil. Add first 3 ingredients. Stir well. Cool. Add oranges and Cool Whip. Chill.

Mrs. Andy E. Yoder

Lime Jell-O Salad

2 pkgs. lime or lemon Jell-O
$1/2$ c. white sugar
$3^1/2$ c. hot water
1 can crushed pineapple, drained,
    with juice reserved
$1/2$ c. nuts
8 oz. cream cheese
1 c. whipped topping
Custard Topping:
reserved pineapple juice plus
    water to make 1 cup liquid
$1/2$ c. sugar
2 Tbsp. flour
3 eggs, well beaten

Mix Jell-O, sugar, and hot water. Add pineapple and nuts. Put in pan. When Jell-O is thick, mix cream cheese and whipped topping and put on top of Jell-O. Mix the custard topping ingredients. Cook together and let it cool. Put on top.

Mrs. Jonathan Raber

Lime Crust Salad

2 c. flour
$1/2$ c. brown sugar
$1/2$ c. nuts, optional
1 c. butter
1 c. lime Jell-O
$4^1/2$ c. hot water
$2^1/2$ c. Rich's topping, whipped
8 oz. cream cheese

Mix flour, sugar, nuts, and butter. Press into a 9 X 13 pan and bake at 350° for 15–20 minutes. While cooling, take a fork and chop the crust to crumbs. Mix Jell-O and water. Mix topping and cream cheese. When Jell-O is slightly thick, add to topping mixture and pour over crust. Refrigerate.

Esta & Vesta Yoder

Grape Jell-O Dessert

$2/3$ c. Jell-O
2 c. boiling water
$1/4$ c. powdered sugar
8 oz. cream cheese
2 Tbsp. sour cream
4 c. whipped topping

Dissolve Jell-O in water. Cool. Beat together cream cheese, powdered sugar, and sour cream. Add whipped topping. Add partially thickened Jell-O. When set, top with solid Jell-O. Any flavor Jell-O may be used, but grape is very good.

Mrs. Wayne Yoder

Orange Salad

2 pkgs. orange Jell-O
2 c. boiling water
4 c. small marshmallows
2 c. cold water
16 oz. cream cheese
1 c. sugar
2 c. whipped topping
2 pkgs. orange Jell-O

Mix 2 pkgs. orange Jell-O and boiling water. Add marshmallows and stir until melted. Add cold water and set aside. Mix cream cheese, sugar, and whipped topping. Add to Jell-O mixture above. Pour into pan to chill. When set, prepare 2 pkgs. orange Jell-O as directed on package. Pour on top of first mixture. Variation: For orange sherbet, omit the Jell-O on top, and freeze.

Mrs. Eli N. Hershberger

Jell-O Pudding

First Layer:
1 pkg. Jell-O
Second Layer:
2 c. whipped topping
8 oz. cream cheese, softened
$^3/_4$ c. sour cream
$^1/_3$ c. sugar
1 Tbsp. ReaLemon
1 pkg. Jell-O
1 c. hot water
Third Layer:
1 pkg. Jell-O

Mix first layer Jell-O as directed on package. Pour into pan. Mix whipped topping, cream cheese, sour cream, sugar, and ReaLemon. Mix Jell-O with hot water. Add to cream cheese mixture. Pour over first layer. Mix third layer Jell-O as directed on package. Pour on top. Variation: Omit sour cream and add vanilla instead of ReaLemon.

Mrs. Arlene Hershberger
Mrs. Levi Yoder

Finger Jell-O

4 Tbsp. unflavored gelatin
2 pkgs. Jell-O
$^1/_2$ c. sugar
2 c. boiling water
1 c. cold water

Soak gelatin in 1 c. cold water. Put Jell-O, sugar, and gelatin in a bowl and add boiling water. Stir. Pour into cake pan. Set and cut.

Mrs. Emanuel J. Miller

3-Layer Finger Jell-O

First Layer:
3 pkgs. Jell-O
3 pkgs. Knox gelatin
4 c. boiling water
Second Layer:
3 pkgs. Knox gelatin
2 c. boiling water
1 can Eagle Brand milk
Third layer:
3 pkgs. Jell-O
3 pkgs. Knox gelatin
4 c. boiling water

Mix first layer. Divide into 2 sheet cake pans. For second layer, dissolve Knox gelatin in cold water, then add boiling water. Cool slightly, then add Eagle Brand milk. Mix third layer ingredients. We like to use red and green Jell-O for Christmas.

Barbara Coblentz
Mary Esther Miller

Aunt Pet's Pineapple Salad

2 pkgs. lemon Jell-O or half orange
3^1/$_2$ c. hot water
1 can crushed pineapple,
   drained with juice reserved
^{1}/$_2$ c. sugar
1 egg, beaten
2 Tbsp. butter
3 Tbsp. flour
reserved pineapple juice with
   water to make 1 c. liquid
8 oz. cream cheese
1 carton Cool Whip

Dissolve Jell-O in hot water and add pineapple. Put mixture in oblong cake pan. Chill. Cook sugar, egg, butter, flour, and juice until thick. Fold in cream cheese. Cool. Add Cool Whip. Spread on top of firm Jell-O. Chill and serve.

Mrs. Levi (Susan) Troyer

Jell-O Mold

2 pkgs. Jell-O, any flavor
1 can Eagle Brand milk
1 c. hot water
16 oz. Cool Whip

Mix together hot water and Jell-O until dissolved and ready to set. Add milk and mix well. Add Cool Whip and mix. Pour into Jell-O mold or bowl.

Mrs. Leroy A. Miller

Patriotic Gelatin Salad

2 pkgs. berry blue gelatin
2 pkgs. strawberry gelatin
4 c. boiling water, divided
2¹/₂ c. cold water, divided
2 pkgs. unflavored gelatin
2 c. milk
1 c. sugar
2 c. sour cream
2 tsp. vanilla extract

In 4 separate bowls, dissolve each pkg. gelatin in 1 c. boiling water. Add ¹/₂ c. cold water to each and stir. Pour 1 bowl of blue gelatin into an oiled 10" fluted tube pan. Chill until almost set, about 30 minutes. Set 3 remaining bowls of gelatin aside at room temperature. Soften unflavored gelatin in remaining cold water. Let set for 5 minutes. Heat milk in a saucepan over medium heat just below boiling. Stir in softened gelatin and sugar until sugar is dissolved. Remove from heat. Stir in sour cream and vanilla until smooth. When blue gelatin in pan is almost set, carefully spoon 1¹/₂ c. sour cream mixture over it. Chill until almost set, about thirty minutes. Carefully spoon one bowl strawberry gelatin over cream layer. Chill until almost set. Carefully spoon 1¹/₂ c. cream mixture over strawberry layer. Chill until almost set. Repeat, adding layers of blue gelatin, cream mixture, and strawberry gelatin, chilling between each. Chill several hours or overnight. This salad takes time to prepare since each layer must be almost set before the next layer is added. Yields 16 servings.

Barbara Coblentz

tid bits

Canned peach juice may be used instead of cold water when making Jell-O. It's already sweetened. For us, the peaches are eaten and the juice is left over, so this way there's no need to throw it away.

Lime Party Salad

2 c. flour
1/2 c. brown sugar
1/2 c. nuts
1 c. butter
1 can crushed pineapple
1 pkg. lime Jell-O
8 oz. cream cheese
1/2 c. sugar
1 can evaporated milk, chilled

Mix flour, brown sugar, nuts, and butter. Press into oblong pan. Bake at 325° for 12–15 minutes. Drain pineapple juice into saucepan. Bring to a boil. Dissolve Jell-O and cool. Cream sugar and cream cheese. Whip chilled milk and add Jell-O, cream cheese, and pineapple. Mix well and pour on top of crust and serve.

Clara Hershberger

Apple Surprise

1 pkg. Jell-O, any flavor
1/2 c. diced apples
1 c. drained pineapple
1/4 c. chopped nuts
1/2 c. whipping cream
1/2 c. chopped celery, optional
1/2 c. chopped dates, optional
mayonnaise
bananas

Prepare Jell-O and cool. When slightly thickened, fold in fruit and whipping cream. Add or subtract ingredients to your taste.

Mrs. Ben R. Hershberger

Creamy Fruit Jell-O

3 oz. cream cheese, softened
1 pkg. lime Jell-O
1 c. boiling water
1/4 c. mayonnaise
1 (15 1/4 oz.) can fruit cocktail, drained
1/2 c. chopped pecans

Beat cream cheese and Jell-O. Add water and stir until Jell-O is dissolved. Refrigerate until thick, about 1 hour, stirring occasionally. Add mayonnaise. Whisk until smooth. Stir in fruit and pecans. Pour into a 1-quart mold that has been coated with nonstick cooking spray. Chill until firm. A double batch fills a Tupperware mold.

Topping for Jell-O

¹/₂ c. pineapple juice
1 egg, beaten
¹/₂ c. sugar
2 Tbsp. flour
3 oz. cream cheese
³/₄–1 c. Rich's topping, whipped

Cook beaten egg, sugar, flour, and
juice until thick. Add cream cheese.
Stir until smooth and cooled. Fold in
whipped topping. Spread on top of
chilled Jell-O.

Mrs. Atlee Hershberger

Yogurt

Heat 2 qt. milk to 150°. Add 1 c. coffee creamer and 2 pkgs. Knox gelatin.
Beat with beater and put on stove again. Beat until 180°. Take off stove
and cool to 120°–125°. Add ¹/₄ c. plain yogurt. Beat again with beater and
put in oven for 7 hours or until thickened, then take a little yogurt out for
next time. Add 1 c. sugar or to suit your taste. Add 1 Tbsp. vanilla.

Mrs. Norman H. Mast

Yogurt

1 gal. milk
2 Tbsp. gelatin
¹/₂ c. cold water
1 tsp. vanilla
4 Tbsp. yogurt
2¹/₄ c. sugar
¹/₂ tube lemon or red raspberry
  pie filling, optional

Heat milk to 190°, then cool to 130°.
Soak gelatin in ¹/₂ c. cold water.
When milk is cool, add gelatin,
vanilla, yogurt, and sugar. Let set in
a gas oven for 8 hours or overnight.
Add pie filling when taking out of
oven. This is a famous recipe.

Ruby Kline
Mrs. Roman Hershberger

tid bits

Never put a cover on anything
that is cooked in milk unless you want
to spend hours cleaning up the
stove when it boils over.

Snacks

Water Chestnuts

2 cans whole water chestnuts
1 pkg. bacon, cut into ¹/₂" strips
2 tsp. Worcestershire sauce
14 oz. ketchup
12 oz. peach preserves

Wrap bacon around water chestnuts. Secure with toothpick. Bake at 350° in broiler pan for 30 minutes. Mix remaining ingredients. Dip each chestnut in sauce. Put in baking pan. Pour remaining sauce all over chestnuts. Bake for 20–30 minutes more.

Mrs. Myron Miller

Ham & Cheese Roll-Ups

5 slices med. sliced ham
8 oz. cream cheese, softened
1¹/₄ c. shredded cheddar cheese
2 Tbsp. butter

Mix cream cheese, butter, and cheese together. Spread on ham. Roll up and refrigerate. Slice and serve with crackers.

Mrs. Myron P. Miller

Vegetable Tortilla Pinwheels

10 flour tortillas
5–6 green onions
chopped carrots
chopped peppers
8 oz. sour cream
8 oz. cream cheese, softened
1 pkg. Italian seasoning or
    Hidden Valley Ranch seasoning

Mix sour cream, cream cheese, and seasoning. Spread on tortillas. Sprinkle with onions, carrots, and peppers. Roll up and refrigerate. Slice.

Mrs. Myron Miller

Vegetable Roll-Ups

10 flour tortillas
2 c. sour cream
8 oz. cream cheese, softened
1 lb. bacon, fried crisp, crumbled
red and green peppers, chopped
shredded cheddar cheese

Mix sour cream and cream cheese. Spread on flour tortillas. Top with peppers, bacon, and cheese or your favorite toppings. Roll up and chill. Slice to serve. Serve with salsa sauce.

Mrs. Wayne R. Weaver

Garden Roll-Ups

1 c. sour cream
8 oz. cream cheese, softened
1 pkg. Hidden Valley Ranch mix
10 flour tortillas
1 c. broccoli
1 c. cauliflower
1 c. fine grated cheese
1 c. crumbled bacon or diced ham

Mix sour cream, cream cheese, and Ranch mix. Spread on tortillas. Top with remaining ingredients. Roll up and chill overnight or 5–6 hours. A SalsaMaster works well to chop vegetables.

Mrs. Delbert Miller

Tortilla Pinwheels

2 c. sour cream
4 oz. cream cheese
1 pkg. Hidden Valley Ranch dip mix
8 flour tortillas
broccoli
cauliflower
onions
grated cheddar cheese
crumbled bacon

Mix sour cream, cream cheese, and dip mix. Spread over tortillas. Top with remaining ingredients. A SalsaMaster works well to chop broccoli and cauliflower. Roll up and chill overnight. Slice 1/2" thick.

Mrs. Wayne Schrock
Mrs. David J. Troyer

Salsa Chip Dip

2 c. sour cream
8 oz. cream cheese
1 c. salsa
cheddar cheese

Mix sour cream and cream cheese. Put salsa on top and top with cheese. Serve with plain corn chips.

Mrs. Arlene Hershberger

Nachos & Cheese

2 cans cheddar cheese soup
1 can nacho cheese soup
1/2 can water
1 c. pasteurized processed cheese
1 lb. ground beef, browned, drained
nacho-flavored tortilla chips

In saucepan, combine soups, water, and cheese. Stir over medium heat until cheese is melted. Add beef. Serve hot with chips. Yields 6–8 cups.

Mrs. Jerry Erb

Taco Delight Layered Dip

8 oz. cream cheese, softened
1 c. cottage cheese
2 c. salsa or picante sauce
1 lb. hamburger, browned
1 pkg. taco seasoning
shredded lettuce
chopped onions
chopped tomatoes
chopped green peppers
1 1/2 c. shredded cheddar cheese

Mix cream cheese and cottage cheese. Spread on large round tray or 2 sm. Tupperware pans. Spread salsa on top. Mix hamburger and taco seasoning. Spread on top of salsa. Layer remaining ingredients on top in order listed. Serve with tortilla chips or Doritos.

Mary Esther Miller

Cheddar Bacon Dip

8 oz. cream cheese, softened
1 c. sour cream
5 green onions, thinly sliced
4 med. tomatoes, chopped
1 lg. green pepper, chopped
1 (16 oz.) jar taco sauce
2 c. shredded cheddar cheese
1 lb. bacon, cooked, crumbled
tortilla or taco chips

In a mixing bowl, beat cream cheese and sour cream. Spread in an ungreased 9 X 13 pan or 12" round plate. Combine onions, tomatoes, and green pepper. Sprinkle over cream cheese layer. Pour taco sauce over vegetables. Sprinkle with cheddar cheese. Refrigerate. Just before serving, sprinkle with bacon. Serve with chips.

Mrs. Atlee (Lizzie) Raber

Easy Cheese Ball

16 oz. cream cheese
6 oz. Velveeta cheese
8 oz. shredded cheddar cheese
1 tsp. salt
1 tsp. onion salt
1 Tbsp. chopped onion
2 Tbsp. Worcestershire sauce
3 tsp. sour cream and onion seasoning
1 Tbsp. ReaLemon

Mix all ingredients except cheddar cheese. After well mixed, add cheese.

Mrs. David J. Troyer

Cheese Dip

1 lb. hamburger
1 pkg. taco seasoning
2 lbs. Velveeta cheese
8 oz. cream cheese
1 c. sour cream

Brown hamburger and add taco seasoning. Melt Velveeta, sour cream, and cream cheese together. Add hamburger. Serve warm with tortilla chips.

Luella Wengerd

Cheese Ball

1 lb. Velveeta cheese
16 oz. cream cheese
2 Tbsp. Worcestershire sauce
3 Tbsp. milk
1 Tbsp. parsley flakes
onions, optional

In double boiler, melt Velveeta and cream cheese. Add remaining ingredients.

Esta & Vesta Yoder

Good Snack Crackers

1 lb. snack crackers
3/4 c. vegetable oil
1/2 tsp. garlic salt
1/2 tsp. celery salt
1 pkg. Hidden Valley Ranch mix

Mix all ingredients except crackers. Pour over crackers and mix well. Do not bake. Store in a tightly closed container. Add more crackers if needed.

Mary Schlabach

Seasoned Crackers

2 (12 oz.) boxes Ritz Crackers
1 c. Wesson oil
1 tsp. dill weed
1 pkg. Hidden Valley Ranch mix
1 tsp. garlic salt

Mix everything except crackers. Pour over crackers and stir. Let set for 1 hour and stir again. Repeat several times.

Mrs. Ben N. Weaver
Susie Kuhns

Snack Crackers

1 lb. soda crackers
1 c. oil
3 Tbsp. sour cream and onion powder

Mix oil and seasoning. Pour over crackers. Bake at 250° for 20 minutes.

Mattie Yoder

Oyster Crackers

11 oz. oyster crackers
oil
1 pkg. Ranch dressing mix
$1/2$ tsp. dill weed
$1/4$ tsp. lemon pepper
$1/2$ tsp. garlic salt
$1/4$ tsp. garlic powder

Combine oil and seasonings. Pour over crackers. Stir to coat. Put on cookie sheet. Bake at 250° for 15–20 minutes. Stir gently halfway through baking time. Cool on paper towels. Enjoy!

Mrs. Susan Miller

Dairy State Fudge

8 oz. cream cheese
2 Tbsp. butter
2 lbs. white chocolate
1–$1^1/2$ c. nuts

In a mixing bowl, beat cream cheese until fluffy. Set aside. In double boiler, melt butter. Add white chocolate. Heat until melted. Pour over cream cheese. Beat until glossy, about 7–10 minutes. Stir in nuts. Pour into 9" square greased pan. Yields 64 pieces.

Mrs. David A. Yoder

Creamy Cheese Mints

6 oz. cream cheese
$1^1/2$ lbs. powdered sugar
food coloring, optional
$1/4$ tsp. oil of peppermint

Combine ingredients in a large bowl until mixture is smooth and creamy. I put it in a big cookie sheet. Melt chocolate for first layer and on top. Cut before too hard.

Mrs. Eli J.S. Barkman

Caramel Dip for Apples

8 oz. cream cheese, softened
1 tsp. vanilla
³/₄ c. brown sugar

Great for an after school snack!

Erma Mast

Fruit Dip

1 c. pineapple juice
1 pkg. miniature marshmallows
8 oz. cream cheese

Melt together. Cool. Add 8 oz. Cool Whip. Serve with fresh fruit.

Mrs. Mahlon R. Yoder

Fruit Dip

1 egg, beaten
¹/₂ c. white sugar
2 Tbsp. ReaLemon
8 oz. cream cheese
1 c. whipped topping

Combine egg, sugar, and ReaLemon. Boil 6 minutes. Stir while boiling. Cool. Add cream cheese and whipped topping.

Barbara Hershberger
Mrs. Mattie Miller

Fruit Dip

2 c. pineapple juice
2 Tbsp. clear jel
¹/₂ c. sugar
8 oz. Cool Whip
8 oz. cream cheese

Combine juice, clear jel, and sugar. Cook until thick. Cool. Add Cool Whip and cream cheese.

Mrs. John E. Troyer

Trail Mix

2 lbs. dry roasted peanuts
2 lbs. cashews
1 lb. raisins
1 lb. M&M's
¹/₂ lb. flaked coconut

Combine all ingredients in a large bowl. Store in an airtight container. Yields 6 quarts.

Mrs. Lovina Schlabach

Sugar-Coated Pecans

1 Tbsp. egg whites
2 c. pecan halves
$^1/_4$ c. sugar
2 tsp. cinnamon

In bowl, beat egg whites until foamy. Add pecans and toss until well coated. Combine cinnamon and sugar. Sprinkle pecans and toss to coat. Spread in a single layer on an ungreased cookie sheet. Bake at 300° for 30 minutes or until browned. Cool on waxed paper.

Mrs. Atlee Mast

Munchies

3 c. Rice Chex
3 c. Corn Chex
3 c. Cheerios
2 c. pretzel stick pieces
1 c. cashews
1 lb. M&M's
$1^1/_2$ lb. white confectioner's coating

Melt coating. Mix slightly with cereal mixture. Add M&M's and mix. Dump on wax paper until cool, then break into pieces.

Mrs. David E. Beachy

Party Mix

15 oz. Honey Nut Cheerios
18 oz. Honeycomb
1 pkg. French toast cereal
7 oz. potato sticks
2 pkgs. bugles
1 pkg. ABC pretzels
1 c. butter, melted
2 c. vegetable oil
3 tsp. seasoned salt
6 Tbsp. Worcestershire sauce
1 tsp. garlic salt
24 oz. peanuts
2 pkgs. honey-roasted sesame sticks
16 oz. miniature M&M's
3 pkgs. cheese Ritz bits sandwiches

Combine first 6 ingredients in a large bowl. Mix butter, oil, seasoned salt, Worcestershire sauce, and garlic salt. Pour over cereal mixture. Bake at 250° for $1^1/_2$ hours, stirring every 15 minutes. Cool, then add remaining ingredients.

Mrs. Roman E. Raber

Cheerios Crunch

½ c. butter
⅔ c. brown sugar
4 c. Cheerios
1 c. peanuts, optional

Melt butter in saucepan. Blend in brown sugar and cook until thick and smooth, stirring constantly. Stir in Cheerios and nuts. Cook and stir a few minutes over low heat until Cheerios are coated. Spread in thin layer on baking sheet. Crumble when cool.

Mrs. Roy E. Mast

Peanut Butter Popcorn

12 c. warm, lightly salted popcorn
¼ c. margarine
3 Tbsp. sugar
2 Tbsp. peanut butter
1 Tbsp. Karo

Mix margarine, sugar, Karo, and peanut butter. Pour over popcorn and mix. Chocolate chips are also good with this.

Crunchy Popcorn

1½ gal. popped corn
¼ c. margarine
16 lg. marshmallows
¾ c. brown sugar
dash salt
¼ c. crunchy peanut butter

Combine margarine, marshmallows, brown sugar, and salt in saucepan. Cook over low heat until dissolved. Add peanut butter. Stir; pour over popcorn. Stir until evenly coated.

Mrs. Henry J.C. Yoder

Popcorn Balls

popped corn
1 pkg. marshmallows
1 pkg. Jell-O, any flavor
½ c. margarine

Melt marshmallows, margarine, and Jell-O together. Pour over popcorn. Mix well and shape into balls.

Mrs. Henry J.C. Yoder

Cinnamon Candy Popcorn

8 qts. popped corn
1 c. butter
1/2 c. light corn syrup
9 oz. cinnamon candy

Put popcorn in large roaster. Melt butter, corn syrup, and candy until it starts to boil. Pour over popcorn. Bake in a warm oven at 250° for 1 hour, stirring every 15 minutes. This is a famous recipe under various names.

Momy Mast

Quick Cinnamon Popcorn

1/2 c. corn
1/2 c. cinnamon candy
oil

Put all in a large popper. Stir all the time while popping.

Momy Mast

Party Mix

1 pkg. Crispix cereal
1 pkg. pretzel sticks
1 can mixed nuts
1 can potato sticks
1 pkg. Bugles
4 c. Cheerios
2/3 c. butter
2 Tbsp. Worcestershire sauce
1 tsp. garlic salt
1 tsp. seasoned salt

Melt butter. Add Worcestershire sauce, garlic salt, and seasoned salt. Pour over remaining ingredients. Bake at 250° for 2 hours, stirring every 30 minutes.

Mrs. Monroe N. Miller

tid bits

Before melting chocolate, rub side of pan it is to be melted in with butter. The chocolate will not stick to the pan.

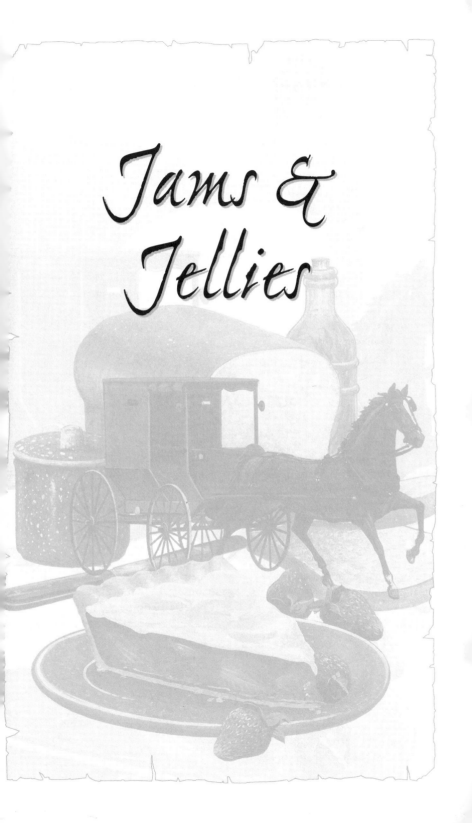

Jams & Jellies

Peanut Butter Spread

10 c. brown sugar
5 c. water
1 1/4 c. Karo
2 tsp. maple flavoring
7 1/2 lbs. peanut butter
4 qt. marshmallow creme

Combine brown sugar, water, Karo, and maple flavoring. Cook. Cool, then add remaining ingredients.

Anna Troyer

Church Spread

2 lg. c. brown sugar
1 lg. c. sweet cream
1/2 gal. light Karo
1/4 tsp. salt
1 tsp. maple flavoring

Combine sugar and cream. Cook until it bubbles. Add remaining ingredients.

White Sugar Spread

2 c. brown sugar
4 c. light Karo
5 egg whites, beaten stiff
3/4 Tbsp. maple flavoring, optional

Combine sugar and Karo. Cook for 2 minutes. When cool, but not cold, add egg whites and stir until cold. Add flavoring.

Mattie Yoder

Strawberry Jam

4 c. mashed strawberries
4 c. sugar, divided

Mix berries and 2 c. sugar. Cook for 5 minutes. Add remaining sugar. Cook for 10 minutes. Put into jars and seal. This jam will not separate.

Mrs. Fannie Mae Barkman

Elderberry Jam

3 lbs. white sugar
2 c. light Karo
2 c. strong juice from cooked fruit

Cook until thick, about 30 minutes.

Amanda Mast

Freezer Jam

4 c. strawberries, mashed
4 c. sugar
$1/3$ c. plus 2 Tbsp. instant clear jel

Mix clear jel and sugar well. Add to strawberries and stir until sugar is dissolved. Freeze.

Mrs. Aden E. Schlabach

Zucchini Jam

6 c. zucchini, peeled, seeded, and ground or grated fine
6 c. sugar
2 Tbsp. lemon juice
2 (6 oz.) pkgs. apricot Jell-O
20 oz. crushed pineapple, drained
1 c. water

Mix water and zucchini. Cook for 6 minutes. Add sugar, lemon juice, and pineapple. Cook for 6 minutes. Add Jell-O. Cook for 6 minutes more, stirring constantly. Put in jars. Seal.

Barbara Coblentz

Fake Raspberry Jelly

6 c. red beet juice
2 pkgs. Sure-Jell
$1/2$ c. lemon juice
8 c. sugar
1 (6 oz.) pkg. red raspberry Jell-O

Heat beet juice, Sure-Jell, and lemon juice. Bring to a boil, then add the sugar and Jell-O all at once. Cook for 5 minutes. Put in jars. Seal.

Ada Nisley

Grape Molasses

5 c. grape juice
5 c. sugar
3 c. light Karo

Cook together.

Mrs. H.C.Y.

Grape Butter

5 c. homegrown grapes
$1/2$ c. water
4 c. sugar
2 Tbsp. lemon juice

Cook grapes and water. Put through a food mill to produce 4 c. juice. Add sugar and lemon juice. Cook for 20 minutes. Put in hot jars. Seal.

Katie Hershberger

Apple Butter

8 bu. Grimes or non-acid
    apples for 25 gal. cider
4 bu. any kind apples for sauce
50 lb. sugar
2 gal. light Karo
2 Tbsp. cinnamon
2 Tbsp. allspice

Using a copper kettle, cook cider down halfway, then add applesauce. Cook halfway down again, then add sugar and Karo. Just before removing from heat, add spices. Yields 20 gal.

Mrs. Dan. E. Mast

Apple Butter

3 gal. apples, cut up
1 gal. light Karo
8 lbs. sugar

Cook together for 3 hours, covered. Do not take off lid while cooking. Put through sieve. Add cinnamon. Put in jars. Seal.

Mattie Yoder

Pear Butter

2 qts. pear pulp
2 lbs. sugar

Put in roaster in oven at 350° for 3 hours. Stir occasionally. Put in hot jars. Seal.

Amanda Mast

Mint Jelly

1¹/₂ c. firmly packed tea
    leaves and stems
3¹/₂ c. water
green food coloring
4 c. sugar
1 pkg. Sure-Jell

Combine tea leaves and water. Bring to boil. Remove from heat and allow to steep for 10 minutes, covered. Remove tea leaves. Add green food coloring to 3 c. juice. Pour into a 6–8 quart saucepan. Add Sure-Jell and stir. Bring to a full boil over high heat, stirring constantly. Add sugar and bring to a full rolling boil. Cook hard for 1 minute, stirring constantly. Turn off heat. Skim off foam and ladle quickly into jars and seal or let set in jars until cold, then seal with paraffin.

Barbara Coblentz

Salsas, Sauces, & Seasonings

Homemade Mild Salsa

20 lg. or 40 bell tomatoes
4 lg. onions
4 carrots, grated
3 green peppers
3 hot peppers
1/2 c. parsley
6 Tbsp. sugar
1 tsp. black pepper
3 Tbsp. basil
2 Tbsp. salt
1 tsp. cumin
2 cans tomato paste

Put vegetables through a Salsa-Master. Cook over low heat for 2 hours. Add spices and tomato paste. Put in jars. Add 1 Tbsp. lemon juice on top of each jar. Cold pack for 35 minutes.

Mrs. Dennis (Rosie) Yoder

Chi-Chi Taco Salsa

20 lg. tomatoes
4 lg. onions
4 carrots, grated
3 green peppers
4 hot peppers
8 jalapeño peppers (4 without seeds)
1/2 c. parsley
6 Tbsp. sugar
1 tsp. black pepper
3 Tbsp. basil
2 Tbsp. salt
1 tsp. cumin
1 Tbsp. lemon juice

Cut everything up with a knife or put through SalsaMaster. Mix all together. Bring to a boil and cook for 15–20 minutes. Add a clear jel thickening to the thickness you desire. Cold pack for 30 minutes.

Mrs. Aden Yoder

Salsa

12 c. peeled, cubed tomatoes
5 lg. onions
9 hot or mild peppers
2 bell peppers
3/4 c. sugar
1/4 c. salt
1 c. vinegar
1 c. tomato paste

Grind peppers and onions. Mix with tomatoes and remaining ingredients. Cook for 30 minutes. Add clear jel, if desired. Put in jars. Cold pack for 30 minutes. Yields 6–8 pints.

Mrs. Abe A. Yoder

Chunky Salsa

14 lb. tomatoes
2 1/2 lb. onions
10 green peppers
6–11 hot peppers
3 garlic buds
3 Tbsp. chili powder
2 tsp. oregano
1 1/2 tsp. cumin
1 c. vinegar
7/8 c. brown sugar
1/4 c. salt

Put tomatoes in hot water to take the skin off. Cut tomatoes into big chunks. Cut onions and peppers into medium chunks. Mix all together and cook for 45 minutes. Thicken slightly with 1 c. clear jel mixed with a little water. Cold pack for 20 minutes. Yields 17–18 pints.

Mrs. Roman E. Raber

Pizza Sauce to Can

10 lbs. tomatoes
2 lg. onions
1 tsp. Tabasco sauce
4 tsp. salt
2 tsp. oregano leaves
1 tsp. pepper or
   all-purpose seasoning
2 tsp. garlic powder
1 c. vegetable oil
1 c. sugar
6 Tbsp. clear jel (heaping)

Cook tomatoes and onions and put through a Victorio strainer. To 4 qts. tomato juice, add remaining ingredients except clear jel. Bring to a boil and thicken with clear jel. Pour into clean jars. Cold pack for 35 minutes. Yields 8–9 pints.

Mary Schlabach

Pizza Sauce

½ bu. tomatoes
5 lg. onions, chopped
2 hot peppers or
　2 tsp. hot pepper sauce
1 c. oil
1½ c. sugar
½ c. salt
1 Tbsp. basil leaf
1 Tbsp. oregano
1 Tbsp. garlic powder
1 Tbsp. Italian seasoning
5 (12 oz.) cans tomato paste

Cook tomatoes and drain off water. Add remaining ingredients. Bring to a boil and cook for 15 minutes. Put in jars. Cold pack for 20 minutes.

Mrs. Wayne R. Weaver

Italian Pizza Sauce

½ bu. tomatoes, juiced
3 hot peppers or
　1½ Tbsp. hot pepper sauce
3 lbs. onions
4 (12 oz.) cans tomato paste
4½ Tbsp. oregano
3 Tbsp. paprika
2 tsp. black pepper
3 tsp. garlic powder
4½ Tbsp. Italian seasoning
2½ c. Italian dressing
½ c. salt
1½ c. sugar
3 c. Crisco oil

Heat tomato juice. Mix remaining ingredients together and add to juice. Bring to a boil. Cook for 10 minutes. Thicken with 4 c. Perma-Flo mixed with enough water to make a paste. Cold pack 1½ hours.

Mrs. Jonas M. Miller

Spaghetti or Pizza Sauce

1 lg. onion, shredded fine
1 c. white sugar
1 tsp. garlic salt
3 tsp. oregano
1 tsp. basil
1 can mushroom soup
6 (6 oz.) cans tomato paste
2 cans tomato soup
3 qts. tomato juice
2 green peppers, diced fine or
   cooked with tomatoes

Stir all together in a large bowl. Put
in jars and cold pack 30 minutes.
Yields 12 pints.

Katie Mae Troyer

Spaghetti Sauce

35 buds garlic
10 green peppers, chopped
10 onions, chopped
10 qts. tomato juice
120 oz. tomato paste
5 tsp. black pepper
7^1/$_2$ tsp. oregano
7^1/$_2$ tsp. paprika
10 tsp. chili powder
4 Tbsp. salt
oil to sauté
Italian seasoning

Heat oil. Add garlic, peppers, and
onions. Add tomato paste and
tomato juice. Heat until almost
boiling. Add spices. Cook about 15
minutes. Cold pack for 20 minutes.
Yields 18 qts.

Mae Mast

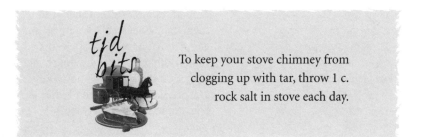

tid bits

To keep your stove chimney from
clogging up with tar, throw 1 c.
rock salt in stove each day.

Spaghetti Sauce

5 lb. hamburger, browned
2 c. chopped onion
1 c. chopped green pepper
9 c. tomato juice
4 (6 oz.) cans tomato paste
2 Tbsp. brown sugar
2 Tbsp. parsley
1 1/2 Tbsp. salt
1 Tbsp. oregano
1/2 tsp. black pepper
1/2 tsp. ginger
1/2 tsp. allspice
2 Tbsp. vinegar

Brown hamburger. Add onions and peppers. Cook until tender. Add remaining ingredients and simmer until thick enough for serving. Fill jars. Pressure can at 10 lbs. for 1 hour and 15 minutes. Note: Drain liquid before putting tomatoes through strainer. You won't need to simmer long.

Mrs. Wayne R. Weaver

Ketchup

4 qts. tomato juice
1 tsp. Tabasco sauce
3 c. white sugar
1/2 pkg. ketchup mix
1 Tbsp. salt
1/2 c. vinegar
1 Tbsp. ketchup spice
3 Tbsp. cornstarch
1/2 c. water

Mix cornstarch with water. Mix all together and cook for 1 hour. Cold pack for 15 minutes.

Mrs. Eli N. Hershberger

Tomato Ketchup

15 qt. tomato juice
11 onions
10 c. white sugar
6 Tbsp. salt
1 c. vinegar
1 Tbsp. black pepper
2 Tbsp. cinnamon
3 oz. pickling spice

Cook onions and tomatoes together. Put through strainer, then drain in a cloth for about 1 hour. Put thick pulp in stainless steel canner. Add sugar, salt, vinegar, black pepper, and cinnamon. Put pickling spice in a small cloth bag. Tie shut with string and put into ketchup. Simmer for 1–2 hrs. Gives good flavor. Remove bag. Put in jars. Seal. Yields 12–15 pints.

Mrs. Myron J. Miller

Barbecue Sauce

2 onions, chopped
1 c. brown sugar
$^{1}/_{4}$ c. vinegar
$^{1}/_{2}$ c. ReaLemon
1 c. water
$^{1}/_{4}$ c. oil
$^{1}/_{4}$ c. Worcestershire sauce
$^{1}/_{4}$ c. mustard
1 c. chopped celery
4 c. ketchup

Yields $^{1}/_{2}$ gal.

Mrs. Allen R. Troyer

Barbecue Sauce

1$^{1}/_{2}$ pt. ketchup
$^{1}/_{3}$ c. Karo
1$^{1}/_{4}$ c. brown sugar
$^{1}/_{2}$ Tbsp. Worcestershire sauce
2 Tbsp. McNess BBQ concentrate
1 Tbsp. mustard
$^{1}/_{2}$ Tbsp. ReaLemon
1 onion, finely chopped

This is a good sauce to marinate pork ribs, etc. for a day or two before being prepared for a meal.

Martha A. Hershberger

Tangy Barbecue Sauce

1 c. ketchup
2 Tbsp. lemon juice
2 Tbsp. cider vinegar
$^{1}/_{4}$ c. brown sugar
2 tsp. prepared mustard
1 tsp. salt
$^{1}/_{2}$–1 tsp. hot pepper sauce
1 bay leaf
1 garlic clove, minced
$^{1}/_{2}$ c. water
2 tsp. Worcestershire sauce

Combine all ingredients in a small saucepan and bring to a boil, stirring occasionally. Reduce heat. Cover and simmer for 30 minutes. Discard bay leaf. Use this sauce for basting when grilling chicken, pork, or beef. I use it on meatloaf. Very good.
Yields 1$^{1}/_{2}$ cup.

Hot Dog Relish

2 c. ground onions
10 green tomatoes
6 sweet red peppers
1 med. head cabbage
12 green bell peppers
$^1/_2$ c. salt
6 c. sugar
4 c. vinegar
$1^1/_2$ tsp. turmeric
2 Tbsp. mustard seed
1 Tbsp. celery seed
2 c. water

Grind vegetables coarsely. Sprinkle with salt. Let set overnight. Rinse and drain. Combine remaining ingredients and pour over vegetables. Heat to boiling and simmer for 3 minutes. Can. Yields 8 pts.

Katie Mae Troyer

Hot Pepper Relish

36 hot peppers
1 qt. mustard
1 qt. vinegar
6 c. sugar
$1^1/_4$ c. flour
$1^1/_2$ c. water

Mix first 4 ingredients and bring to a boil. Mix flour and water well. Add to pepper mixture. Cook for 5 minutes. Put in jars. Note: For mild relish, remove pepper seeds. Yields $7^1/_2$ pts.

Mrs. Roy A. Troyer

Marinade

20 oz. Worcestershire sauce
15 oz. A-1 sauce
$^1/_3$ c. Spike
$^1/_3$ c. vinegar
1 Tbsp. Lawry's seasoned salt
2 tsp. garlic
$^1/_2$ tsp. black pepper
Indo
15# steak or pork chops

Mix first 7 ingredients. Sprinkle meat with Indo before marinating. Use leftover sauce when grilling. Note: Spike and Indo can be purchased at Nature's Paradise.

Mrs. Norman H. Mast

Pineapple Sauce for Ham

1 lg. can pineapple juice
2 c. water
2 c. brown sugar
2 Tbsp. dry mustard
1/4 c. vinegar
3 Tbsp. clear jel
pinch salt

Bring to a boil. Put a layer of ham in a roaster, then cover with sauce. Repeat until done. This is enough sauce for 25 lbs. ham.

Lovina Raber

Coney Sauce

oil
1/2 c. chopped onions
1/2 c. chopped celery
2 c. ketchup
1 c. tomato juice
2 Tbsp. brown sugar
2 Tbsp. cornstarch
salt
pepper

Sauté onions and celery in oil. Stir in remaining ingredients. Simmer until thickened. Brown 1 lb. hamburger. Add to sauce. Serve over hot dogs.

Mrs. David E. Beachy

Sauce for Hamburgers

1 c. ketchup
2 tsp. mustard
2 Tbsp. vinegar
1/2 c. sugar
3/4 tsp. salt

Stir all together and pour over hamburgers. Bake at 350° for 1/2–1 hour.

Mrs. Mattie D. Miller

Cheez Whiz

6 lbs. Velveeta cheese
3 1/2 c. cream or evaporated milk
1 qt. milk
1/2 c. butter or margarine

Melt all together in a double boiler or an 8-quart Lifetime kettle on low heat. Cold pack 30 minutes. Very good! Yields 9–10 pints.

Mrs. Leroy (Barbara) Erb

Melt-Away Cheese Spread

5 lbs. white American cheese, diced
1½ lbs. sharp cheddar cheese, diced
1 c. butter
8 c. milk
2 tsp. baking soda

Melt butter in double boiler. Add cheese. Heat milk in another saucepan to boiling point. Add baking soda and dissolve. Add to cheese, stirring with wire whisk until cheese is all melted. Remove from heat. Set in a cool place, stirring every 5 minutes to keep a skin from forming, until mixture is thickened.

Esta & Vesta Yoder

Chocolate Syrup

6 c. sugar
2 c. cocoa
3 c. water
1 c. light Karo
pinch salt
4 tsp. vanilla

Cook for 8–10 minutes.

Mrs. Raymond D. (Edna) Miller

Esther's Hot Fudge Sauce

1 c. sugar
2 Tbsp. cornstarch
2 Tbsp. cocoa powder
1 c. hot water
½ c. butter

Mix together dry ingredients. Add hot water. Cook until thickened, stirring constantly. Cool a little and add butter. This is wonderful for hot fudge brownie sundaes!

Mrs. Edwin N. (Ruth) Weaver

Sweetened Condensed Milk

1 part white sugar
2 parts milk

Cook together until thickened—225° or "jelly" on a thermometer. Use in cookies or wherever you wish.

Mrs. Mose E. Beachy

Taco Seasoning Mix

1 Tbsp. chili powder
1 tsp. garlic powder
1 tsp. paprika
1 tsp. oregano
$^1/_2$ tsp. salt
2 tsp. onion powder
1 tsp. cumin powder
1 tsp. sugar

Combine all ingredients and blend well. Store in airtight container. This equals a $1^1/_4$ oz. pkg. seasoning. Yields 3 Tbsp.

Mrs. Roman E. Raber
Mrs. Albert Barkman

Chicken Seasoning

1 c. bread flour
2 tsp. celery salt
2 tsp. paprika
2 tsp. onion salt
$^1/_2$ tsp. salt
$^1/_4$ tsp. pepper

Mix all together. Can be used for frying chicken, fish, steak, or any other meat.

Fish Seasoning

2/3 c. eggs, beaten
1/3 c. buttermilk
Crumbs:
1 c. cornmeal
1/2 c. flour
1/2 c. cornflake crumbs
1/2 c. cracker crumbs
1 Tbsp. salt
1 Tbsp. garlic
1 Tbsp. onion powder
Seasoning:
2 1/2 Tbsp. paprika
2 Tbsp. salt
2 Tbsp. garlic powder
1 Tbsp. onion powder
1 tsp. cayenne pepper
1 Tbsp. oregano
1 Tbsp. thyme
1 Tbsp. black pepper

Mix eggs and buttermilk. Combine crumb ingredients in a separate bowl. Dip fish pieces in egg mixture, then roll in crumb mixture. Season and deep fry. This can also be used with chicken.

Mrs. Roy L. (Arlene) Miller

Homemade Drinks

Eggnog

1 egg
4 Tbsp. sugar
2 c. milk
1/8 tsp. salt
1/2 tsp. vanilla
1/2 tsp. nutmeg

Beat egg with egg beater until fluffy. Add sugar, milk, salt, and vanilla. Beat mixture again. Sprinkle nutmeg on top. Yields 2 servings.

Hot Cocoa

1 Tbsp. cocoa
1 Tbsp. sugar
dash salt
1/4 c. water
1 c. milk
vanilla

Use listed amount for each serving. Mix cocoa, sugar, salt, and water. Cook until thickened. Add milk and heat until scalded. Add a few drops vanilla. Top with a marshmallow or marshmallow creme.

Katie B. Yoder

Hot Chocolate Mix

Large Batch:
6 boxes dry milk
4 containers creamer
3 boxes Nestlé Quik
3 lbs. powdered sugar
Small Batch:
2 boxes dry milk
1 1/3 container creamer
1 box Nestlé Quik
1 lb. powdered sugar

Yields 5 gallons mix.

Mrs. Melvin Mast

Hot Chocolate Mix

1½ lb. dry milk
1½ lb. Cremora (nondairy creamer)
1½ lb. Nestlé Quik
½ c. sugar

Mix all together. To serve, mix ⅓ c.
mix with 1 c. hot water.

Katie Hershberger

Cappuccino

8 oz. French vanilla CoffeeMate
1½ c. hot chocolate mix
1 c. dry milk
½ c. instant coffee
1 c. powdered sugar
½ c. white sugar

Mix all together. To serve, put 3
heaping tsp. in a mug and fill with
hot water. Good with Cool Whip on
top.

Mrs. Junior A. Troyer
Mrs. David A. Yoder
Mrs. Roy A. Troyer

Cappuccino Mocha Mix

4 c. nondairy coffee creamer
2½ c. nonfat dry milk
2 c. sugar
⅔ c. cocoa
¾ c. instant coffee
½ c. chocolate drink mix
½ c. powdered sugar
dash salt
1 lg. pkg. instant vanilla pudding
2 lb. French vanilla cappuccino

Mix in a large bowl. Store in an
airtight container. To serve, mix 3
heaping tsp. mix with 1 c. boiling
water. Stir well. May add a small
handful of marshmallows and ¼ tsp.
vanilla when serving. Enjoy!

Mrs. Allen Jay Beechy

Coffee for Church

1 canner cold water
1 sm. can coffee

Put coffee in a loose cloth and put it
in water while it's cold. Heat until
almost boiling.

Susie Kuhns

Iced Tea Concentrate

4 qts. water
2 c. sugar
4 c. fresh tea leaves

Bring water to a boil. Add sugar and tea leaves. Let set 15 minutes. To serve, mix 1 part concentrate with 2 parts water. Concentrate may be frozen.

Mrs. David E. Beachy

Tea Concentrate

4 c. tea leaves
³/₄ c. sugar
4 c. water

Cook water and sugar. Add tea and simmer for a few minutes. Let set overnight. Strain and add 3 qts. water. Can also freeze concentrate and then add water.

Mrs. Ben N. Weaver

Iced Tea

3 oranges, sliced
3 lemons, sliced
4 c. sugar
18 orange pekoe red rose tea bags
4 qts. boiling water
1 bag crushed ice

Mix oranges, lemons, and sugar in a 13-qt. mixing bowl. Add tea bags and pour boiling water over all. Let set until water is dark. Remove tea bags. Immediately pour in ice.

Mrs. Roy E. Mast

Mennonite Wine

1 c. Sunny Delight orange juice
1 (12 oz.) can frozen grape juice
1 (2 liter) bottle ginger ale
¹/₄ c. ReaLemon
1¹/₂ c. water
1 c. sugar

Cook together sugar and water. Cool. Mix remaining ingredients. Add to sugar water. Mix and add ice cubes. Enjoy!

Katie Mae Troyer

Refreshing Punch

1 qt. pineapple juice
1 qt. orange juice
1 c. lemonade drink mix
20 oz. punch mix or
    strawberry Kool-Aid
1 liter 7-Up

Mix all together and add water to
make 2 gallons.

Mrs. Aden Chupp

Punch

1 pkg. cherry Kool-Aid
1 pkg. strawberry Kool-Aid
1 1/2 c. sugar
3 qts. water
1 (6 oz.) can frozen orange juice
1 (6 oz.) can frozen lemonade
1/2 lg. can pineapple juice
1 qt. 7-Up

Yields 1 1/2 gallon.

Mrs. Arlene Hershberger
Mrs. Raymond D. (Edna) Miller

Refreshing Raspberry Punch

2 pkgs. raspberry Kool-Aid
2 c. sugar
1 gal. warm water
1 can frozen orange juice
1 qt. 7-Up
1/2 gal. raspberry sherbet

Dissolve sugar in warm water. Cool.
Add orange juice and Kool-Aid. Just
before serving, add 7-Up and
sherbet. Yummy!

Mrs. Dennis (Rosie) Yoder

Party Punch

1 pkg. cherry Kool-Aid
1 pkg. strawberry Kool-Aid
6 oz. frozen orange juice
6 oz. frozen lemonade
2 c. sugar
3 qts. water
2 c. 7-Up

Mrs. Andy E. Yoder

Golden Punch

3 lg. cans frozen orange
  juice concentrate
2 lg. cans frozen lemonade
  concentrate
2 qts. pineapple juice
1/2 c. sugar
4 qts. 7-Up

Mix concentrates as directed on can.
Stir in remaining ingredients. Mix
well and chill. Hint: Pour some in
muffin tins or ice cube trays and
freeze. Use instead of ice to chill the
punch.

Mrs. Philip L. Yoder

Punch

1 lg. can pineapple juice
1 (12 oz.) can frozen orange juice
4 bananas, mashed
4 c. white sugar
2 qts. water
1 lg. bottle 7-Up or Sprite

Mix all except 7-Up. Freeze. Do not
thaw completely. Add 7-Up when
ready to serve.

Anna Troyer

Frozen Drink

6 oz. Jell-O, any flavor
4 c. hot water
2 c. sugar
8 c. cold water

Mix well and put in freezer. When
ready to serve, fill glasses 3/4 full and
fill with Mt. Dew, Slice, or 7-Up.

Mrs. Aden B. Miller

Rhubarb Punch

2 qts. rhubarb, diced
2 c. pineapple juice
$^1/_2$ c. lemon juice
$2^1/_4$ c. white sugar
2 Tbsp. sugar-free strawberry Jell-O
2 c. hot water

In a saucepan, cover rhubarb with water and cook for 10 minutes. Drain in a colander for 1 hour. If not enough juice, add water to make 2 qts. Combine sugar and Jell-O with hot water. Add remaining juices. Cold pack 15 minutes or freeze. Add 7-Up when ready to serve. For 2 qts. rhubarb punch, use 2 liters 7-Up.

Mrs. Dan Mast
Marlene Troyer

Cheery Cherry Punch

3 pkgs. cherry Jell-O
2–3 c. sugar
6 c. boiling water
1 (46 oz.) can unsweetened
    pineapple juice
1 (12 oz.) can frozen orange juice
1 (12 oz.) can frozen lemonade
1 gal. cold water
2 (2 liter) bottles 7-Up

Dissolve Jell-O and sugar in boiling water. Add pineapple juice, cold water, and concentrate. Mix well. Freeze. Just before serving, add 7-Up and mix well.

Mrs. Roy A. Troyer

Drink Slush

3 pkgs. Jell-O, any flavor
9 c. hot water
4 c. white sugar
4 c. water
2 (46 oz.) cans pineapple juice
2 liters 7-Up

Mix Jell-O and hot water. Cook sugar and water. Add to Jell-O mixture. Add pineapple juice. Freeze. Stir in 7-Up while it thaws. This is also good refrozen.

Mrs. Ray Raber

Mr. Misty

1 pkg. Jell-O
1 qt. hot water
$^1/_2$ qt. cold water
$^1/_2$ c. pineapple juice
$^3/_4$ c. sugar

Freeze. When ready to serve, mix
2–3 freezer boxes punch with 2 liters
lemon-lime pop.

Mrs. Andrew A. Troyer

Grape Juice

5 c. grapes (heaping)
12 c. water
$2^1/_4$ c. sugar

Cook grapes and water until grapes
are light in color. Drain. Add sugar.
Bring to a boil again. Put in jars and
seal. Very good.

Mrs. Myron J. Miller

Grape Juice to Can

$1^1/_2$ c. sugar
4 c. grapes

Put in a 2-quart jar and fill with
warm water. Cold pack 20 minutes.
Dilute with water when opening.

Mrs. Mattie D. Miller

Tomato Cocktail

1 peck tomatoes
2 bunches celery
2 green peppers
6 sm. onions
1 bunch parsley
1 c. sugar
$^1/_4$ c. salt
1 tsp. pepper

Combine first 5 ingredients and cook
until tender. Press through sieve and
add remaining ingredients. Cook for
10 minutes and put into jars. Seal.

Mrs. Henry Mast

Tomato Cocktail

1/2 bu. tomatoes
3 Tbsp. lemon juice
2 c. sugar
1/2 tsp. cloves
1/2 onion
celery
salt

Cook all together for 30 minutes.
Put through a food mill, then can.

Mrs. Eli A. Mast

V8 Tomato Juice

1 peck ripe tomatoes
3 lg. green peppers
1 stalk celery
2 onions
2 tsp. salt
1 1/2 c. white sugar
1 tsp. garlic
1 tsp. parsley

Cook tomatoes, peppers, celery, onions,
garlic, and parsley. Put through sieve
or juicer. Heat, then add salt and
sugar. Cold pack 15 minutes.

Mrs. Eli A. Mast

Grape Wine

6 c. sugar
2 qts. unwashed grapes

Combine grapes and sugar. Squeeze
and mash with hands, then use a
potato masher to mash well. Let set
1 week. Stir once a day to make sure
sugar is dissolved. Add 1 gallon
lukewarm water and drain through
organdy or cloths. Add 4 c. sugar to
a gallon of juice or wine. Put into
jugs. Do not put cap on tightly for at
least 2 weeks, then turn on tightly.

Mrs. Mattie Miller

Dandelion Wine

1 gal. dandelion blossoms
1 gal. boiling water
1 lemon, sliced
3 oranges, sliced
4 lbs. sugar
2 Tbsp. yeast

Pour boiling water over blossoms. Let set 3 days. Add sugar. Simmer 15 minutes. When warm, add lemon and oranges. Add yeast. Let set 1 week, then strain and bottle.

Verna Yoder

Punch

1 (46 oz.) can pineapple juice
2 (12 oz.) cans frozen lemonade
1 (12 oz.) can frozen limeade
2 qts. 7-Up
5 (12 oz.) cans water
1 c. sugar or to taste

Mix everything except 7-Up. Freeze. When ready to serve, mash slightly and add 7-Up.

Mrs. John Yoder

tid bits

For coffee or tea stains, pour boiling water over spot before washing.

Don't make coffee water boiling. It has a better flavor if you don't boil it.

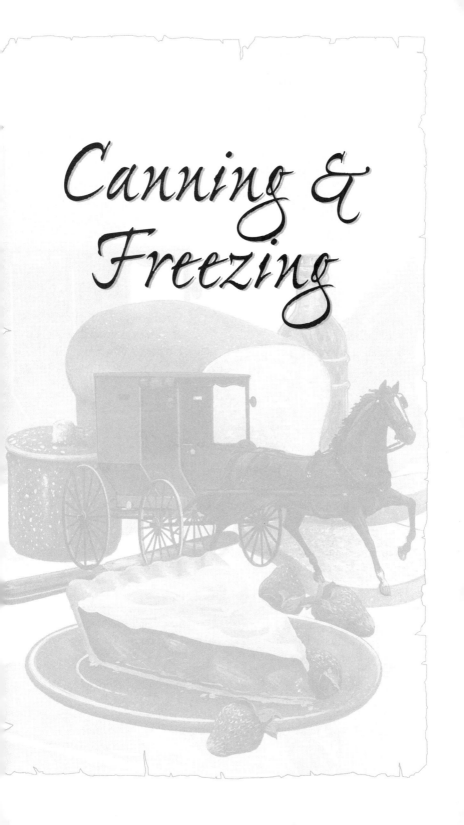

Canning & Freezing

Tender Beef Chunks

16 lb. beef chunks
1 c. brown sugar
³/₄ c. salt
1 tsp. saltpeter
2 tsp. soda
1 gal. water

Combine sugar, salt, saltpeter, soda, and water. Bring to a boil. Cool. Pour over meat. Add water to cover meat. Let set 4 days. Drain and rinse meat. Add ¹/₄ tsp. salt and 1 c. water to each quart. Cold pack for 2 hours.

Savilla Mullet
Mrs. John L. Erb

Canning Beef Chunks

1 gal. cold water
1 lb. Tender Quick
4–5 gal. beef chunks

Marinate 2–3 days. Drain. Put in jars. Fill with clear water. Do not add salt. Cold pack 3 hours.

Mrs. Emanuel J. Miller

To Can Meat

Bologna: Add 1 tsp. salt to 1 qt. bologna. Fill with water. Cold pack 2¹/₂ hours.

Bologna without casing: Press into jars. Cold pack 3 hours. Very good to slice and fry.

Hamburger and beef chunks: 2 tsp. salt to 1 qt. meat. Do not add water. Cold pack 3 hours.

Fried, crumbled hamburger: Cold pack 2 hours.

Steaks: Mix 1 gal. water, 1 c. brown sugar, and 1 c. salt. Divide liquid into 15 quart jars. Fill with steaks. Cold pack 2¹/₂ hours. This is also good for beef chunks.

Cooked, diced chicken: Add 1 tsp. salt to 1 pint meat. Do not add water. Cold pack 1¹/₂ hours.

Chicken broth: Add 1 tsp. salt to 1 pint broth. Cold pack 1 hour.

Mrs. Eli N. Hershberger

Cured Ham

1 1/2 c. Tender Quick
2 c. brown sugar
1 Tbsp. black pepper
6 c. water
1/4 c. Liquid Smoke

Cut 1 ham in chunks to fit in jars. Combine ingredients and pour over ham. Let set for 6 days. Wash with cold water before putting into jars. Cold pack 2 hours.

Mrs. Felty L. Raber

Pickled Tongue & Heart

1 1/4 c. water
1 c. vinegar
1/3 c. brown sugar

Place tongue into boiling water and cook for 5–10 minutes. Pull off skin. Cut tongue and heart into small strips. Cook in salt water until soft. Add ingredients and cook a little longer.

Mrs. Mattie Miller

Trail Bologna

100 lbs. hamburger
4 lbs. Tender Quick
2 c. brown sugar
2/3 c. salt
2 Tbsp. saltpeter (scant)
2 Tbsp. black pepper
8 qts. water

Mix and let set 2–3 days. Grind twice. Put in jars and cold pack 3 hours.

Miriam Mast

Sausage Mix

5 gal. meat
1 c. salt
1/2 c. black pepper
1/2 c. dry mustard

Mix and grind. Put into stuffing or casing.

Henry Masts

Sloppy Joe to Can

12 lbs. hamburger
1 c. chopped onions, optional
salt
pepper
6 c. oatmeal
8 c. ketchup
4 c. water
1 c. brown sugar
1 1/2 c. vinegar

Fry hamburger and onions. Salt and pepper to taste. Add remaining ingredients. Put in jars and cold pack 1 1/2 hours.

Mrs. Paul E. Miller

Pickled Red Beets

2 c. sugar
2 c. vinegar
2 c. water
1 tsp. allspice
1 Tbsp. cinnamon
1 tsp. cloves
1 tsp. pickling spice

Cook beets. Slip off skins and cut in chunks. Heat syrup to boiling. Add beets and bring to a boil. Pack in jars and seal. Note: I use red beet juice instead of water. I also use whole spices to avoid the settling in the bottom. When cooking, I like to leave the spices in syrup for a while. Five batches yields 15 quarts.

Savilla Mullet

Red Beets

8 qts. cooked beets
7 c. sugar
7 c. beet juice
1 3/4 c. vinegar
pinch salt

Cook beets with salt. Save juice. Mix sugar, beet juice, vinegar, and salt. Pour over beets. Let set overnight. Put in jars and seal. Cold pack 15 minutes.

Mrs. Mahlon R. Yoder

Red Beets to Can

6 qts. beets
Syrup:
4$^{1}/_{2}$ c. sugar
2$^{1}/_{2}$ Tbsp. salt
1$^{1}/_{2}$ c. vinegar
1$^{1}/_{2}$ c. water
1$^{1}/_{2}$ red beet water

Cook beets until soft. Peel off skin. Cut beets into bite-sized pieces. Put into 6 jars and pour syrup over them. Cold pack 10–15 minutes.

Mrs. David J. Troyer

To Can Peppers

1 tsp. vegetable oil
1 tsp. salt
Syrup:
2 c. vinegar
3 c. water
3 c. sugar

Mix syrup ingredients and bring to a boil. Fill quart jars with peppers. Add 1 tsp. oil and 1 tsp. salt to each quart. Pour syrup over peppers while boiling hot. Cold pack to boiling point.

Verna Yoder

Canned Hot Peppers

2 qt. white vinegar
1 qt. water
2 c. sugar
1 Tbsp. pickling salt
1 Tbsp. oil per quart

Combine first 4 ingredients. Bring to a boil. Fill hot quart jars with peppers. Add oil to each quart. Pour boiling syrup into hot jars so they will seal. Do not cold pack. These are very good on pizza or sandwiches.

Mrs. Paul J. Hochstetler

tid bits

A rule to remember:
Left is loose and right is tight.

Sweet Dill Pickles

1 qt. vinegar
2 c. water
$^1/_4$ c. salt
4 c. sugar
4 onions, cut up
2 tsp. dill seed per quart
1 tsp. garlic salt per quart

Slice cucumbers. Put cucumbers, dill seed, and garlic salt in jar. Bring liquid to rolling boil. Pour over cucumbers. Set jars in boiling water long enough so they will boil. Yields 4 quarts.

Mrs. Alvin I. Yoder

Bread & Butter Pickles

1 gal. thinly sliced cucumbers
2 green peppers
8 small onions
$^1/_2$ c. salt
Syrup:
5 c. sugar
1 Tbsp. mustard seed
2 c. vinegar (scant)
1 tsp. turmeric
1 Tbsp. celery seed
2 c. water

Slice peppers and onions. Mix in salt. Add cucumbers and cover with water. Let set 3 hours. Drain well. Cook syrup ingredients until clear. Pour over cucumbers and can.

Mrs. John D. Miller

Banana Pickles

1 c. vinegar
$1^1/_2$ c. water
3 c. sugar
1 tsp. salt
1 Tbsp. celery seed
1 Tbsp. turmeric
1 Tbsp. mustard seed

Bring to boil and pour over cucumbers in jars. Cucumbers need to be peeled and cut into long strips. Cut out seeds and put into jars. Cold pack 10 minutes. This is a good way to use up pickles that got too big. A bonus on a hot dog or sausage sandwich. Our family's favorite.

Mrs. Andrew A. Troyer

Hamburger Pickles

1 gal. thinly sliced cucumbers
Salt Brine:
1 gal. hot water
1 c. salt
Alum Water:
water
1 Tbsp. alum
Syrup:
2 c. vinegar
2 c. water
3 lbs. sugar
Spice Mix:
1 Tbsp. celery seed
1 Tbsp. whole cloves
1 Tbsp. allspice
1 Tbsp. cinnamon sticks

Soak cucumbers in salt brine for 3–5 days. Drain and wash in clear water 4 times. This step is very important! Cook in alum water for 10 minutes. Pour syrup over cucumbers. Put spices in a bag. Put the bag in syrup and cucumbers and cook until clear. Can and seal.

Mose Ada

Cold Packing Fruit in Quart Jars

Peaches: 7–10 minutes   Cherries: 15 minutes
Pears: 15 minutes   Raspberries: 10 minutes
Applesauce: 10 minutes

Don't throw juice out from pears and peaches—use for Jell-O or thicken as a fruit glaze.

Peaches & Glaze to Can

4 c. water
3 c. pineapple juice
7 c. sugar
$^1/_3$ c. peach Jell-O
$1^3/_4$ c. clear jel
$5^1/_2$–6 qts. peaches

Mix first 4 ingredients. Thicken with clear jel. Add to peaches. Cold pack 20 minutes.

Rachel Yoder

Peach Fruit Thickening to Can

10 c. water
1 1/2 c. instant clear jel
4 c. sugar
3 Tbsp. lemon juice
1 tsp. salt

Mix in a large bowl and fill with fresh peaches. Cold pack 15–20 minutes. This makes the peaches a little more special for lunches. Can also add fresh fruit when opened or use for pie filling.

Mrs. Ben N. Weaver

To Can Peaches

6 qts. sliced peaches
3 c. pineapple juice
3 c. water
7 c. sugar
2 pkgs. apricot Jell-O
2 c. clear jel or Perma-Flo
1 1/2 c. water

Combine pineapple juice, water, and sugar. Bring to a boil. Mix clear jel and water. Add and cook until thick. Add Jell-O. Add sliced peaches and put in jars. Cold pack 20 minutes. I often add pineapple, grapes, or other fruit after opening. Yields 8–9 quarts.

Susie Kuhns

Cinnamon Tapioca Pears to Can

1 1/4 c. minute tapioca
2 1/4 c. sugar
1 c. red hots
2 1/2 qts. water
salt
pears, diced

Mix first 4 ingredients in a 6-quart kettle and bring to a boil. Boil and stir until red hots are melted. Remove from heat and fill kettle with pears. Put in jars and cold pack 20 minutes. Add Rich's topping to serve. Very handy for unexpected company. Do not keep for more than 1 year.

Mrs. Eli N. Hershberger

To Freeze Peaches

16 qts. peaches, sliced
24 oz. frozen orange juice
   concentrate
1/2 c. sugar per quart

Mix all together. Let set a little, then put into boxes and freeze.

Mary Hostetler

For Freezing Fruit

2 1/2 c. water
1/3 c. Sure-Jell
1 1/4 c. sugar
8–10 qts. strawberries

Combine water and Sure-Jell. Bring to a boil and cook for 2 minutes, stirring constantly. Remove from heat and add sugar. Cool, covered. Mix with strawberries.

Katie Yoder

Freezing Strawberries

4 c. sugar
2 c. mashed strawberries
10 c. sliced or mashed strawberries
1 pkg. Sure-Jell
3/4 c. water

Add sugar to the 2 c. mashed berries. Cook Sure-Jell and water for 1 minute. Add to the sugar mixture. Stir until sugar is dissolved. Add the remaining strawberries. Freeze. Yields 4 quarts.

Mrs. Roman E. Raber

Freezing Corn with Sauce

5 qts. corn
2 c. water
4 1/2 tsp. salt
1 c. sugar

Mix all together and cook 5 minutes. Cool before freezing.

Mrs. Edward M. Hershberger
Mrs. Nelson L. Miller

Freezer Sweet Corn

4 qts. fresh cut sweet corn
1 qt. hot water
²/₃ c. sugar
¹/₂ c. butter
2 tsp. salt

Put everything together and simmer 5–7 minutes. Cool quickly. Freeze.

Mrs. Aden Schlabach

Notes

Home &
Garden

Cookware Cleanser

1 c. lye
1 c. bleach, optional
1 c. laundry detergent

Fill your stainless steel canner $^3/_4$ full of warm water. Add ingredients. Heat to almost boiling. Dip all your stainless steel cookware and silverware. They will shine like new! It works!

Mrs. Ivan Hershberger

Stain Solution

Use 1 tsp. baking soda and 2 c. water to remove stains from Tupperware and plastic kitchenware. It will also soak up burned food from kettles if left to soak overnight, using 2–3 tsp. soda to a cup of water.

Sediment Remover

1$^1/_2$ c. apple cider vinegar
1$^1/_2$ c. water
3 Tbsp. salt

Put in teakettle and boil for 15 minutes. Let set overnight. This will boil over if burner is turned on high.

Homemade Soft Soap

2$^1/_2$ gal. rain or soft water
7 c. melted lard (lukewarm)
1 c. ammonia
2 c. borax
3 c. Wisk
1 c. lye

Put water in a 5-gallon bucket. Mix in borax and Wisk until dissolved. Dissolve lye in warm water before adding. Add remaining ingredients. Fill pail with water. Stir for a few minutes several times a day for a a week or so. It will start to thicken after 2–3 days. This can be used for any clothes.

Onion Salve

1 handful ground horseradish
1 handful ground poke root
1 handful ground comfrey root
3 wool kraut hearts, ground
3 onions, ground
1 qt. lard

Simmer and fry in lard until brown.
This is a very good drawing salve for
chest cold.

Mrs. Lizzie Raber

Cold Salve

1 oz. camphor gum
8 oz. petroleum jelly or Vaseline
1 oz. menthol crystals

Put in pan until melted, then put in
jars.

Mrs. John D. Miller

Plant Food

1 Tbsp. Epsom salt
1 Tbsp. baking powder
1 Tbsp. household ammonia
1 Tbsp. saltpeter
1 gal. water

Mix all together. To keep your houseplants healthy and free from bugs,
give them this once a month.

Mrs. Levi (Susan) Troyer

Plant Food

1 tsp. baking powder
1 tsp. Epsom salt
1 tsp. saltpeter
$^1/_2$ tsp. ammonia
1 gal. water

Add to watermelons and muskmelons
when you plant them and about 4
times during the summer to prevent
bugs from coming to roots and
vines. Also use on your houseplants.

Fly Spray

3 c. water
2 c. white vinegar
1 c. Avon Skin-So-Soft
1 Tbsp. citronella or eucalyptus oil

Put in a jar and shake well. Use as a wipe or spray. It lasts 2–3 days to keep flies and mosquitoes away.

Mrs. Roman R. Miller

Baby Wipes

1¹/₂ c. boiling water
3 Tbsp. baby bath
1 Tbsp. baby oil

Cut 1 roll Bounty paper towels in half. Remove center cardboard. Place upright in an airtight container and pour mixture over towels. Cover tightly and it's ready to use in 30 minutes. The wipes can be pulled up from center and torn off at any length. Note: May use soft soap instead of baby bath, and Skin-So-Soft instead of baby oil.

Mrs. Levi Yoder
Katie Mae Troyer

Baby Wipes

1 roll Bounty paper towels
1 Tbsp. Melaleuca bath and
    shower gel
2 Tbsp. baby oil
2 c. boiling water

Cut paper towel roll in half. Put in a plastic container with lid. Mix boiling water, baby oil, and bath gel, then pour over towels. Let set 1 hour, then they are ready to use.

Mrs. Norman H. Mast

Play Dough

2 c. flour
$^1/_2$ c. cornstarch
1 Tbsp. powdered alum
2 c. water
1 c. salt
1 Tbsp. salad oil

Place all ingredients in saucepan. Stir constantly over low heat until mixture thickens into consistency of dough. Remove from heat and let cool until it can be handled. Knead like bread dough until smooth. Add food coloring if you wish. Store in airtight container. Keeps for a month. This gives children something to do on winter days.

Mrs. Vernon Mast

Gooey Slime

$^1/_8$ c. borax laundry detergent
$1^1/_2$ c. hot water
1 c. white Elmer's school glue
1 c. hot water

Mix borax with hot water. Stir until dissolved. Mix glue and water. Put $^1/_2$ c. plus 2 Tbsp. of glue mixture in a medium Ziploc bag and add 2 drops food coloring. Add $^1/_4$ c. borax mixture. Squish the bag to mix the ingredients well. Soon you'll have a slime. Put in small containers over-night. Children have a lot of fun playing with it and it's not messy.

Mrs. Roman Hershberger
Katie Yoder

Rock Garden

$^1/_2$ c. water
$^1/_2$ c. salt
$^1/_2$ c. liquid bluing
1 c. ammonia

Put a washed coal into a shallow glass pan. Mix all ingredients. Pour over coal. Drop food colorings over it, then watch it grow.

Soap Bubbles

1/3 c. dishwashing detergent
1 1/2 c. water
2 tsp. sugar
1 drop food coloring

Combine in a bottle.

Mrs. Roy E. Mast

Bird Feed

1 c. lard
1 c. peanut butter
1/3 c. sugar
1 c. whole wheat flour
2 c. oatmeal
2 c. cornmeal

Melt and mix peanut butter and lard. Add remaining ingredients. Put in cake pan. Cut to size.

Mrs. Dan E. Mast

Weights & Measures

1 pound of:	Equals:
all-purpose flour	4 cups
granulated sugar	2 cups
powdered sugar	3 1/2 cups
brown sugar	2 1/4 cups
syrup (molasses, etc.)	1 1/3 cups
butter	2 cups
grated American cheese	4 cups
oatmeal	6 1/4 cups
walnuts	4 cups
raisins	3 cups

Substitutions

1 Tbsp. cornstarch = 2 Tbsp. flour for thickening gravies.
1 tsp. baking powder = 1/4 tsp. soda plus 1/2 tsp. cream of tartar
1/2 tsp. baking powder = 1 egg

 Index

SOUPS & SALADS

CAKES

PIES

COOKIES & BARS

DESSERTS

HOME & GARDEN

VOLUME I

Cooking with the Horse & Buggy People

A Collection of Over 600 Favorite Recipes from the Heart of Holmes County

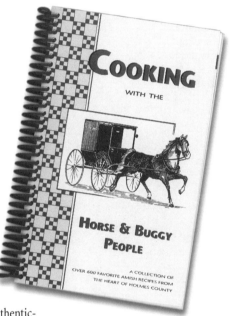

From mouth watering Amish style main dishes to kitchen dream desserts, this one has it all. Over 600 made-from-scratch recipes that please the appetite and are easy on the food budget. You'll get a whole section on canning and food preparation. The Amish, long known for their originality in the kitchen, share their favorites with you. If you desire originality, if you respect authenticity, if the Amish style cooking satisfies your taste palate—**Cooking With The Horse & Buggy People** is for you.

Contains 14 Complete Sections:
Breads, Cakes, Cookies, Desserts, Pies, Salads, Main Dishes, Soups, Cereal, Candy, Miscellaneous, Drinks, Canning, Home Remedies & Preparing Wild Game, Index.

$9.95

· $5^1/_2$" x $8^1/_2$" · 275 pp · Spiral Bound · Laminated Cover
· Convenient Thumb Index · ISBN 1-890050-16-4

In Its 18th Printing, Over 100,000 sold!

Mary Yoder's Candy & Confections Cookbook

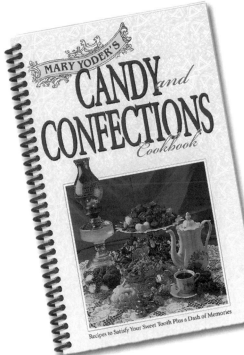

Mary Yoder

Ready for a really special treat …one that will satisfy your sweet tooth? Dripping chocolates, dreamy fudges, reach-for-more mints, and over 100 other sweet secrets—the homemade way. Mary has over 30 years' experience in making candy and confections—for her family as well as commercially. In this book she shares her own secret recipes, never before published.

Mary Yoder's Candy and Confections Cookbook is even more! Take a good look, for example, at the 24 color photos of the author's childhood memories and unique hobbies. You'll enjoy a walk down memory lane with her through the photos of her home, gardens, and hobbies. 70 illustrations in her own original pencil art are scattered throughout the book.

The next time you need a treat so special, so unique, so mouthwatering that it can't be bought, reach for Mary Yoder's Candy and Confections Cookbook. You'll add that personal touch that's just right.

You'll make that special moment even sweeter!

$9.95

· 5¹/₂" x 8¹/₂" · 126 pp · Spiral Bound · 24 Color Photographs
· 70 Original Pencil Illustrations by Mary Yoder · ISBN 1-890050-36-9

The Wooden Spoon Cookbook

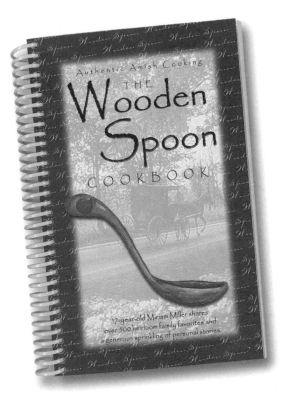

M eet 17-year-old Miriam Miller in the Wooden Spoon Cookbook. In addition to sharing her own, her mother's, and her grandmother's favorite recipes, Miriam shares childhood memories, stories, and personal details of her life as a young Amish girl.

$9.95

· 5¹/₂" x 8¹/₂" · 194 pp · Spiral bound · Laminated cover · Double indexed
· ISBN 1-890050-41-5

Cooking with Wisdom

Cooking Naturally—from the Amish Community

Cooking with Wisdom gives you 450 ideas on how to prepare good wholesome food. You'll enjoy food that contains no white flour, sugar or hundreds of other ingredients. Cooking with Wisdom contains recipes that are recommended for persons suffering with candida. The natural foods resource guide (included with the book) is great for beginners who need help in finding the healthy alternatives used throughout the book. The recipes are practical, made-from-scratch foods that are easy on the budget, but still exciting to the palate. Healthy ice cream and yogurt recipes as well as a section on food preparation make this a standard in natural foods cookbooks.

Contains 14 complete sections:
Breads, Breakfasts, Main Dishes, Salads & Dressings, Cookies, Cakes, Pies, Desserts, Ice Cream & Frozen Desserts, Wholesome Snacks, Yogurt, Food Preservation, Natural Food Resources, Index.

$9.95

· 8½" x 8" · 224 pp · Spiral Bound · Illustrated with 78 Pen & Ink Drawings
· ISBN 0-9642548-7-5

TO ORDER COOKBOOKS

Check your local bookstore or call **1-800-852-4482.**

2673 TR 421
Sugarcreek, OH 44681

Carlisle Press
WALNUT CREEK